# MASTER THE

# TOEFL® CBT

## 2 0 0 3

PATRICIA NOBLE SULLIVAN
GAIL ABEL BRENNER
GRACE YI QIU ZHONG

## TEACHER-TESTED STRATEGIES AND

## TECHNIQUES FOR SCORING HIGH

*TOEFL is a registered trademark of Educational Testing Service (ETS).
This book is not endorsed or approved by ETS.

THOMSON

ARCO

Australia • Canada • Mexico • Singapore • Spain • United Kingdom • United States

An ARCO Book
ARCO is a registered trademark of Thomson Learning, Inc., and is used herein
under license by Peterson's.

**About The Thomson Corporation and Peterson's**
With revenues of US$7.2 billion, The Thomson Corporation (www.thomson.com) is a leading
global provider of integrated information solutions for business, education, and professional
customers. Its Learning businesses and brands (www.thomsonlearning.com) serve the needs
of individuals, learning institutions, and corporations with products and services for both
traditional and distributed learning.

Peterson's, part of The Thomson Corporation, is one of the nation's most respected providers
of lifelong learning online resources, software, reference guides, and books. The Education
Supersite℠ at www.petersons.com—the Internet's most heavily traveled education resource—has searchable databases and interactive tools for contacting U.S.-accredited institutions and programs. In addition, Peterson's serves more than 105 million education consumers annually.

*Master the TOEFL CBT* is published with a CD. The CD will allow you to practice what you
have learned using state-of-the-art computer software. The software was created by Cambridge Educational Services, 2720 River Road, Ste. 36, Des Plaines, IL 60018.

For more information, contact Peterson's, 2000 Lenox Drive, Lawrenceville, NJ 08648; 800-
338-3282; or find us on the World Wide Web at www.petersons.com/about.

ISBN (book only): 0-7689-0897-3
ISBN (book with CD-ROM): 0-7689-0896-5
ISBN (Prep Kit with Tapes): 0-7689-0898-1

Printed in the United States of America

10 9 8 7 6 5 4 3    04 03 02

# CONTENTS

## ABOUT THE AUTHORS

**PATRICIA NOBLE SULLIVAN** is an English Language Officer with the U.S. State Department. She was formerly a lecturer at the University of California, Santa Cruz. She has a Ph.D. in Education with a focus in language, literacy, and culture from the University of California, Berkeley. She also has taught English, teacher training, and TOEFL in California, China, Taiwan, Afghanistan, Vietnam, and Turkey.

**GAIL ABEL BRENNER** is an instructor for the English Language International Program at the University of California, Santa Cruz, where she teaches English, TOEFL, pronunciation, and American culture. She has trained foreign professionals in medical and business English and business communications at Santa Cruz–based companies International Health Programs and Silicon Systems. She holds a graduate degree in education from the University of California, Santa Cruz.

**GRACE YI QIU ZHONG** is the vice president and cofounder of AbleSys Corporation in Hayward, California. She came to the United States from Shanghai, China, in 1984 and received a Master of Arts degree in Sports Psychology from California State University, Sacramento, in 1987.

## ACKNOWLEDGEMENTS

**To Mick, Rebecca, Adam, Josh, John, and Jesse for their love and support.**

Several people helped in the writing of this book. Some helped by prewriting questions and proofing new material; others helped by evaluating test questions. Thanks to Lori Buehring for her excellent work in writing new questions for this edition. Thanks also to Le'a Lieux who helped field test the questions. In addition we thank the students at English Language International, University of California Extension, Santa Cruz, California who took practice tests and gave valuable feedback to us.

# ABOUT THIS BOOK

This book is designed to help you attain high scores on either the computer-based or paper-based TOEFL test by helping you increase your language skills, improve your testing speed, and learn test-taking strategies. Part 1, "The Test of English as a Foreign Language," gives up-to-date information about both the computer-based and paper-based formats, and Part 2, "Sample Questions and Test-Taking Strategies," includes sample questions and test-taking strategies for both test formats, and illustrations of how test questions appear on a computer screen. Part 3, "Four Practice TOEFL Tests," consists of full-length practice tests, and Part 4, "Transcripts for Practice Tests," gives the transcripts for the listening sections of the practice tests. This book, will help you prepare by familiarizing you with the format and test questions for both the computer-based and paper-based versions, while helping you to increase the language skills needed for a high score. If you have purchased the CD version of this book or the Preparation Kit, you can listen to the audio components of the practice exams to better simulate the test-taking experience. In addition, if you have the CD version, you have access to additional TOEFL practice.

You will find the following throughout the book:

**NOTE**

A Note highlights critical information about the TOEFL test.

**TIP**

A tip draws your attention to valuable concepts and advice about the English language.

# The Test of English as a Foreign Language

# An Overview of the TOEFL Test

## WHAT IS THE TOEFL TEST?

The letters "TOEFL" stand for "Test of English as a Foreign Language."
The purpose of the test is to evaluate the English proficiency of nonnative
speakers of English who wish to study in colleges and universities where
English is the language of instruction. TOEFL scores are used by more than
2,400 institutions in the United States and Canada. For many of these
institutions, you must send in your TOEFL score with your application.
TOEFL scores also might be requested for employment in some companies
where advanced English language skills are needed.

There are two versions of the TOEFL test: one version is taken on a
computer, and the other is a paper-and-pencil (or paper-based) test. Each
version has a separate Information Bulletin. For the computer test, the
bulletin is called *Information Bulletin for Computer-Based Testing*. For the
paper-based test, the bulletin is called *Information Bulletin for Supplemental TOEFL Administrations*. You must take the version that is available in
the area in which you live. In most parts of the world, the TOEFL is given
via computer. The supplemental administrations are all paper-based tests
and are offered in places where computer-based testing is limited. In this
book, we refer to the computer-based test as the CBT and the supplemental
administrations (the paper-based test) as the PBT.

The CBT has four sections: (1) Listening, (2) Structure, (3) Reading, and
(4) Writing. The PBT also has four sections: (1) Listening Comprehension,
(2) Structure and Written Expression, (3) Reading Comprehension, and (4)
Test of Written English (TWE).

On both versions of the TOEFL, the listening sections test your ability to
understand English as it is spoken in the United States and Canada. The
structure sections test your ability to recognize standard written English.
The reading sections test your ability to understand reading passages on
nontechnical subjects. The writing section and the TWE test your ability to
write standard academic English.

## ROAD MAP

- *What Is the TOEFL Test?*
- *What Is the TOEFL CBT?*
- *What Is the TOEFL PBT?*
- *How is Writing Tested?*
- *How Do the CBT and PBT Compare?*
- *How Do I Register?*
- *When and Where Are the Tests Given?*
- *How Much Does It Cost to Take the TOEFL?*
- *How Long Are the Tests?*
- *What About Scoring?*

**NOTE**
Check to see which version of the TOEFL is given in your area. The CBT is given in most countries in the world. However, some countries offer a supplemental TOEFL administration in the paper-based format. You must check the TOEFL Information Bulletin (available in libraries, U.S. commissions and foundations, and binational centers) to see which version is given in your area. If you have access to a computer, visit the TOEFL Web site at www.toefl.org for the latest information.

No single "passing score" is given for the TOEFL. Some schools, especially those with special English language classes, might accept a score below 175 (CBT score) or 500 (PBT score). On the other hand, many universities require a score of over 210 (CBT score) or 550 (PBT score). For graduate school programs, you might need a score above 250 (CBT score) or 600 (PBT score). Check with your institution to see what score is admissible.

## WHAT IS THE TOEFL CBT?

The letters "CBT" stand for "computer-based test." The CBT is not simply a pencil-and-paper test reformatted for the computer; it is different in the way that some of the questions are written, answered, and rated. The CBT uses two different types of question formats: computer adaptive and linear.

In the computer adaptive sections (listening and structure), the computer selects a specific range of questions that is matched to the test taker's level. The test taker's answer to any one question determines the difficulty level of the next question. In this section, you can view only one question at a time. You must answer each question as it appears on the screen, and you cannot skip a question or change answers to previous questions.

In the linear section (reading), questions are selected randomly without consideration of the test taker's ability level. Within this section, you are allowed to review or change your previous answers.

## WHAT IS THE TOEFL PBT?

The Supplemental Administration of the TOEFL is the paper-based version of the TOEFL test that is given in places that have limited access to computers. The letters "PBT" stand for "paper-based test." The paper-based version is also the version used for the institutional TOEFL test, that is, the TOEFL test that is given by particular institutions for which you receive only an unofficial score. On the PBT, all questions are selected randomly without consideration of PBT test takers level of ability.

## HOW IS WRITING TESTED?

Both the CBT and the PBT include a 30-minute essay. The essay questions reflect the type of writing that is required in colleges and universities. You can see example essay questions in the TOEFL Information Bulletins. For the CBT, the essay can be written either by hand or on the computer. The essay is scored separately, and then the score is combined with the Structure score for a total Structure/Writing score. For the PBT, the Test of Written English (TWE) can only be written by hand. The TWE score is not combined with the TOEFL score but is given as a separate score.

# HOW DO THE CBT AND PBT COMPARE?

The following table illustrates the main differences in the format of the two versions of the TOEFL test.

| COMPUTER-BASED TOEFL TEST | PAPER-BASED TOEFL TEST |
| --- | --- |
| **Listening Section**<br>1. 30–50 questions<br>2. Overall time: 40–60 minutes (15–20 minutes for answering questions, self-paced)<br>3. Part A = short conversations<br>Part B = long conversations and talks<br>4. Test includes charts, diagrams, and pictures of the speakers.<br>5. Test taker hears and sees the questions.<br>6. Each question must be answered before going on to the next; test taker cannot go back. | **Listening Comprehension**<br>1. 50 questions<br>2. Overall time about 30 minutes (10–12 seconds to answer each question)<br>3. Part A = short conversations<br>Part B = long conversations<br>Part C = talks<br>4. There are no pictures, charts, or diagrams.<br>5. Test taker hears but cannot see the questions.<br>6. Test-taker can go back to previous answers. |
| **Structure Section**<br>1. 20–25 questions<br>2. Time limit: 15–20 minutes<br>3. Sentence Completion and Error Identification questions are mixed. | **Structure and Written Expression**<br>1. 40 questions<br>2. Time limit: 25 minutes<br>3. The first part has 15 Sentence Completion questions; the second part has 25 Error Identification questions. |
| **Reading Section**<br>1. 44–55 questions<br>2. Time limit: 70–90 minutes<br>3. Some questions have two or more answers. | **Reading Comprehension**<br>1. 60 questions<br>2. Time limit: 55 minutes<br>3. All questions have one answer. |
| **Writing Section**<br>1. 1 question<br>2. Time limit: 30 minutes<br>3. Essay can be written on the computer or by hand. | **TWE**<br>1. 1 question<br>2. Time limit: 30 minutes<br>3. Essay must be written by hand. |

# HOW DO I REGISTER?

To register for both the CBT and the PBT, you first must obtain the current TOEFL Information Bulletin. Different bulletins are available for the CBT and the PBT; check the TOEFL Information Bulletin or the TOEFL Web site to see which test format is used in your area. Copies of the bulletins are generally available in libraries, language schools, United States commissions and foundations, and binational centers. If you cannot find the bulletins in your area, you may request one from:

TOEFL/TSE Publications
P.O. Box 6151
Princeton, New Jersey 08541
USA
Telephone: 609-771-7100
TTY: 609-771-7714
Fax: 609-771-7500

You can register for the CBT by mail, by telephone, or by fax. For the PBT you can only register by mail. The TOEFL Information Bulletins contain all the information and forms you need. You can also find current information about registration by checking the TOEFL Web site at www.toefl.org.

1. **By mail**—If you are taking the test in the United States, Canada, or U.S. Territories, mail in a CBT voucher request form along with your payment. You will be mailed a confirmation of your appointment. If you are taking the TOEFL outside the United States, mail in the scheduling form that is in the bulletin, along with your payment, and your confirmation will be mailed or faxed to you.

2. **By phone**—You can register by phone for the CBT. Complete the appropriate registration form in the TOEFL Information Bulletin for Computer-Based Testing. You will receive your test date by phone.

3. **By fax**—For CBT testing outside the U.S., Canada, and U.S. Territories, you can register by fax. Fill out and fax the appropriate information from the bulletin, and include your credit card number for payment. Your test date confirmation will be sent to you.

## CAN I CANCEL OR RESCHEDULE MY TEST DATE AFTER I REGISTER?

The policies for canceling or rescheduling the test vary depending on whether you are taking the CBT or PBT; however, you can usually receive a partial refund if you cannot go to the test center. If you are taking the CBT, you can reschedule the test, but you must pay an additional fee. If you have registered for the PBT, you cannot change your test date, but you can get a partial refund and register again for a new date. For details, read the Information Bulletin carefully.

## WHEN AND WHERE ARE THE TESTS GIVEN?

The CBT is individually scheduled on any date that is available in your area. Tests are administered at locations such as testing centers, ETS field offices, binational centers, and specified universities. The PBT dates and locations are listed in the *TOEFL Information Bulletin for Supplemental TOEFL Administrations*. You can also get information from the TOEFL Web site at www.toefl.org. Consult the current Information Bulletin or the Web site for current information.

# HOW MUCH DOES IT COST TO TAKE THE TOEFL?

Both the TOEFL CBT and the TOEFL PBT cost U.S. $110. You can send your payment in U.S. dollars or in the equivalent currencies of certain countries. See the *Information Bulletin for Computer-based Testing* or the *TOEFL Information Bulletin for Supplemental Administrations* for a list of accepted currencies. Forms of payment may include:

> Visa, MasterCard, American Express
>
> Check
>
> Money order
>
> U.S. postal money order
>
> Bank draft
>
> UNESCO coupons
>
> Eurochecks

**NOTE**

Some tests centers might charge you more to take the TOEFL. Check with your local test center for exact fees. In some cases, the fee can vary due to local conditions.

# HOW LONG ARE THE TESTS?

The CBT and PBT are somewhat different in length. On the CBT, the total number of questions can range from approximately 94–130. The number of questions and the types of questions vary according to your skill level. The CBT takes about 4 hours, which includes a self-paced computer tutorial. The PBT has about 150 questions, and it takes about 3 hours to complete.

# WHAT ABOUT SCORING?

The CBT and PBT use different scoring systems. The CBT gives you four scaled scores: Listening (0–30), Structure/Writing (0–30), Reading (0–30), and a total converted score of 0–300. The essay first is rated separately on a scale of 0–6 and then is later figured into the total Structure/Writing score. When you take the CBT, you can view your unofficial score for Listening and Reading immediately after you finish the test. You will see a range for your Structure/Writing score because your essay will not have been scored yet. An official score report—including your scores on the individual sections, your essay rating, and your total score—will be mailed to you approximately fourteen days after the test.

The PBT gives you three scaled scores: Listening Comprehension, Structure and Written Expression, and Reading Comprehension. The total score range is 310–677. The TWE score range is 0–6, and this is given as a separate score. You receive an official score report in the mail approximately five weeks after taking the test.

Although the scoring systems for the CBT and the PBT differ, they are similar in what they measure. The Information Bulletin includes a concordance table that gives a comparison of scores for each type of test.

## Summary of Test Times and Questions for the CBT

| Section | Test Times (minutes) | Approximate Number of Test Questions |
| --- | --- | --- |
| Tutorial | 40 (self-paced) | Variable |
| Listening | 15–25* | 30–50 |
| Structure | 15–20 | 20–25 |
| Reading | 70–90 | 44–55 |
| Essay | 30 | 1 |

Total time at the computer: Approximately $3\frac{1}{2}$ to 4 hours

* The clock does not run while you are listening to the conversations and talks, so the 15–25 minutes is the time given for answering the questions. The total time given for the Listening section is 40–60 minutes.

## Summary of Test Times and Questions for the PBT

| | Test Times (minutes) | Approximate Number of Test Questions |
| --- | --- | --- |
| Filling out forms | 30 (approximately) | |
| TWE | 30 | 1 |
| Listening Comprehension | 30 (approximately) | 50 |
| Structure and Written Expression | 25 | 40 |
| Reading Comprehension | 55 | 60 |

Total time at the test center: Approximately 3 hours

# Summary: General Information About the TOEFL

- The TOEFL is given in two forms: a computer-based version (CBT) and a supplemental paper-based version (PBT). The CBT has replaced the paper-based version in most areas of the world. Check the Information Bulletin to see which form is given in your area.

- Two TOEFL Bulletins of Information are available: one for the CBT (*Information Bulletin for Computer-based Testing*) and one for the PBT (*TOEFL Information Bulletin for Supplemental Administrations*). The registration materials are included in the Bulletins. You can get a TOEFL Bulletin at various institutions such as libraries, language schools, U.S. Commissions and foundations, and binational centers. The bulletins are free. You can also download them from the Internet at www.toefl.org.

- To take the CBT, you schedule an appointment by mail, telephone, or fax. Each test center has its own schedule of available times and dates. To take the PBT, you register for a specific test date by mail. The PBT is given about once a month on Saturdays. See the Bulletin for a list of possible days.

- For both the CBT and PBT, you will be in the test center for approximately 3 or 4 hours. Both forms cost U.S. $110.

- The CBT has four sections: Listening, Structure, Reading, and Writing. Two of the sections, Listening and Structure, are computer adaptive, which means that you are given particular questions based on your skill level. You cannot skip any question or go back to questions you have already answered. You listen to the Listening sections with headphones. The Reading section is not computer adaptive, which means that it is similar to the paper-based test. You read a passage and answer several questions about it. You can go back and forth between the passages in the Reading section.

- The PBT has four parts: Listening Comprehension, Structure and Written Expression, Reading Comprehension, and the Test of Written English (TWE). You can work on only one section at a time. For the Listening Comprehension section, you listen to a cassette tape.

- There is no single passing score for the TOEFL test. Institutions that require a TOEFL score have their own guidelines and minimum score requirements for admittance. You must contact your institution to find out what score is required.

# General Preparation for the TOEFL CBT

## LEARN THE "FORMATS" OF THE CBT

Some aspects of taking the TOEFL are like playing a game. To play a game well, you need to know the rules of the game and be able to apply the rules without spending a lot of time thinking about them. Understanding the rules of a game is similar to understanding the way the TOEFL CBT is formatted. If you understand the format of the test, you will feel more comfortable about taking the test. This chapter provides information about the format of the computer-based TOEFL test.

1.  You need to have a few basic computer skills. The CBT begins with a self-paced tutorials, so if you have never used a computer, you can learn the basic skills before you begin the actual test. The basic skills that you need to know are how to use a mouse, how to point and click, how to scroll up and down, and how to select icons. Forty minutes is an average time for tutorials. Studies conducted by the Educational Testing Service on test takers with similar skill abilities indicate that after taking the tutorial, those with no prior experience with computers have scores that are similar to test takers who are familiar with computers.

2.  The CBT sections have different formats. The Listening and Structure sections are computer adaptive, which means the questions you are presented with will vary depending on your individual skill level. You might get different questions than other people taking the test at the same time as you. In the Listening and Structure sections, you must answer each question before the computer will allow you to go on to the next question. You cannot go back to change any of your answers.

3.  The Reading section is not computer adaptive. The selection of passages and questions is not based on your skill level. This format is similar to the paper-based test. In this section, you can answer questions in any order. However, it is best to answer the questions in the order that they are given in case you don't have time to scroll back.

4.  In the Reading section, you cannot begin answering the questions until you have scrolled to the end of the passage. So, for each new passage, first read or skim to the end. You can then refer back to the passage as you answer the questions.

## ROAD MAP

- *Learn the "Formats" of the CBT*
- *Tips for Taking the CBT*
- *On the Day of the Test*

5. Some of the question types in the CBT are different than those in the PBT. See Part 2 of this book, "Sample Question and Test-taking Strategies," for examples of these types of questions.

6. You can write the essay either on the computer or by hand. Decide on the format that makes you feel the most comfortable. Once you decide which format to use, you cannot change your mind.

7. No penalty is given for a wrong answer. If you are running out of time, click on the answers very quickly, even if you have to guess.

8. If you are very unhappy with the quality of your answers on the test, you have two options:

   • You can decide not the send your score to any college or university. If so, indicate this at the end of the test when the computer asks you where you want your scores sent. The scores will only be sent to you.

   • You can decide to cancel the whole test; however, this is not advised and is unnecessary except in unusual situations. If you do decide to cancel, indicate this at the end of the test when the computer asks you if you want to cancel the test. If you do cancel your test, it will not be scored, so no score will be sent to you or to any institution. You cannot get your money back, but you can take the test again after one month, if you choose.

## TIPS FOR TAKING THE CBT
### GENERAL HINTS

1. Practice working at a computer for more than four hours at a time so that you are accustomed to it.

2. If you wear glasses, be sure that they are appropriate for the distance of reading a computer screen.

3. Use earplugs when you work on the Structure, Reading, and Writing sections so that you are not bothered by noises in the room.

4. There is a 5-minute break between the Structure section and the Reading section. Take advantage of this break by walking around to relax your body and mind. Also, rest your eyes by looking out a window, if possible. You might try massaging your eyes, especially if they are tired from looking at the computer screen.

### LISTENING SECTION

5. If you find yourself distracted by the visual images shown during the listening section, concentrate on the speaker's words. Don't close your eyes or look away from the images, however, because you might be shown a diagram or chart that is important.

## STRUCTURE SECTION

6. A lot of questions in the Structure section focus on your ability to use correct word forms (nouns, verbs, adjectives, and adverbs). Practice these using the material in Part 2 of this book, and also consult your own grammar books.

## READING SECTION

7. Practice reading various information on a computer to get used to this format.

## WRITING SECTION

8. Practice writing 30-minute essays on a computer if you decide to use the computer rather than paper. Use the sample questions that the Educational Testing Service publishes in the TOEFL Information Bulletin as well as the ones in this book.

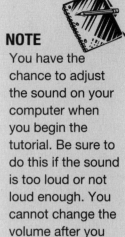

**NOTE**
You have the chance to adjust the sound on your computer when you begin the tutorial. Be sure to do this if the sound is too loud or not loud enough. You cannot change the volume after you begin the test.

# ON THE DAY OF THE TEST

Arrive at the test center 15 – 30 minutes before the scheduled time. Bring your appointment confirmation, your CBT voucher number (if you have one), and your passport or proper identification. (See the Information Bulletin for details on proper ID.)

If you want to have your test score sent to one or more institutions, bring a list of these institutions to the test center along with the state or province and country for each one. You will find this information in the TOEFL bulletin, and they also will appear on the computer screen after you finish taking the test.

Do not bring any paper, pencils, beepers, pagers, cell phones, calculators, books, dictionaries, translators, or food with you to the testing center.

Sit down and take some deep breaths to relax before the test begins.

**TIP**

A 5-minute break is offered during the CBT between the Structure and the Reading sections. Taking advantage of this time to rest can help you keep your concentration during the Reading section.

# Summary: What You Need to Know About the CBT

- You need to use a computer to take the test. You will need to learn basic computer skills such as how to use a mouse, how to point and click, and how to scroll.

- Each test begins with a tutorial that teaches you how to use the computer and the mouse and how to answer the questions. You will be given time at the beginning to learn these skills. Most people who are not familiar with computers take about 40 minutes for the tutorial.

- Some types of questions in the Listening section and the Reading section of the CBT do not appear on the PBT.

- You will have a 5-minute break between the Structure and Reading sections.

- You can choose to write the essay either by hand or on the computer, but once you choose, you cannot change your mind.

- If you are very unhappy with your work on the test, you can decide not to have your score sent to any institution.

- To prepare for the test, it helps to practice using a computer for at least four hours at a time. However, if it is not possible for you to use a computer, don't worry. Studies show that those who are familiar with computers and those who are not do not differ in their relative scores.

# General Preparation for the TOEFL PBT

## LEARN THE RULES OF THE PBT

There are rules for taking the PBT. If you are familiar with the rules, you will feel less anxious and will be better able to concentrate on the test itself. You will also increase your speed in answering the questions. As you take the practice tests in this book, apply the rules below.

This list gives some of the key rules of the paper-based TOEFL.

1.  You may work on only one section at a time. During the time limit for one particular section, you may not turn back to the previous section or turn ahead to the next section.

2.  You may not turn the page and read ahead while the Listening Comprehension directions are being read.

3.  You may not make any marks in your test booklet or on your answer sheet (except for filling in the answer ovals).

4.  No penalty is given for choosing the wrong answer. You should take advantage of this by answering every question, even if you have to guess.

5.  Only one answer is allowed for each question. If you mark two answers for one question, you get no credit for that question.

6.  There is no rest break during the test. If you have to leave to use the restroom or for any other reason, you may do so, but you lose valuable test time.

7.  When the stop time is called, you must stop writing immediately and close your test booklet. If you do not stop writing, you risk getting no credit for the entire test and having to repeat the TOEFL at another time.

8.  Mark your answer sheet in the correct way. There is only one correct way to mark your answers on the answer sheet. Look at the following examples of the correct and incorrect ways to fill in the answer spaces.

## ROAD MAP

- *Learn the Rules of the PBT*
- *Mark Your Answer Sheet in the Correct Way*
- *Tips for Taking the PBT*
- *On the Day of the Test*

# MARK YOUR ANSWER SHEET IN THE CORRECT WAY

There is only one correct way to mark your answers on the answer sheet. Look at these examples of the correct and incorrect ways of filling in the answer spaces.

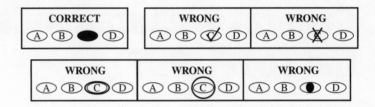

Each time you take a PBT practice test, use the special answer sheets in this book to record your answers, and practice filling in the ovals correctly. This way, you will become comfortable with marking your answers correctly and will do it automatically when you take the real test.

# TIPS FOR TAKING THE PBT

When you take the test, you need to go back and forth between your test booklet and your answer sheet. This is sometimes difficult to do. You do not want to lose time by having to search for your place on the answer sheet. You certainly do not want to make an error by marking your answer in the wrong place.

To avoid these mistakes and to save time, practice using both hands to mark your place. If you are right-handed, keep your left hand on the question in your test book, and use your right hand to mark your place on the answer sheet. After you mark your answer, keep your pencil on that place without moving it until you are ready to mark your next answer. With one hand on the question and one hand on the answer sheet, you will be able to keep track of where you are at all times. If you practice this procedure while you take the practice tests in this book, it will seem comfortable to you when you take the real test.

# ON THE DAY OF THE TEST

Arrive at the test center 15–30 minutes before the scheduled time. Bring your admission ticket and your passport or proper identification. (See the TOEFL Information Bulletin for details on proper ID.) Bring two sharpened no. 2 pencils.

Do not bring paper, cell phones, pagers, beepers, watches that make noise or have a flashing light, calculators, books, dictionaries, translators, or food with you to the testing center.

Sit down and take some deep breaths to relax before the test begins.

# Summary: What You Need to Know About the TOEFL Paper-Based Test

- You can work on only one section at a time. Do not try to read ahead or go back to a previous section.
- You cannot take any notes, underline any words, or make any marks in the test booklet or on the answer sheet.
- You should answer all questions because there is no penalty for an incorrect answer.
- If you mark two answers by mistake, you will not get any credit for that question.
- Mark all answers by filling in the oval on the answer sheet completely.
- There is no rest break during the test.
- On the day of the test, bring your admission ticket, your passport, two sharpened medium-soft (no. 2) black-lead pencils, and an eraser.

**NOTE**
The identification requirements for taking the TOEFL are very strict. You must have all the correct documents, including proper identification. If you do not arrive at the test center with the correct documents, you will not be allowed to take the test.

# Sample Questions and Test-Taking Strategies

# PART 2

# PREVIEW

# Choosing an Answer

## STRATEGIES FOR CHOOSING ANSWERS

A number of effective strategies can help you in choosing your answer. Try the following strategies as you take the practice tests in this book. These strategies are the same for both the CBT and the PBT. If you practice them every time you take a practice test, they will become automatic and it will be easy for you to apply them as you take the real test.

## TRUST YOUR INTUITION

You probably know more than you think you do and have more knowledge about English stored in your mind than you realize. So, if an answer seems right, even if you are not sure why, it might be best to trust that impression. The same applies if an answer seems wrong—eliminate it and choose a different answer.

This strategy might not work for you every time, of course. It also does not imply that you should use only your feelings to answer the questions. But many test takers have found that, when in doubt, their feeling or intuition about an answer is often right.

## YOUR FIRST CHOICE MIGHT BE THE BEST

For many people, their first answer choices are more often correct than the answers that they have reconsidered and changed. This might seem strange: it is logical to assume that the changed answer would be better because you had more time to think about it. But often in test taking, the first impression is the best. So, unless you are sure that your first answer is wrong, it is better not to change your first choice. This knowledge will also help you move more quickly through the test, as you spend less time reanalyzing and changing answers.

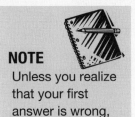

## ELIMINATE INCORRECT ANSWER CHOICES

If you do not immediately see the answer you think is correct, begin by eliminating the ones you know are *not* correct. On the TOEFL, there is no penalty for choosing an incorrect answer; therefore, you should answer every question, even if you have to guess. If you randomly guess one answer out of four choices, your chance of getting that answer correct is 25 percent. If you randomly guess one answer out of three choices, your chance of getting that answer correct is 33 percent. If you randomly guess one answer out of two choices, your chance of getting a correct answer is 50 percent. This means that if you can eliminate two of the answer choices, you increase your chance of being correct from 25 percent to 50 percent.

Some of the new question types on the computer-based TOEFL might have more (or less) than four answer choices, but the strategy of eliminating incorrect answers still can be applied. The following are some ways to eliminate answer choices if you do not know the correct answer:

1. Look at all the answer choices, and eliminate those that seem wrong—even if you do not know the reason they are wrong. Then choose your answer from among the answer choices that are left.

2. Try to figure out the testing point and apply the strategies that are in this book.

3. If you are running out of time and do not know the answers, or if you have no time to read the questions, just mark or click on one letter for all remaining questions. This strategy is only advisable if you're running out of time. If you know that you cannot finish in the time you have left, it is better to mark answers than to leave them blank—you might gain a point or two by pure luck.

## WHAT ARE TESTING POINTS?

A *testing point* is the *main point* of a TOEFL question. It is the specific area of English on which you are being tested. The practice tests in this book were written to reflect the testing points represented on previous TOEFL exams. Even though the questions in the real TOEFL are new for each test, many of the testing points remain the same.

An understanding of the major testing points of the TOEFL, therefore, will help you organize your study time and help you prepare for the many different kinds of questions you will see on the real test. When you study with the idea of learning to recognize testing points rather than simply to answer individual questions, you are using a strategy that will help you when you take the real TOEFL. The time you spend learning to recognize and understand the testing points in this book will increase your understanding of English and help you prepare for the TOEFL.

In the following practice sections of this book, you will see examples of different testing points and the way in which they are used in the test questions. Testing points are different in each section of the TOEFL, and there might be several testing points in one question. A testing point might be a grammatical structure, a common vocabulary word, an idiom, an intonation, or a particular type of reading or listening question. When you take the practice tests in this book, you also will be testing yourself to see if you understand the testing point and the test-taking strategies to use with that testing point.

# Summary: What You Need to Know about Choosing Answers and Recognizing Testing Points

- If you are unsure of what answer to choose, trust your first intuition of what sounds right or what seems right. Your first response is more often correct than a changed answer.

- Don't go back and change an answer unless you know that you have made a mistake. If you are not sure, then leave your original response.

- If you have no idea what answer to choose, first try to eliminate the ones that you think are incorrect. Then choose among the ones that are left.

- To help you choose an answer, try to figure out the testing point. Then, use the strategies in the next chapters of this book to guide you.

- Testing points are the categories that are used to develop questions. These can be grammatical structures, vocabulary words, idioms and phrases, intonation or stress patterns, or particular types of questions. Learning to recognize testing points will help you organize your study and react more quickly when you take the test.

- If you run out of time and have not finished the test, go quickly through the questions, just marking one letter for each. This will not help you very much, but it might help a bit by pure luck. This is better than leaving answers blank.

# Listening Section

The Listening section of the TOEFL tests your ability to understand spoken English. This section is divided into two parts in the computer-based test (CBT) and three parts in the paper-based test (PBT). For the CBT, you will see pictures on your computer screen and hear dialogue through individual headphones. For the PBT, an audiotape will be played in the testing room.

## SAMPLE LISTENING QUESTIONS FOR THE CBT

The Listening section includes two parts. In Part A, you hear conversations between two people. Sometimes the people speak only once, and at other times they speak more than once. Each conversation is followed by one question. In Part B, you hear longer conversations and talks. Sometimes the talks are by professors in a classroom; for these, you might hear students in the classroom asking questions, answering questions, or giving comments. Each of the longer conversations and talks is followed by several questions. The conversations and talks usually take place in a university setting among students and professors.

## LISTENING—PART A: SHORT CONVERSATIONS

An image will appear on your computer screen, and you will hear a short conversation between two people. Then you will answer the question based on what is stated or implied in the conversation.

## ROAD MAP

- *Sample Questions for the CBT*
- *Sample Questions for the PBT*
- *Listening Strategies*
- *Testing Points*

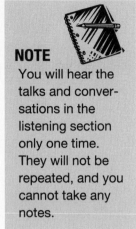

*Example 1*

You will see:

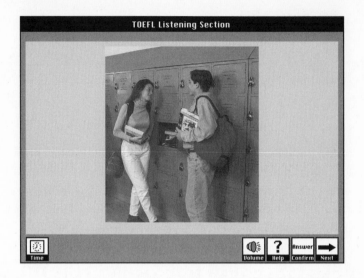

You will hear:

> *Woman:*   That statistics exam was really difficult.
>
> *Man:*   I'll say! I studied for it, but I hardly knew any of the answers.

Then you will see and hear the question:

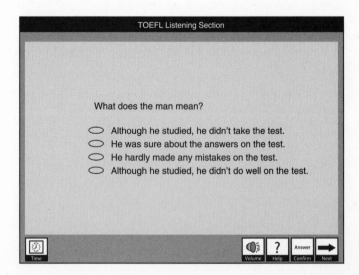

Click on an oval to choose your answer. The oval will darken to indicate your choice. To change your answer, simply click on a different oval. Your old choice will be erased as your new choice is selected. The correct answer is shown below but not shown during the test.

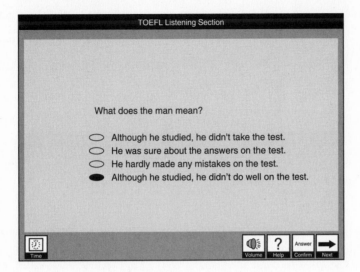

After you have chosen your answer, click Next and Confirm Answer to hear the next conversation.

*Example 2*

You will see:

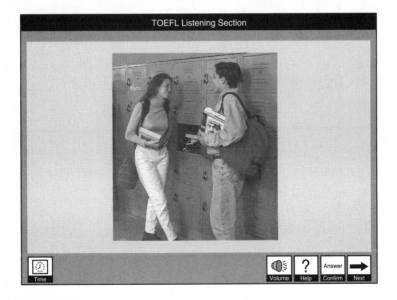

You will hear:

> *Woman:*    Do you know when the computer lab is open? I need to finish my research paper before tomorrow.

> *Man:*    The lab is open Monday through Friday from 8 A.M. to midnight, and on Saturday and Sunday from noon to 5 P.M.

> *Woman:*    Great, I'll go tonight!

Then you will see and hear the question:

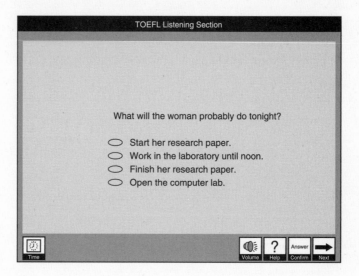

Click on an oval to choose your answer. The oval will darken to indicate your choice. The correct answer is shown below.

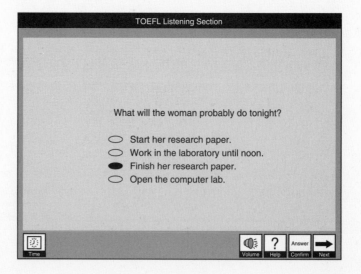

After you have chosen your answer, click Next and Confirm Answer to hear the next conversation.

## LISTENING—PART B: LONGER CONVERSATIONS AND TALKS

For the longer conversations and talks, a series of images will appear on your computer screen while you listen. Each conversation or talk will be followed by several questions, which you will answer based on what is stated or implied.

*Example 3*

The topic of a longer conversation will appear on your screen.

*Narrator:* Listen to part of a class discussion in a zoology class.

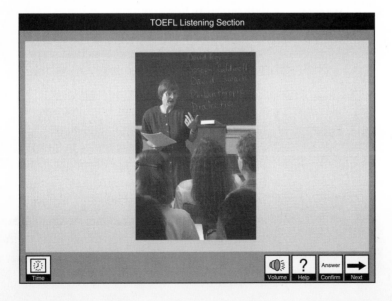

| | |
|---|---|
| *Professor:* | Yesterday we discussed three mammalian strategies that enable animals to survive during periods of food shortage or temperature extremes. We talked about migration, food storing, and changes in fertility resulting in lower birth rates. Today we'll look at another strategy, hibernation, which is common to many mammals like fat-tailed lemurs, bears, bats, ground squirrels, chipmunks, and other rodents. First of all, exactly what do we mean by hibernation? |
| *Woman:* | I know that hibernation is similar to a deep sleep, but I don't understand how it's different from regular sleep. |
| *Professor:* | Well, actually it's different in a number of ways. When a mammal goes into hibernation, its heart rate and breathing slow down greatly, and its body temperature drops, sometimes as low as the surrounding air. In this state, called a torpor, the animal uses very little energy and can live off fat stored in its body. |
| *Man:* | How do animals know when to hibernate? |
| *Professor:* | That depends somewhat on the type of animal. For example, cold-blooded hibernators, like frogs, lizards, and snakes, enter hibernation when cold weather causes their body temperature to drop too low for activity. When the weather warms up, they warm up, too, and become active again. But in mammals who are not so directly or immediately affected by normal climate changes, hibernation is brought on by a chemical found in the blood. This chemical is called HT, or hibernating inducing trigger. And, as the name implies, when it's released into the blood, it induces the animal to enter hibernation. |
| *Woman:* | I've heard that some animals hibernate in the summer. Is that true? |
| *Professor:* | Yes, it is. In fact, there are three basic types of mammalian hibernation. There's winter hibernation, which you're probably most familiar with; there's estivation, or summer hibernation; and there's diurnal hibernation or daytime hibernation. Some mammals, mostly rodents, hibernate in the summer to protect themselves from heat and food shortages caused by drought. Other mammals, like some species of bats, hibernate just during the day to conserve energy and wait for evening when food supplies, such as insects, are most available. So, you can see that hibernation is a very effective strategy for surviving in times of food scarcity or temperature extremes. |

After you hear the conversation, you will read:

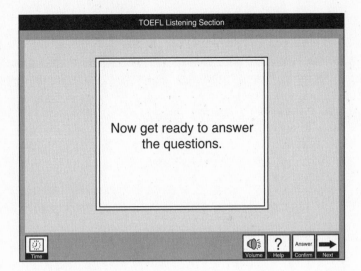

Then you will see and hear the first question:

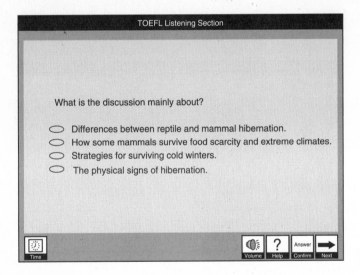

Click on an oval to choose your answer. The oval will darken to indicate your choice. To change your answer, simply click on a different oval. Your old choice will be erased as your new choice is selected. The correct answer is shown on the next screen.

**NOTE**
Usually several pictures go with each talk or conversation. They might include people, charts, or diagrams.

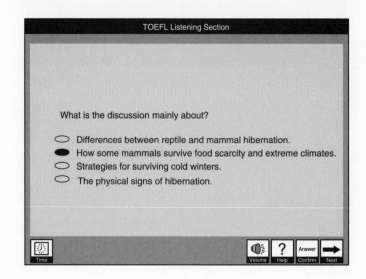

After you have chosen your answer, click Next and Confirm Answer to go to the next question.

Then you will see and hear the second question:

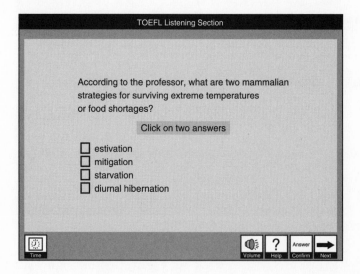

The correct answers are shown on the next screen.

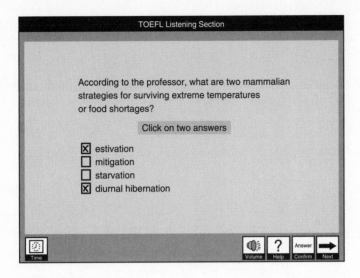

*Example 4*

The topic of a talk will appear on your computer screen.

*Narrator:*    Listen to part of a talk in an English literature class.

**TIP**

Listen for "almost negative" words (such as hardly, barely, and scarcely) which imply that something almost didn't happen, but did. For example, "He barely passed the test" means that he received a low score, but it was just enough for a passing grade. In other words, he *almost* didn't pass the test; his score was very close to failing.

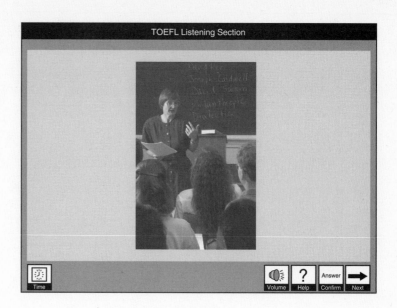

*Professor:*     Although the first books for children written in English appeared as early as the seventh century A.D., the concept of children's literature as a distinct branch of literature did not fully develop until the nineteenth century—more than 1,000 years later! Before the 1800s, few books were written specifically for children and even fewer were designed for their enjoyment. Let's look briefly at the history of this type of literature.

The earliest books were textbooks written in a question-and-answer format and void of illustration. For centuries, this style remained unchanged, and textbooks were the only type of literature available to children. In the 1500s, a series of inexpensive books was published containing much-edited versions of folk tales and ancient legends. But adults considered these books worthless and inappropriate for children. Acceptable books for children were expected to contain school lessons and didactic themes. By *didactic,* I mean that their purpose was to teach important social and moral lessons. Didactic stories and verse extolled the virtues of good behavior and warned of the grave consequenses of disobeying rules. *The New England Primer,* published around 1690 in colonial America, exemplifies this type of didactic literature.

This text, used by many school children in America at the time, contained rhymes for teaching the alphabet, vocabulary, rules for behavior, and stories of Christian saints. In its content and simple illustrations, *The New*

*England Primer* reflected the strict ideals of the Puritans, a prominent and powerful religious group. Puritan ideals strongly influenced the tone and content of children's literature in both England and America for centuries.

Despite this influence, by the mid-1700s there were a number of books that appealed to children's sense of enjoyment and fantasy. Fairy tales, Mother Goose rhymes, and stories like *Gulliver's Travels* were much loved by children. Interestingly, most of this literature was not initially intended for children, but was designed to entertain adults with humor or social commentary. *Gulliver's Travels* was written as a satire on society, and many Mother Goose rhymes are thought to have originated as local lore or tavern songs designed to transmit news about actual people and events. "Tom, Tom the Piper's Son" (who "stole a pig and away he run") is one such rhyme. During the next century, children's literature blossomed with important works in fiction, nonfiction, and poetry. Prominent authors and illustrators specialized in children's books, producing many classic novels, like *Alice's Adventures in Wonderland,* by Lewis Carroll; *Little Women,* by Louisa May Alcott; *Black Beauty,* by Anna Sewell; *Treasure Island,* by Robert Louis Stevenson; and many others. Tomorrow we'll discuss some of these famous works of literature and see what they can tell us about the social climate of the times.

After you hear the talk, you will read:

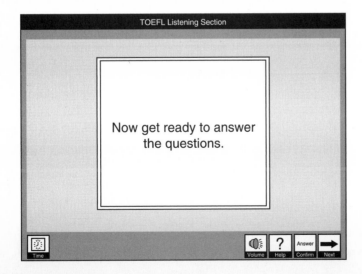

Then you will see and hear the first question:

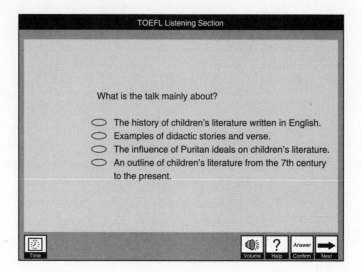

Click on an oval to choose your answer. The oval will darken to indicate your choice. The correct answer is shown below.

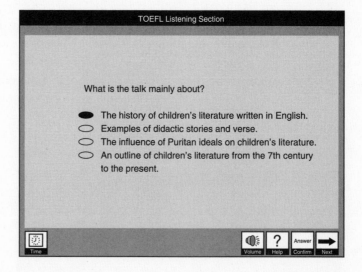

After you have chosen your answer, click Next and Confirm Answer to go to the next question.

Then you will see and hear the second question:

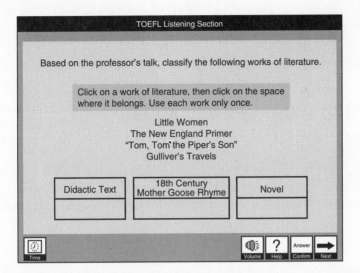

For this type of question, click on a word or phrase, and then click on the space under the category where it belongs. As you do this, the item from the list will appear under the category that you have selected. The correct answer is shown below.

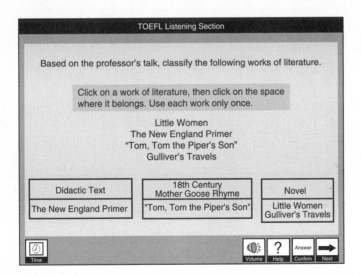

## SAMPLE LISTENING QUESTIONS FOR THE PBT

The Listening Comprehension section for the PBT is divided into three parts:

Part A: Short Conversations—You will listen to a brief conversation between two people and then answer a question about it.

Part B: Long Conversations—You will listen to a longer conversation between two people and then answer approximately four or five questions about what was said.

Part C: Talks—You will listen to a single speaker giving a lecture or talk and then answer approximately four or five questions about what was said.

## PART A: SHORT CONVERSATIONS

*Example:*

On the tape you will hear:

| | |
|---|---|
| *Woman:* | Have you called Pete? |
| *Man:* | I'll call him as soon as I get home. |
| *Narrator:* | Question 1. What does the man mean? |

In your test booklet, you will read:

1. (A) He will call Pete before he goes home.
   (B) He will call Pete after he gets home.
   (C) He called Pete at home.
   (D) He will call Pete tomorrow.

You learn from the conversation that the man will call Pete as soon as he gets home. Therefore, the best answer to the question is choice (**B**), "He will call Pete after he gets home." Indicate your answer by filling in answer space (**B**) for question number 1.

## PART B: LONG CONVERSATIONS

On the tape you will hear:

| | |
|---|---|
| *Narrator:* | Questions 1 and 2 are based on the following conversation between two friends at school. |
| *Man:* | Hi, Joanie. Where are you going? |
| *Woman:* | Oh, hi, Paul. I'm on my way to the library. |
| *Man:* | I just wondered if you wanted to go to a movie with me. |
| *Woman:* | I'd love to, but I can't. I can't believe all the work I have this semester. I only have three classes, but in all of them I have lots of reading, term papers, reports, and essay exams. It's incredible! I feel like I'll never get through everything. |

| | |
|---|---|
| *Man:* | That's terrible. I felt that way last year when I had term papers to write, but this semester seems much easier. I spend a lot of time in class, but most of it is in labs doing experiments. I hated writing all those term papers. Can't I talk you into going to the show anyway? I've heard that the movie over at the East Auditorium is really good. It's a murder mystery. |
| *Woman:* | Oh, now I'm sure I won't go. I might go to a comedy, but I hate murder mysteries. |
| *Narrator:* | Now listen to sample question number 1. Where is the woman going? |

In your test booklet, you will read:

1. (A)  To the cafeteria
   (B)  To the movie theater
   (C)  To her dorm room
   (D)  To the library

The best answer to the question "Where is the woman going?" is choice (**D**), "To the library," because the woman says, "I'm on my way to the library." Therefore, the correct choice is (D), and you should blacken the oval marked D for question number 1.

| | |
|---|---|
| *Narrator:* | Now listen to sample question number 2. Which of the following best describes the man's feeling about his classes? |

In your test booklet you will read:

2. (A)  Term papers are easy for him.
   (B)  He has a lot of essay exams.
   (C)  He finds lab experiments easier than writing term papers.
   (D)  He is busier this semester than last semester.

The best answer to the question is choice (**C**) because the man says that this semester seems much easier because he spends a lot of time in labs doing experiments. Blacken oval C for sample question 2.

## PART C: TALKS

On the tape you will hear:

| | |
|---|---|
| *Narrator:* | Questions 1 to 4 are based on the following announcement: |
| *Woman:* | At this university we offer three different programs for students who have children. For those of you with very young children, we have a day care program that takes |

**NOTE**

In the CBT, you will be able to read the question as well as hear it. In the PBT, you will only hear the question; it will not be written in your test booklet.

infants from 3 months to 24 months. We have another program for children between 2 and 5 years of age. And we also have an after-school program for school-aged children. This program offers sports, crafts, outings, and tutoring during after-school hours. Enrollment in these childcare programs is limited, so early application is essential, since our programs often have waiting lists. The fees are on an hourly basis. If any of you new students need these services, please let me know right away so I can get you an application form.

*Narrator:* Now listen to sample question number 1. What is the main purpose of this announcement?

In your test booklet you will read:

1. (A) To demonstrate tutoring techniques
   (B) To explain school policies
   (C) To recruit childcare workers
   (D) To explain a service

The best answer to the question "What is the purpose of this announcement?" is choice (**D**), "To explain a service." One clue is that, at the end of the talk, the speaker says, "If any of you new students need these services." Indicate your answer by blackening the oval marked D for question number 1.

*Narrator:* Now listen to sample question number 2. What does the speaker recommend?

In your test book you will read:

2. (A) Give your child extra tutoring.
   (B) Take your child to the program today.
   (C) Apply as soon as you can.
   (D) Pay next month.

The best answer to the question "What does the speaker recommend?" is choice (**C**), "Apply as soon as you can," because the speaker says, "Please let me know right away." Blacken oval C for question number 2.

## LISTENING SECTION STRATEGIES

Many TOEFL test takers consider the Listening section to be difficult, in part because the conversations and talks are spoken only once. The talks will not be repeated, and you cannot take notes. Therefore, we suggest practicing the following strategies as you study for the test.

1.  **Do Not Take Notes or Stop the Recording**

    As you take practice tests, do not take notes and do not stop the recording until the end of the test. After you finish the test, check your answers against the anser key.

2.  **Repeat the Test**

    If you missed a lot of questions the first time, listen to the whole test again and answer the questions a second time. Again, do not stop the recording as you take the test. Check your answers again, but this time look at the explanatory answers. This repetition of listening to the recording will help you practice listening comprehension skills.

3.  **Pay Attention to Details**

    As the speakers are talking, pay particular attention to examples, charts, and diagrams on the screen (for the CBT) and to specific names, places, and dates that the speaker mentions. There are often questions about these things.

4.  **Determine the Relationships Between the Speakers**

    If there is more than one speaker, think about the relationship between the speakers. Are they college friends, roommates, or classmates? Are they a professor and a student? Are they students and administrative staff members? Understanding the relationship will help you understand the meaning of the conversation.

5.  **Skim the Answer Choices**

    Although the Listening section is designed to test your ability to understand spoken English, it is also a test of your reading ability because you must read the answer choices. Since time is limited, it is important to read quickly. One way to do this is by skimming. When you skim, you glance quickly over all of the answer choices, rather than reading each line slowly. To do this, let your eyes travel down through the answer choices rather than reading across the lines. When you glance down the answer choices, do the following:

    • Look for words and phrases that are similar in two or more of the answer choices. These similar words give you a clue about the topic and might help you recognize details you heard while listening.

    • Don't just pick an answer simply because it looks (or sounds) similar to words or phrases you heard. Similar-sounding words may have very different meanings.

6.  **Glance at Answer Choices First (only for PBT)**

    The standard procedure is to listen to the recording and then read the answer choices in the test book. However, another technique is to glance at the answer choices before you hear the speaker. By looking very quickly at the answer choices, you get clues about the general topic before you hear the conversation, talk, and questions.

7.  **Scan the Answer Choices as You Listen to the Recording (only for PBT)**

    It may help you focus on the details of the talk or conversation if you look at

**NOTE**
While listening to a class discussion, pay careful attention to students' comments and questions and to how the professor responds to student questions. Information from these student/ teacher interchanges is often in the test questions and answer choices.

the answer choices while the speaker is talking and see if you can match the speaker's words with some of the words in the answer choices. Seeing the answer choices can give you clues about what questions will be asked. You must remember, though, that the answer choices are sometimes very similar, so they might be confusing. If you find that you are losing your place, however, stop reading and focus only on the recording.

# TESTING POINTS

In this section, you will find examples of listening questions and testing points for Part A, short conversations, and Part B/C, long conversations and talks. Each example is followed by an explanation of the testing point.

# PART A: SHORT CONVERSATIONS

In Part A, you first hear two people speak, and then you hear a question. The chart that follows shows common testing points for Part A. Some questions have more than one testing point, and some testing points fit more than one category.

### Testing Points for Part A

| | |
|---|---|
| Vocabulary Word | Tone of voice |
| Idiom/phrasal verb | Similar sounds |
| Verb | |
| Order/sequence | |
| Comparison | |

## Examples of Each Testing Point

In this section are examples of each of the testing points for Part A.

### Vocabulary Word

> *Woman:* How do you like your literature class?
>
> *Man:* I love it; the professor is terrific.
>
> What does the man mean?
> - (A) The teacher is excellent.
> - (B) The professor thinks the new literature book is great.
> - (C) He likes the subject, but he is afraid of the professor.
> - (D) He thinks the class would be better with another teacher.

**The correct answer is (A).** In this question, the testing point is the word *terrific,* which is similar in meaning to *excellent.* The vocabulary words in the Listening section are usually fairly common words, but they are difficult because you only hear the words; you do not see the words written out. When you study new words, therefore, try to listen to the way they are spoken by a native English speaker.

## Idiom/Phrasal Verb

> *Man:*      Did you hear that Kathy just got hired as the new dean?
>
> *Woman:*      Yes. Her effort really paid off.
>
> What does the woman mean?
>
> (A)   Kathy will get paid more as a dean.
>
> (B)   Kathy's hard work had a positive result.
>
> (C)   Kathy could not afford what she wanted.
>
> (D)   Kathy will have more work to do as dean.

**The correct answer is (B).** The phrase that is being tested in this question is "her effort paid off." "To pay off" means to give or receive a full return or a complete benefit for something.

## Verb

> *Man:*      Alice, I expected to see you at the party yesterday.
>
> *Woman:*      If I had known that you were going, I would have gone.
>
> What do we know about the woman?
>
> (A)   She didn't go to the party.
>
> (B)   She didn't remember seeing the man at the party.
>
> (C)   She left the party before the man arrived.
>
> (D)   She didn't want to see the man.

**The correct answer is (A).** The main testing point of this question is the past perfect verb and the past conditional: "If I had known . . . I would have . . . ." In this type of conditional (past/unreal), you need to know that the described event did not happen. Common verb testing points include present perfect tense, passive voice, and conditionals.

## Order/Sequence

| | |
|---|---|
| *Woman:* | Did you have to wait very long before the airplane left? |
| *Man:* | No sooner had we gotten on the airplane than the engine started. |

What does the man mean?

(A) They didn't have enough time to get their seats on the plane.

(B) The pilot had trouble starting the engine.

(C) The engine started as soon as they got on the plane.

(D) They were delayed in the airport.

**The correct answer is (C)**, which restates the man's comment. In this example, you must understand the order of the two things that are happening: First, "we got on the airplane," and second, "the engine started." This question also tests the past perfect verb *had gotten* and the phrases "no sooner than" and "as soon as." The phrase "no sooner" goes with a past tense or past perfect tense and is followed by a comparison beginning with *than*.

## Comparison

| | |
|---|---|
| *Woman:* | I like to play tennis as a way to exercise. |
| *Man:* | I used to feel that way too, but now I think that walking is a better way to exercise. |

What can we infer about the man?

(A) He would rather exercise by walking than by playing tennis.

(B) He doesn't like to walk as much as he likes to play tennis.

(C) His ability to play tennis has improved since he started walking.

(D) He quit playing tennis because it was not enough exercise.

**The correct answer is (A).** This question is classified as "comparison" because of the use of the word *better* and the comparison between playing tennis and walking. This question also tests the modals "used to" and "would rather," and the word *but*, which introduces a contrast. When you hear the word *but*, listen carefully for a change in the thought that follows.

## Tone of Voice

| | |
|---|---|
| *Woman:* | They don't know the news yet. |
| *Man:* | They don't? |

What does the man imply?

(A)   They don't want to hear the news yet.

(B)   He already told them the news.

(C)   He is surprised that they don't know the news.

(D)   They don't have any way to hear the news.

**The correct answer is (C).** Some TOEFL conversations require you to understand the meaning of a speaker's intonation. In this example, the man's tone of voice would go up on the word *don't*. His repetition of the woman's words indicates that he is questioning the woman and is surprised at the woman's comment. We can assume that he expected that "they" already knew the news. If his voice went down instead of up, he might be confirming the woman's comment rather than questioning it.

## Similar Sounds

| | |
|---|---|
| *Woman:* | Why are you taking all these notes? |
| *Man:* | So that I can remember all the new information. |

What does the man mean?

(A)   He is a member of the computer information club.

(B)   He doesn't want to forget what he just learned.

(C)   He is organizing the information by number.

(D)   He is leaving with his notes.

**The correct answer is (B).** In this sentence, the word *remember* sounds like *member*. It also sounds a little like *number*. Any TOEFL listening question might use words in the answer choices that sound like words in the spoken part of the question. To answer this question you must know that *remember* means the same as "not forget," so this question might also be categorized as vocabulary. You also need to know that "taking notes" is very different from "taking something away" or "leaving."

## PART B: LONG CONVERSATIONS AND TALKS

Part B of the Listening section of both the PBT and the CBT includes longer conversations between two people. After each conversation ends, you are asked three or four questions about what was said. You cannot take any notes while you listen to the conversation, so you must listen carefully for the main ideas. Some people taking the PBT like to look at the answer choices in the

**TIP**

Listening for intonation is as important as listening to the words that are being spoken. A rising tone often indicates a question, and a falling tone often indicates agreement.

test booklet while they are listening to the conversation. Other people like to close their eyes and concentrate on the conversation, trying to imagine who is speaking and where they are. If you are taking the PBT, try both of these techniques when you take the practice tests so that you can find out which technique works best for you. If you are taking the CBT, do not close your eyes because you might miss valuable visual information.

The major testing points for Listening Parts B and C are listed next. Most of the questions that follow these long conversations are restatement questions. The next most common question type is inference. Only a few questions ask about the main idea, the preceding or following topics, or the location. The restatement questions may seem easy when you can read the conversation as you can in this example, but these questions are much more difficult when you only get to hear the conversation. Two of the testing points (classification and choose two) are only on the CBT.

### Types of Questions for Long Conversations and Talks

Main idea

Restatement

Inference

Classification (only on CBT)

Choose two (only on CBT)

## Examples of Each Question Type

*Conversation No. 1:* Answer questions 1–4 on the basis of the following conversation between two students.

| | |
|---|---|
| *Man:* | Hello, Lena. |
| *Woman:* | Hi, Kurt. How are you? It's been a long time since I've seen you. Don't you live in the dorm anymore? |
| *Man:* | No, I moved out at the beginning of last semester. |
| *Woman:* | Where are you living now? |
| *Man:* | I moved to the Oak Creek apartments. I'm sharing a unit with three other people: one from Brazil, one from Japan, and one from Hong Kong. |
| *Woman:* | That sounds interesting. How are you getting along with your roommates? |
| *Man:* | Everything is working out just fine, at least up to now. They all share the cooking, and I do the shopping since I have a car. |
| *Woman:* | I guess that would work out. You must have all kinds of |

foods from different countries.

Man:       That's right. I'm really enjoying mealtime! But we've had a few problems.

Woman:     Like what?

Man:       Well, one was that we got confused when the first month's telephone bill came.

Woman:     What happened?

Man:       We couldn't remember who had called each number, so we didn't know how much each person owed. After a lot of discussion, we each ended up paying for the calls we were sure of and dividing the rest equally. Now we all jot down the number whenever we make a call, especially the long-distance calls, and we have no more telephone problems.

Woman:     Hope it stays that way. I'd love to come over and meet your roommates sometime.

Man:       OK. How about coming for dinner? I'll ask them about it and let you know.

Woman:     Great.

## Inference

Where did the man live before?

    (A)   In Oak Creek apartments

    (B)   In a student dorm

    (C)   In a residential house

    (D)   In a fraternity house

**The correct answer is (B).** The woman says, "Don't you live in the dorm anymore?" From this question, we can infer that the man used to live in the dorm.

**TIP**
When a speaker uses a conditional phrase in a sentence, that person may be implying that the opposite of what was said is true. Example: If there were some bread, I would make a sandwich. (This means there is no bread, so I can't make a sandwich.)

## Restatement

> Where do two of the man's roommates come from?
> - (A) Italy and Japan
> - (B) Hong Kong and Singapore
> - (C) Japan and Malaysia
> - (D) Brazil and Japan

**The correct answer is (D).** The man says that his roommates come from Brazil, Japan, and Hong Kong.

## Restatement

> What problem did the roommates have?
> - (A) They didn't know how much each person owed for telephone calls.
> - (B) They couldn't understand each other because they speak different languages.
> - (C) They had difficulty deciding who should cook.
> - (D) They had different lifestyles.

**The correct answer is (A).** The man says that they had a problem remembering who had made each call on their telephone bill.

## Inference

> What can we infer about the woman?
> - (A) She is looking for a new house to rent.
> - (B) She likes to cook.
> - (C) She would like some new roommates.
> - (D) She is friendly.

**The correct answer is (D).** Although all the other answers might be true, the best answer is that the woman is friendly because she says that she would like to meet the man's roommates.

*Conversation No. 2:* Answer questions 5–8 on the basis of the following conversation between two students.

> *Man:* Hi Anna. I haven't seen you around the lab lately. Are you still working here?
>
> *Woman:* Oh, hi George. I am still working for Professor Johnston, at least as much as I can. The trouble is that I'm so busy with my own classes that I don't have enough time for her lab work.

| | |
|---|---|
| *Man:* | Do you have much to do? |
| *Woman:* | Well, not too much at the moment. I'm trying to pull together my data from my work last summer. Professor Johnston is giving a paper about the project in two months, and she needs to include my final results. It's not too much work, but I've got this deadline so that's why I'm here. |
| *Man:* | Are you going to continue working with Professor Johnston next semester? |
| *Woman:* | I hope so. I really like the work, and next semester I'll have more time. She has said that she'd like me to continue with the project. |
| *Man:* | Sounds good. Hey, I've got to get back to my own work now, but it was good running into you. I hope I'll see you around more often. |
| *Woman:* | OK. I hope I see you, too. Bye for now. |

## Inference

Why has the woman come to this place?

(A)   To work on a project

(B)   To see the man

(C)   To talk with Professor Johnston

(D)   To prepare for her presentation

**The correct answer is (A).** The woman says that she is in the lab to "pull together her data" because the professor needs her results. Later she says that Professor Johnston wants her to continue working on the project. From all this, we can infer that she is in the lab to work on the project. Although she is talking to the man, we can also infer that she did not come to the lab in order to see the man, so choice (B) is incorrect. Professor Johnston, not the woman, is going to give a presentation, so choice (D) is wrong.

## Restatement

What does the woman hope to do next semester?

(A)   Take another lab course

(B)   Work for Professor Johnston

(C)   Teach a lab course

(D)   Write up her project

**The correct answer is (B).** The woman says that she hopes to work for Professor Johnston next semester.

**TIP**
Statements with a denial and a negative are difficult because they can have various meanings. For example, the sentence, "I didn't say he wasn't smart" might mean, "I didn't say anything about him" or "I said he was smart."

*Talk No. 1:* Questions 1–5 are based on this talk by a professor on the first day of a class.

I want to begin this class on the history of filmmaking with a discussion of a filmmaker who is known to people throughout the world. You've all heard of Walt Disney. No one has ever delighted more children or adults than Walt Disney, the winner of 31 Academy Awards. Almost everyone has heard of Mickey Mouse and Donald Duck, and his other popular characters like Minnie Mouse, Pluto, and Goofy.

Walt Disney started creating cartoon animations in 1920, but it was in 1928 when his best-known character, Mickey Mouse, came to life. Disney also created the first sound cartoon, which he called *Steamboat Willie*. It was in this cartoon that he introduced Mickey to the public. In 1937, Walt Disney made movie history again with the first full-length cartoon film, *Snow White and the Seven Dwarfs*. In the 1950s, Walt Disney created a series of nature films. He was always planning something new. In 1955, he opened Disneyland, the "magic kingdom," in Anaheim, California. Even at his death in 1966, he was planning another massive project: Florida's Walt Disney World. Since Walt Disney's death, his film company has continued to grow and attract the public, even producing new cartoons by computer animation.

## Main Idea

What is the speaker mainly discussing?
- (A)    The life and times of Walt Disney
- (B)    Famous Disney characters
- (C)    Walt Disney's work
- (D)    The importance of Disney's industry

**The correct answer is (C).** The speaker continues to refer to Walt Disney's work: his cartoon characters, his nature films, and his amusement parks.

## Restatement

In which year did Walt Disney first begin creating cartoon animations?
- (A)    1920
- (B)    1928
- (C)    1950
- (D)    1955

**The correct answer is (A).** The speaker says that Walt Disney first started creating cartoon animation in 1920.

What was the name of Disney's first full-length cartoon film?

(A)    Steamboat Willie

(B)    Snow White and the Seven Dwarfs

(C)    Disney World

(D)    Mickey Mouse

**The correct answer is (B).** The speaker says that the name of the first full-length cartoon film was *Snow White and the Seven Dwarfs*.

## Inference

Which of the following was NOT planned by Walt Disney himself?

(A)    Mickey Mouse

(B)    Nature films

(C)    Disneyland

(D)    Computerized cartoons

**The correct answer is (D).** The speaker says that computerized cartoons were developed after Disney's death.

## Classification

This type of question, for which you classify items in boxes, is found on the CBT, not the PBT.

Based on the talk, classify the following Disney titles. Click on the title and then click on the space where it belongs.

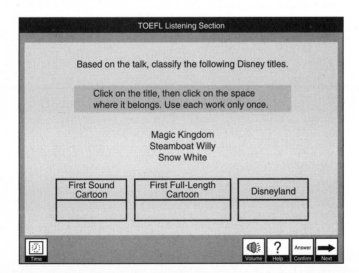

The answer is shown on the next screen.

**NOTE**

In the PBT Listening section, there are three parts: A, B, and C. The CBT, however, contains only two parts: A and B. Part B of the CBT includes questions that are in B and C of the PBT.

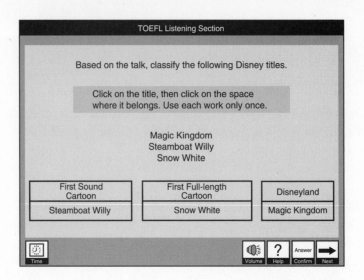

*Talk No. 2:* Questions 6–8 are based on this lecture to an architecture class.

Now that you've put some time into the practical work of this course, drawing house plans, let's go back to our continuing discussion of famous architects. Today's architect is Samuel McIntire, a man from Salem, Massachusetts, who lived during the latter half of the eighteenth century, just as the United States was beginning to become a nation. McIntire had very little formal training; he learned his skill from his father, a carpenter-builder, and from architectural books. Besides doing carpentry and architectural work, McIntire became a very skilled wood sculptor, which was demonstrated in his work throughout his life.

Samuel McIntire was honored as the architect of Salem since he designed so many of the town buildings and residences. His first important commission, for the Pierce-Nichols House, came when he was only 22 years old. When this house was completed in 1782, it had more classical details than any other house in town, and it established McIntire as an up-and-coming young architect among the affluent merchants of the growing town. The exteriors of McIntire's houses were influenced by other architects of his time, but McIntire's interiors were unique. They demonstrated his love of and his skill in decorative carving.

## Restatement

How did McIntire learn his skill?

    (A)    From affluent merchants

    (B)    From his father

    (C)    From classes at school

    (D)    From his coworkers

**The correct answer is (B).** The speaker says that McIntire learned his skill from his father.

## Inference

> What was unique about McIntire's houses?
>
> (A)    The wood exteriors
>
> (B)    The classical designs
>
> (C)    The inside wood carvings
>
> (D)    The decorative gardens

**The correct answer is (C).** The speaker says that McIntire's interiors were unique. Then he says that they demonstrated McIntire's love of and skill in decorative carving. Since the speaker talks about the decorative carving after he says that McIntire's interiors were unique, we can assume that the decorative carvings are what is unique.

## Choose Two

This type of question, in which two answers are asked for, is found on the CBT, not the PBT.

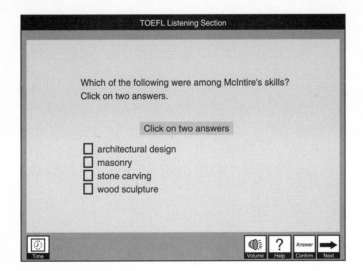

The answer is indicated here. The speaker said that McIntire designed buildings and was a skilled wood sculptor.

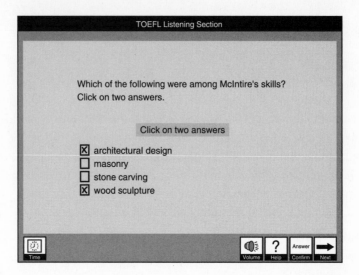

# Summary: What You Need to Know About the TOEFL Listening Section

- The Listening section tests your ability to understand conversations and talks in English.

- The TOEFL CBT and PBT are slightly different. The CBT has two parts: Part A (Short Conversations) and Part B (Long Conversations and Talks). The PBT has three parts: Part A (Short Conversations), Part B (Long Conversations), and Part C (Talks).

- In the CBT, the Listening section is computer adaptive. This means that you must answer each question when it is given on the screen. Once you answer a question, you cannot go back to view it again.

- The Short Conversations consist of two speakers with one question following the dialogue.

- The Long Conversations consist of conversations or between two or more speakers followed by several questions.

- The Talks consist of a single speaker's talk, followed by several questions. Often, the talks are lectures by a professor and questions, responses, or comments by several students.

- For the CBT, you see pictures on the computer screen during the Listening section, and you listen through individual headphones. You will both see and hear the questions. You cannot take any notes. The pictures, diagrams, or charts on the computer give valuable information that helps you remember facts on which you might be tested.

- For the PBT, you will hear the taped recording from a cassette tape player in the testing room. You cannot take any notes.

- The testing points for Part A include vocabulary words, idioms or phrasal verbs, order or sequence of events, comparison, intonation, and similar sounds.

- The question types for Part B (and Part C in the PBT) include main idea, restatement, inference, classification, and choose-two.

# Structure Section

The Structure section of the TOEFL includes two different types of questions, sentence completion and error identification, each with its own special directions. Both question types measure your ability to recognize standard written English and correct grammatical form. On the CBT, the two question types are mixed together, so just one section contains both types of questions. On the PBT, these two sections are separated into Part 1 and Part 2.

## SAMPLE STRUCTURE QUESTIONS FOR THE CBT

This section consists of two different question types: sentence completion and error identification.

## SENTENCE COMPLETION QUESTIONS

For sentence completion questions, the directions and question will appear on your computer screen, followed by four answer choices.

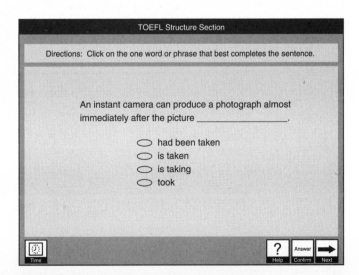

Click on an oval to choose your answer. The oval will darken to indicate your choice. To change your answer, simply click on a different oval. Your old choice will be erased as your new choice is selected. The correct answer is shown on the next screen.

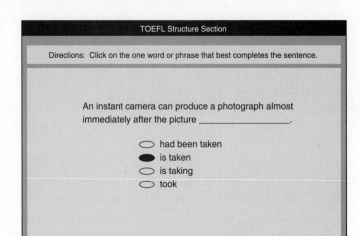

After you have chosen your answer, click Next and Confirm Answer to go to the next question.

## ERROR IDENTIFICATION QUESTIONS

For error identification questions, the directions and a sentence with four underlined words or phrases will appear on your screen.

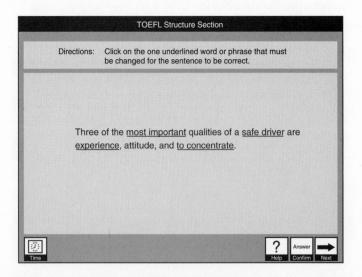

Clicking on a word or phrase will darken it, indicating your answer choice. To change your answer, simply click on a different word or phrase. Your old choice will be erased as your new choice is selected. The correct answer is shown on the next screen.

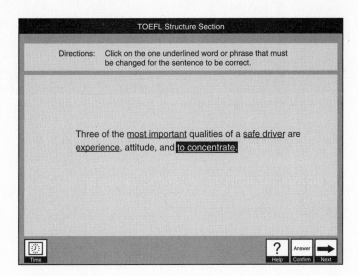

After you have chosen your answer, click Next and Confirm Answer to go to the next question.

# SAMPLE STRUCTURE QUESTIONS FOR THE PBT

The Structure and Written Expression section of the PBT includes two different types of questions, sentence completion and error identification, each with its own special directions. Both question types measure your ability to recognize standard written English.

## PART 1: SENTENCE COMPLETION QUESTIONS

The sentences in this part are not complete. One or more words are left out of each sentence. Under each sentence you will see four words or phrases marked (A), (B), (C), and (D). Choose the one word or phrase that completes the sentence correctly. Then, on your answer sheet, find the number of the question and fill in the oval that corresponds to the letter of your answer choice.

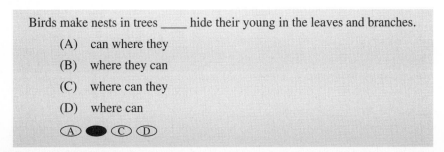

The sentence should read, "Birds make nests in trees where they can hide their young in the leaves and branches." Therefore, you should select choice **(B)**.

Sleeping, resting, and _____ are the best ways to care for a cold.

   (A)   to drink fluids

   (B)   drank fluids

   (C)   one drink fluids

   (D)   drinking fluids

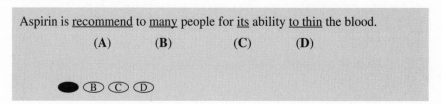

The sentence should read, "Sleeping, resting, and drinking fluids are the best ways to care for a cold." The three words should all be parallel; therefore, you should select choice (**D**).

# PART 2: ERROR IDENTIFICATION QUESTIONS

In this part, each sentence has four underlined words or phrases that are marked (A), (B), (C), and (D). Choose the one word or phrase that must be changed for the sentence to be correct. On your answer sheet, find the number of the question and fill in the oval that corresponds to the letter of your answer choice.

Aspirin is <u>recommend</u> to <u>many</u> people for <u>its</u> ability <u>to thin</u> the blood.
          (A)         (B)         (C)      (D)

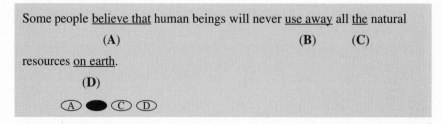

The sentence should read, "Aspirin is recommended to many people for its ability to thin the blood." The verb in this sentence should be in the passive voice. Therefore, you should select choice (**A**).

Some people <u>believe that</u> human beings will never <u>use away</u> all <u>the</u> natural
          (A)                          (B)     (C)

resources <u>on earth</u>.
      (D)

The sentence should read, "Some people believe that human beings will never use up all the natural resources on earth." Therefore, you should select choice (**B**). The correct two-word verb "use up" is an idiom meaning "use all of something until it is gone."

**NOTE**

Look for the main subject and verb. Many test questions can be answered more easily after you have identified the main subject and verb.

# STRUCTURE SECTION STRATEGIES

The two types of questions in the Structure section have different test-taking strategies. These strategies are described next.

## SENTENCE COMPLETION STRATEGIES

1. Look for the main subject and verb of the sentence. If there is no complete subject or verb phrase, you know that you need to find these in the answer choices.

2. To help you see the main subject and verb, simplify the sentence by taking out the prepositional phrases (a preposition plus article, adjective, and/or noun).

   Simplifying a sentence is like taking the leaves off a tree so that you can see the trunk clearly. When you simplify a sentence, you can see the testing point more clearly. You also save time because you don't waste time trying to figure out the meanings of words that you might not need in order to find the answer.

3. Decide what kind of structure the sentence needs. Use the testing points in this chapter to help you decide what is needed.

4. Read the sentence to see if it makes sense and sounds correct.

## ERROR IDENTIFICATION STRATEGIES

1. Read the sentence through quickly to see if you recognize the error. Use the testing points in this chapter of this book to help you identify possible errors.

2. If you do not see the error immediately, then simplify the sentence, focusing on the main subject, verb, and maybe the object of the sentence.

3. Look at the underlined words to see what part of speech they are and how they relate to the main subject and verb.

4. Think through the testing points listed in this book, checking each underlined word or phrase to see if it is correct.

# TESTING POINTS

This section gives lists and examples of common testing points for the questions in the Structure section of the TOEFL.

**NOTE**
You do not need to know the meaning of every word in each sentence in the Structure section to answer the question correctly. If you do not know the meaning of some words in the sentence, don't worry about it. Try to focus on the general meaning and the structure of the sentence.

## PART 1: SENTENCE COMPLETION

### Testing Points for Sentence Completion Questions

| | |
|---|---|
| Noun phrase | Adverb phrase/clause |
| Word order | Comparison |
| Subject + verb | Infinitive/gerund |
| Verb/verb phrase | Preposition/prepositional phrase |
| Adjective phrase/clause | Superlative |
| Conjunction | Negative |
| Parallel construction | Conditional |
| | Pronoun |

## Examples of Each Testing Point

### Noun Phrase

A noun phrase or a single noun are common testing points. The nouns might be the subject of the sentence, the object of a verb, or the object of a phrase in the sentence.

> For people with mouth or gum problems, the dentist might prescribe _____ twice a day as partial treatment.
>
> (A)   if irrigate
>
> (B)   irrigates
>
> (C)   irrigates
>
> (D)   irrigation

To simplify, take out the prepositional phrases:

(For people) (with mouth or gum problems), the dentist might prescribe _____ twice a day (as partial treatment).

The main subject is "the dentist," and the verb phrase is "might prescribe."

This sentence needs a noun phrase after the verb "prescribe." The noun tells what the dentist might prescribe. This sentence is an example of the regular pattern in English: subject, verb, object.

> _____ the economy's performance, strengths, and weaknesses are the tables, charts, and data published by public and private agencies.
>
> (A)   Analyzing
>
> (B)   The tools for analyzing
>
> (C)   The analysis of
>
> (D)   There are tools of

**TIP**

To prepare for the TOEFL, you must do two things: increase your test-taking skills and increase your knowledge of the English language. To increase your test-taking skills, go through the practice tests as quickly and carefully as you can. To increase your knowledge of English, go back to the practice tests after you have taken them, and study the words and structures that were difficult for you.

To simplify, take out the prepositional phrase:

_____ the economy's performance, strengths, and weaknesses are the tables, charts, and data published (by public and private agencies).

The main verb is "are." This sentence needs a noun phrase to complete the subject.

For this sentence, try each answer to see if it makes sense.

> **TIP**
>
> A noun clause sometimes can be the subject of a sentence. For example, look at the sentence "That you have purchased this book indicates your desire to do well on the TOEFL." In this sentence, the main subject is the noun clause "that you have purchased this book," and "indicates" is the main verb.

    (A)    The word "analyzing" could be a subject, but it does not make sense.

    (B)    This is the correct answer: The tools . . . are analyzing . . . tables, charts, . . . .

    (C)    This does not make sense. An analysis is not a table. An analysis is performed from or results in a table or chart.

    (D)    The simplification of the sentence shows that it already has a main verb, so this noun + verb is not correct.

## Word Order

In this type of testing point, the four answer choices contain the same words or similar words, but in different order. This category of testing point also tests your knowledge of verb phrases, noun phrases, adjectives, and adverbs.

> Duplicating the recent history of airborne achievements, the galleries of the National Air and Space Museum _____.
>
>     (A)   exhibit a collection fascinating
>
>     (B)   fascinate an exhibit collection
>
>     (C)   collection a fascinating exhibit
>
>     (D)   exhibit a fascinating collection

To simplify, take out the prepositional phrases:

Duplicating the recent history (of airborne achievements), the galleries(of the National Air and Space Museum) _____.

The main subject is "the galleries." The sentence needs a verb phrase.

Try all answers to see which is correct.

    (A)    This answer begins with a verb but is incorrect in the order of adjective and noun: "collection fascinating" is incorrect. The adjective should come before the noun.

    (B)    This choice does not make sense. Though the galleries may be fascinating, they must be fascinating to people, not to a collection.

**NOTE**
Always read the entire question sentence, not just the answer choices. Most answer choices are correct by themselves and incorrect only when they are used in the particular sentence.

(C)    This answer does not have a verb, and this sentence needs a verb.

(D)    Although the word "exhibit" is often a noun, in this sentence it is a verb.

## Subject + Verb

In this type of testing point, the subject and the verb are in the answer choices. Both are needed to complete the sentence.

_____ all summer, sipping nectar and collecting pollen from flowers.

(A)    Bumblebees are the busy

(B)    Busy bumblebees are

(C)    Being busy bumblebees

(D)    Bumblebees are busy

To simplify, take out the prepositional phrase:

_____ all summer, sipping nectar and collecting pollen (from flowers.)

There is no main subject or main verb. The verb phrases "sipping" and "collecting" describe the main subject.

Try all the answers.

(A)    The article "the" is incorrect in front of "busy" because there is no noun after the word "busy."

(B)    This answer would need an object after "are" to describe the bees.

(C)    This answer has no main verb.

(D)    This answer is correct. It provides a subject ("bumblebees") and a main verb ("are").

## Verb Phrase

Many different testing points can fall into this category. You need to check the answer choices to be sure the verb is in the right tense, that it agrees with the subject in number (singular or plural), and that it is in the right voice (active or passive). When you simplify the sentence, be sure you know which verb should agree with which noun.

The batteries in cordless handheld vacuum cleaners _____ hundreds of times.

(A)    can be recharged

(B)    recharging

(C)    recharged

(D)    was recharged

To simplify, take out the prepositional phrases:

The batteries (in cordless, handheld vacuum cleaners) _____ hundreds (of times.)

Try each answer.

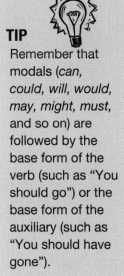

- (A)    This is the correct answer. The sentence describes a fact and uses passive voice and the modal "can."

- (B)    This choice is incorrect because it leaves the sentence without a verb.

- (C)    This is not correct because the verb must be passive.

- (D)    This is incorrect because the verb is singular instead of plural.

The main subject is "batteries." There is no main verb.

## Adjective Phrase/Clause

The testing point in this category might be a relative pronoun, a relative clause, or an adjective participle. You can sometimes find the answer if you ask the question "what kind of . . . ?"

> Societies must often adapt to changes _____ political or economic factors.
>
> (A)   which may be brought on by
>
> (B)   to which are brought
>
> (C)   for bringing on
>
> (D)   can be brought by

The main subject is "societies" and the verb phrase is "must often adapt to." The sentence needs an adjective clause to describe the changes.

Try each answer.

- (A)    This is the correct answer. It supplies a clause that tells what kind of changes.

- (B)    This is incorrect because it means "factors are brought to changes" and this does not make sense.

- (C)    It does not make sense to say "changes for bringing on political and economic factors."

- (D)    The sentence needs the word "which" as a relative pronoun to refer to "changes."

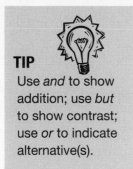

**TIP**

Use *and* to show addition; use *but* to show contrast; use *or* to indicate alternative(s).

## Conjunction

Common conjunctions are the following:

| | |
|---|---|
| and | both . . . and |
| or | either . . . or |
| but | neither . . . nor |
| for | |

This category also includes connective words such as these:

| | |
|---|---|
| because | so . . . that |
| in order to | however |

> Most libraries have general collections of reference works, such as periodicals, pamphlets, _____ books.
>
> (A)   for
>
> (B)   yet
>
> (C)   but
>
> (D)   and

To simplify, take out the prepositional phrase:

Most libraries have general collections (of reference works,) such as periodicals, pamphlets _____ or books.

The subject is "libraries" and the main verb is "have."

The sentence needs the conjunction "and" to indicate that all three items are included. The answer is choice (**D**).

## Parallel Construction

Words or phrases used in a series should be the same part of speech. Usually a comma separates the words or phrases.

> After you have turned over the soil, weeded, and _____ , you'll be ready to plant.
>
> (A)   cultivating
>
> (B)   cultivation
>
> (C)   cultivated
>
> (D)   cultivate

There are two clauses in this sentence. The main subject and verb are in the second clause: the subject is "you" and the verb phrase is "will be ready to plant." The first clause has three verbs separated by commas. This is a common clue for a parallel construction testing point. The correct answer is choice (**C**), a verb form that is in the past, like "turned over" and "weeded."

## Adverb Phrase/Clause

This category includes single adverbs or adverbial phrases or clauses. The words often answer the questions *how, when, where,* or *why.*

> Arlington National Cemetery was built _____ and other war heroes during the American Civil War.
>
> (A)   according to honor
>
> (B)   for honor of soldiers
>
> (C)   in order to honor soldiers
>
> (D)   to soldiers that were honored

To simplify, take out the prepositional phrase:

Arlington National Cemetery was built _____ and other war heroes (during the American Civil War.)

The main subject is "Arlington National Cemetery," and the main verb phrase is "was built."

The sentence needs an adverb phrase to modify the verb "built." The adverb phrase answers the question "Why was it built?"

Look at each choice:

(A)   This is incorrect because it makes no sense to say "to honor and other war heroes."

(B)   The preposition "for" is incorrect. It is incorrect to say "was built for honor of."

(C)   This is the correct answer.

(D)   The word "to" is incorrect. It is incorrect to say "was built to soldiers."

## Comparison

In a comparison question, you will often see these phrases:

the more _____, the more

more _____ than

_____ rather than

_____ the same as _____.

> Espresso coffee makers require more attention than _____.
>
> (A)   drip coffee makers are
>
> (B)   drip coffee makers
>
> (C)   are other drip coffee makers
>
> (D)   so do the other coffee makers

**TIP**

Some verbs are commonly followed by infinitives, such as *want, wish, hope, ask, offer, promise, pretend, intend, begin, attempt, decide, learn, desire, agree, choose, expect,* and *need.* Therefore, we say "I want to go," not "I want going."

This sentence has no prepositional phrase.

The main subject is "coffee makers," and the main verb is "require."

The sentence is comparing espresso coffee makers with drip coffee makers. It needs a noun phrase to be parallel with the noun phrase "espresso coffee makers." Choice (**B**) is correct. The other answers add an unnecessary verb.

## Infinitive/Gerund

This category includes both infinitives and gerunds. Sometimes you are asked to choose between an infinitive, a gerund, and another verb form.

> Walruses use their long tusks to pull themselves out of the water and _____ themselves.
>
> (A)   protecting
>
> (B)   to protect
>
> (C)   protected
>
> (D)   was protected

To simplify, take out the prepositional phrase.

Walruses use their long tusks to pull themselves out (of the water) and _____ themselves.

The main subject is "walruses" and the main verb is "use."

**The correct answer is (B).** An infinitive must follow the verb phrase "use their tusks." The word "to" means "in order to." The two infinitives "to pull" and "to protect" must be parallel.

## Preposition/Prepositional Phrase

The testing points in a prepositional phrase might be the preposition, the noun, or the article.

> President Lincoln was assassinated in Ford's Theater _____ the night of April 14, 1865.
>
> (A)   on
>
> (B)   at
>
> (C)   by
>
> (D)   in

To simplify, take out the prepositional phrases.

President Lincoln was assassinated (in Ford's Theater) _____ the night (of April 14, 1865.)

The main subject is "President Lincoln," and the main verb is "was assassinated."

**The correct answer is (A),** "on the night of April 14, 1865."

**TIP**

Some verbs are commonly followed by gerunds, such as *suggest, finish, avoid, can't help, mind, enjoy, postpone, put off, delay, advise, consider, deny,* and *miss.* Therefore, we say, "I finished doing my homework," not "I finished to do my homework."

## Superlative

The testing point might be the word "the" before the superlative form, or it might be the phrase "one of the x."

> Franklin Delano Roosevelt was one of _____ Presidents in American history.
>
>     (A)   such an energetic
>
>     (B)   most energetic
>
>     (C)   energetic
>
>     (D)   the most energetic

This answer for this sentence is part of the prepositional phrase.

The main subject is "Franklin Delano Roosevelt" and the verb is "was."

The phrase "one of . . ." is a clue that you need a superlative construction.

The correct form is "one of the most" + adjective. **The correct answer is (D).**

## Negative

Common words in this testing point are *no, not, none, nothing,* and *nobody.*

> Beer contains _____ live yeast when it leaves the brewery.
>
>     (A)   no
>
>     (B)   not
>
>     (C)   none
>
>     (D)   neither

There is no prepositional phrase in this sentence.

The main subject is "beer" and the verb is "contains."

**The correct answer is (A).** In this sentence, the word "live" is an adjective that rhymes with "alive" or "dive." It describes something that is living. The word "no" comes before the noun phrase "live yeast."

## Conditional

There are three types of conditional sentences:

1. Real (present/future) conditional
2. Unreal (present) conditional
3. Unreal past conditional

---

**TIP**

Learn to recognize common endings of nouns, adjectives, and adverbs.

- Nouns often end in the letters -ion, -tion, -sion, -ment, -ness, -ity, -ence, or -ance (such as *nation, impression, kindness, intelligence*).
- Nouns that refer to people often end in the letters -er, -ist, -ian, or -or (such as *teacher, typist, beautician, supervisor*).
- Adjectives often end in the letters -ic, -ish, -ive, -y, -ous, or -al (such as *athletic, childish, native*).
- Adverbs often end in -ly (such as *happily*).

---

**TIP**

Negative words such as *no, not, none,* and *neither* can be confusing.

- Use "no" to make a noun negative: No person can do this job alone.

- Use "not" to make a verb or adjective negative: He did not receive the letter.

- Use "none" when there is no noun after it: He and I have one, but she has none.

- Use "neither" with "nor": Neither he nor she has much money.

_____ travelers checks, you may not need to carry money.

    (A)   If you carry

    (B)   To carry

    (C)   If he had carried

    (D)   For carrying

This sentence has no prepositional phrase.

The main subject and verb are in the second part of the sentence. The subject is "you" and the main verb is "may not need."

This sentence is an example of a real (present/future) conditional. **The correct answer is (A).** The other answers make sense in the first part of the sentence, but they do not logically fit with the second half.

## Pronoun

Any type of pronoun might be the testing point: subject, object, demonstrative, or relative pronoun.

The opposite of love is hate, an emotion directed toward any disturbing factor, whatever _____ may be.

    (A)   that

    (B)   those

    (C)   them

    (D)   they

To simplify, take out the prepositional phrase:

The opposite (of love) is hate, an emotion directed toward any disturbing factor, whatever _____ may be.

The main subject is "the opposite" and the main verb is "is."

**The correct answer is (A).** The pronoun "that" refers to the single noun "factor." Choices (B) and (D) are plural, so they are incorrect. Choice (C) is incorrect because it is an object pronoun, not a subject pronoun.

## PART 2: ERROR IDENTIFICATION

### Testing Points for Error Identification Questions

| | |
|---|---|
| Word form | Preposition |
| Verb | Reversed words |
| Pronoun | Conjunction |
| Parallel construction | Infinitive/gerund |
| Singular/plural noun | Comparative |
| Mistaken words | Superlative |
| Unnecessary word | Article |
| Omitted word | |

## Examples of Each Testing Point
### Word Form

Incorrect word forms are the most common testing point in error identification problems. This category refers to words that are written in the wrong form; that is, a noun might be written as an adjective, or an adjective might be written as an adverb. When two or more words are written in a series, they must be written in the same form. The series of words might be nouns, verbs, and/or adjectives.

> A comfort running shoe has good arch support and enough room for toes.
> (A)                    (B)        (C)                        (D)

The word "comfort" is incorrectly written as a noun, but this sentence already has a main noun. The correct word should be "comfortable," an adjective that describes the noun "shoe." The answer is (**A**).

> A full-sized tripod is the most effectively way to steady a camera.
> (A)            (B)      (C)              (D)

The subject and verb are fine. The answer is (**C**). The word "effectively" is an adverb; it should be the adjective "effective" to modify the noun "way."

> Oils left in a pan after cooking can turn rancid affects the food that is cooked
> (A)              (B)                            (C)          (D)
> next.

The subject and verb are correct. The answer is (**C**). The word "affects" should be "affecting," in order to begin an adverb phrase that describes what happens after oils become rancid.

## Verb

This category includes errors in verb tense, verb agreement, and voice.

> Whether you ride your bike 30 miles a day or 30 miles a year, a helmet, adjusted
>                                          (A)                              (B)
> for a snug fit, should be wear on every ride.
>                          (C)        (D)

**The correct answer is (C).** The subject, "helmet," is receiving the action; therefore, the verb should be in the passive voice: "should be worn."

Clothes <u>made of</u> polyester fabric <u>needs</u> <u>little</u> or no <u>ironing</u>.
    (A)                      (B)  (C)      (D)

The subject is "clothes" and the main verb should be plural, "need." The answer is (**B**). The phrase "made of polyester fabric" describes the main noun, "clothes."

## Pronoun

This category includes subject, object, possessive, or relative pronouns.

Never <u>use</u> a drug <u>prescribed</u> for someone else just because <u>its</u> symptoms
      (A)         (B)                             (C)

<u>appear</u> similar.
  (D)

The subject of this sentence is not written. It is the word "you," which is the unwritten subject of the verb "use." This part of the sentence is correct. The error is choice (**C**). The pronoun "its" refers to an object, which in this sentence would be the word "drug." This is not logical, however. The drug does not have symptoms. The correct pronoun is "your."

## Parallel Construction

Words that are written in a series must all be the same part of speech. This type of error may also be categorized as word form.

A <u>good</u> worker <u>is</u> conscientious, <u>reliable</u>, and <u>efficiency</u>.
 (A)      (B)                 (C)       (D)

The answer is (**D**). All three words describe a good worker. They must all be adjectives. The word "efficiency" is incorrect in this sentence because it is a noun. The correct word is "efficient."

## Singular/Plural Noun

For this testing point, a plural noun might be written as singular or with the wrong plural ending. A singular noun may be written as plural or it might have an unnecessary s. Mass nouns can be plural without adding an s.

Studies <u>have shown</u> that you can <u>exercise in</u> many different ways at a
      (A)                       (B)

moderate <u>paces</u> and <u>still</u> gain good results.
     (C)     (D)

The subject and verb are correct in this sentence, so you need to look at the words that describe what the studies have shown. The phrase "at a moderate paces" must be incorrect because of the combination of the word "a" and a plural noun. The answer is (**C**).

## Mistaken Words

This category includes words that are commonly confused, such as *make* instead of *do*, *little* instead of *few*, *separate* instead of *apart*, or *listen* instead of *hear*.

> Much children like to get their faces painted with bright colors at community
> (A)          (B)      (C)      (D)
> fairs.

The subject and verb in this sentence are correct, but the noun "children" must be preceded by the word "many" because it is a countable noun. The plural of the countable noun "child" is "children." The answer is (**A**).

## Unnecessary Words

Sometimes a word that should not be in a sentence is added to the sentence. This might result in a double subject, a double negative, a repeated similar adjective or adverb, or an unnecessary preposition.

> While push-ups build your arms, shoulders, and chest, sit-ups they
> (A)                                                          (B)
> strengthen your abdominal muscles.
>        (C)              (D)

The answer is (**B**). The word "they" after "sit-ups" is an unnecessary word. It results in a double subject. The correct phrase is "sit-ups strengthen your . . . muscles."

## Omitted Words

In this category, a necessary word is left out of a sentence. It is often a preposition or an article.

> Yosemite National Park is most well known its beautiful spouting geysers of
>                          (A)      (B)        (C)
> all sizes.
>     (D)

**TIP**
Whenever you see the singular "a" or "an" that is not underlined, you know the noun that follows must be singular. Look carefully at articles that are not underlined, and use them as a clue to help you decide whether the noun that comes after the article is written correctly.

**TIP**
Use the word *many* to modify a countable noun. Use the word *much* to modify an uncountable noun.

**NOTE**

The category called Omitted Words category is a very difficult category because it is harder to think of something that is missing than it is to pick out a mistake that you can see. Read the whole sentence to yourself to see if one of the words sounds strange but seems correct. If you think a word is missing, choose the underlined word that is next to the missing word.

The subject and verb are correct. You must look at the rest of the sentence. The answer is (**B**) because the word "known" in this sentence must be followed by "for."

## Prepositions

Any preposition might be used incorrectly.

| Surprisingly, a feeling of tiredness may result of a lack of exercise. |
| --- |
| (A)         (B)               (C)     (D) |

The answer is (**C**). After the verb "result," there should be the preposition "in" or "from." Each of these words gives a different meaning to this sentence, but both could be correct in this context. With "result in," the sentence means that a person does not exercise because he or she feels tired. With "result from," a person feels tired because he or she does not exercise. Because the sentence begins with the word "surprisingly," then "result from" probably is the expected correct preposition.

| When having difficulties, many people try for get help from a |
| --- |
| (A)         (B)        (C)     (D) |
| professional. |

The answer is (**C**). In this sentence, after the verb "try," you need the preposition "to."

## Reversed Words

In this category, two words are in the wrong order; that is, an adjective might be written after a noun instead of before the noun.

| Specialization in industry creates workers lack who versatility in their ability |
| --- |
| (A)         (B)        (C)          (D) |
| to step in to other jobs. |

The subject and verb are correct. The answer is (**C**). The words "lack who" should be "who lack." The word "who" describes the "workers" in this sentence.

## Conjunctions

Some common conjunctions are the following: *and, or, but, both, for, neither . . . nor,* and *not only . . . but also.*

<u>A</u> sailing vessel is not only a vehicle <u>for</u> work and play <u>and</u> also a wind-driven
(A)                                                     (B)                         (C)

work <u>of</u> art.
(D)

The first part of the sentence contains the words "not only," so you should look for the words "but also." The correct answer is (**C**). The word "and" should be "but."

Neither the <u>revolution in</u> industry <u>and</u> <u>that</u> in agriculture could have proceeded
                         (A)                        (B) (C)

without the <u>progress in</u> communication and transportation.
                         (D)

The answer is (**B**). The word "neither" goes with "nor." The correct sentence is "Neither the revolution in industry nor that in agriculture could have proceeded without . . . ."

## Infinitive/Gerunds

Except <u>in cases of</u> extreme emergency, police officers <u>are</u> required <u>obeying</u>
              (A)                                                              (B)             (C)

all traffic <u>laws</u>.
                (D)

The main subject and verb are correct. The word "required" in this sentence must be followed by an infinitive, "to obey." The answer is (**C**).

## Comparatives

The specific testing points might be the ending -er or the phrase *more . . . than* or a construction like *as . . . as*.

Disneyland was Walt Disney's <u>special</u> dream <u>for</u> more <u>as</u> twenty years before it
                                             (A)              (B)        (C)

<u>became</u> a reality.
   (D)

The main subject and verb are correct. The answer is (**C**). The word "more" should be followed by "than."

## Articles

The words *a, an*, and *the* are often used incorrectly.

> Scientists have gained <u>the</u> great deal of information about the large animals
>                      (A)
>
> <u>called</u> dinosaurs <u>that</u> lived <u>millions of</u> years ago.
>  (B)            (C)          (D)

The answer is (**A**). The phrase "a great deal of" means "a lot" or "much."

## Superlatives

In this category, you might be tested on the word *the* or *most* or the ending -est in a superlative phrase.

> <u>The staff</u> is often the most <u>importantest</u> of all the <u>resources</u> of an institution <u>or</u>
>   (A)                         (B)               (C)           (D)
>
> business.

The subject and verb are correct. The answer is (B). The correct superlative phrase is "the most important."

# Summary: What You Need to Know About the TOEFL Structure Section

- The Structure section tests your ability to recognize standard written English.

- The Structure section is similar in both the CBT and the PBT. It includes two types of questions: sentence completion and error identification. In the PBT, the questions are separated into two parts. In the CBT, they are mixed.

- In the CBT, the structure section is computer-adaptive. This means that you must answer each question when it is given on the screen. Once you answer a question, you cannot go back to view it again. Also, you will be given questions based on your ability level, so you might have questions that are different from anyone else in the testing room.

- To help you choose the correct answer in the sentence completion questions, look for the main subject and verb of the sentence. To help you find these, simplify the sentence by mentally removing the prepositional phrases.

- For the error identification sentences, read through the sentence quickly to see if you recognize an error. Look at the main subject and verb, prepositions, word forms, tenses, and plural forms. It might not be necessary to understand the meanings of all words in the sentence in order to identify the error.

- Common testing points for sentence completion questions include the ability to use the following correctly: noun phrases, word order, subjects and verbs, verb phrases, adjective phrases or clauses, conjunctions, parallel construction, adverb phrases or clauses, comparison, infinitives, gerunds, prepositions, superlative, negatives, conditionals, and pronouns.

- Common testing points for error identification questions include word forms, verbs, pronouns, parallel construction, plural nouns, mistaken words, unnecessary words, omitted words, prepositions, reversed words, conjunctions, infinitives and gerunds, comparatives, articles, and superlatives.

- It is important to study the many prepositions that follow verbs.

# Reading Section

This section of the TOEFL measures your comprehension of standard written English. It includes approximately five reading passages, each of which may be followed by up to 12 questions. The total number of questions may range from 44 to 55.

## SAMPLE READING QUESTIONS FOR THE CBT

A reading passage will appear on your computer screen. As you read, scroll down using the scrollbar to view the complete passage. Several types of questions follow the passage.

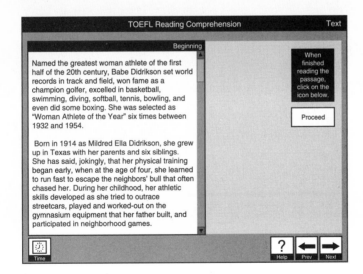

## ROAD MAP

- *Sample Reading Questions for the CBT*
- *Sample Reading Questions for the PBT*
- *Reading Comprehension Strategies*
- *Vocabulary Learning Tip*
- *Testing Points*
- *Examples of Each Question Type*

When you have finished reading, click on Proceed to see the questions about the passage. Both the passage and the question will appear on your screen. Answer the questions based on what is stated or implied in the passage.

For this type of question, choose the best of four answers.

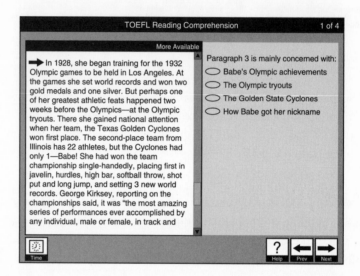

Click on an oval to choose your answer. The oval will darken to indicate your choice. To change your answer, simply click on a different oval. Your old choice will be erased as your new choice is selected. The correct answer is shown on the next screen.

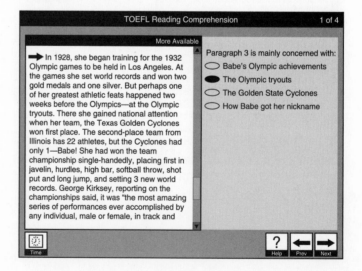

Click on Next to view the next question. You can click on Prev at any time to see previously answered questions, and you can change your answers.

For this type of question, you will choose your answer by clicking on a word or phrase in the passage.

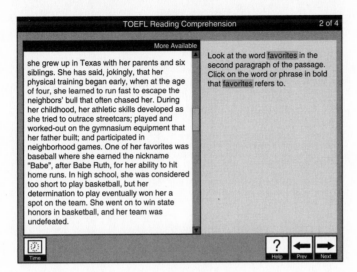

You can click on any part of the word or phrase, and it will darken to indicate your choice.

The correct answer is shown on the next screen.

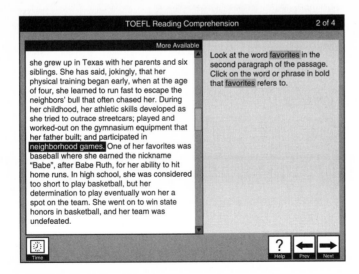

Click on Next to view the next question.

Some questions are answered by clicking on a sentence.

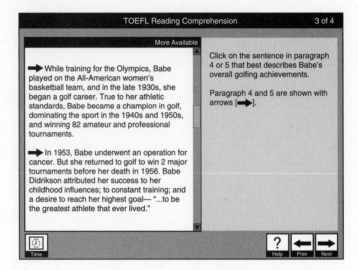

Clicking on any part of the sentence will darken it to indicate your answer choice.

The correct answer is shown on the next screen.

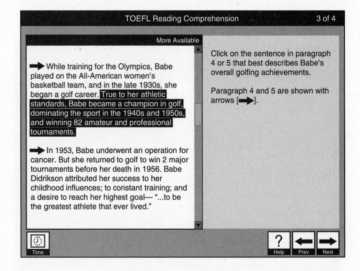

Click on Next to view the next question.

Some questions are answered by clicking on a square in the passage to add a sentence.

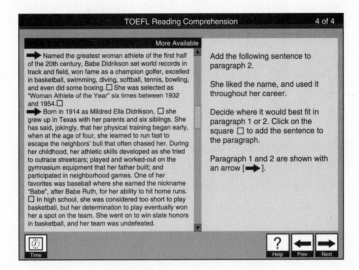

When you click on the square, the sentence will appear in the passage in the place you have chosen. If you want to change your answer, click on another square to move the sentence to a different place.

The correct answer is shown here.

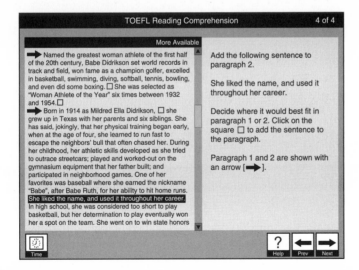

## SAMPLE READING QUESTIONS FOR THE PBT

In the Reading Comprehension section, you will read several passages. Each passage is followed by questions about it. You must choose the best answer to the questions based on what is stated or implied in the reading passage.

## SAMPLE PASSAGE

A new hearing device is now available for some hearing-impaired people. This device uses a magnet to hold the detachable sound-processing portion in place. Like other aids, it converts sound into vibrations. But it is unique in that it can transmit the vibrations directly to the magnet and then to the inner ear. This produces a clearer sound. The new device will not help all hearing-impaired people—only those with a hearing loss caused by infection or some other problem in the middle ear. It will probably help no more than 20 percent of all people with hearing problems. Those people who have persistent ear infections, however, should find relief and restored hearing with this device.

What is the author's main purpose in writing this passage?

(A) To describe a new cure for ear infections

(B) To inform the reader of a new device

(C) To urge doctors to use a new device

(D) To explain the use of a magnet

The author's main purpose is to inform the reader of a new device for hearing-impaired people. Therefore, you should choose answer (B).

The word "relief" in the last sentence means:

(A) Less distress

(B) Assistance

(C) Distraction

(D) Relaxation

● (B) (C) (D)

The phrase "less distress" is similar in meaning to "relief" in this sentence. Therefore, you should select choice (A).

# READING COMPREHENSION STRATEGIES

TOEFL reading passages can be on any topic, but you are not being tested on your knowledge of a particular topic. You are being tested only on your reading skills. All the answers you need are in the passages. The best way to prepare is to read as much as you can on a variety of topics, since you will comprehend what you read more quickly if you are familiar with a topic. Being a good reader in your native language will also help you read in English.

To practice reading comprehension testing skills, try the following two strategies to see what works best for you:

## STRATEGY 1: READ FIRST

Read the passage all the way through slowly and carefully, then answer the questions.

## STRATEGY 2: SKIM FIRST

Read the first sentence of each paragraph carefully, and skim the rest of the passage. Read the last sentence carefully. As you skim, pay particular attention to the names of people and places and to times and events. Then, begin answering the questions, going back to read more carefully whenever needed.

## VOCABULARY LEARNING TIP

The reading section has many questions about the vocabulary that is used in the passages. If you do not know the meaning of a word, you can sometimes guess if you know the prefix or the root of the word. A few examples of these are listed below:

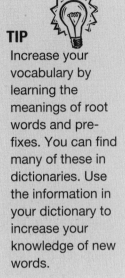

**TIP**

Increase your vocabulary by learning the meanings of root words and prefixes. You can find many of these in dictionaries. Use the information in your dictionary to increase your knowledge of new words.

### Examples of Prefixes

| Prefix | Meaning | Example |
|--------|---------|---------|
| a-, an- | no, not, or without | anesthesia (without feeling), asymptomatic (without symptoms) |
| ante- | before | antedate (come before) |
| anti- | against, opposite | antiwar (against war) |
| circum- | around | circumvent (circle around) |
| intra- | within | intrastate (within the state) |
| inter- | between | interstate (between states) |

### Examples of Roots

| Root | Meaning | Example |
|------|---------|---------|
| chronos | time | chronology (arrangement of events in time order) |
| lingua | tongue, language | multilingual (speaking many languages) |
| phon, phone | sound | symphony (harmony of sounds) |
| struct | build | construction (process of building) |
| therm | heat | thermometer (instrument for measuring heat) |
| ten | hold | tenacious (holding firmly) |

## TESTING POINTS

In this section, you will find examples of topics and types of questions that are common in the TOEFL reading comprehension passages.

**TIP**

The best way to increase your vocabulary is by reading in English. Read as much as you can, whenever you can. This will also help you increase your knowledge of grammar and your reading comprehension skills. As you read, write down new words and look them up later in your dictionary. Make vocabulary cards with a sentence on one side, and the definition and part of speech on the other. Keep these cards with you to practice whenever you have time.

# TOPICS

Although the reading comprehension passages cover a variety of topics, many of the passages focus on some aspect of science or natural history. Some of the most common, general topics are listed here:

1. General science, natural history, and human physiology
2. North American history, government, or geography
3. Art, literature, and music
4. Biographies of famous people

# TYPES OF QUESTIONS

The following types of questions have appeared frequently on previous TOEFL exams. An explanation of each question type and examples are given in this section.

### Reading Comprehension Question Types

| | |
|---|---|
| Main idea | Author's attitude/opinion/purpose |
| Inference | Preceding/following topic |
| Restatement | Sentence insertion (CBT only) |
| Vocabulary | Paragraph focus |
| Negative question | Line Focus |
| Referent | |

# EXAMPLES OF EACH QUESTION TYPE

*Reading Passage 1*

Not much is known about the early history of printing with movable type. There is evidence, however, that hand-set printing with movable type was first invented in China and Korea. At a later time, it was
(5) developed in Europe. In the 1400s, Laurens Janszoon Koster, of Holland, and Pamfilo Castaldi, of Italy, are thought to have made the first European use of printing with movable type. It is Johann Gutenberg's name, however, that is now associated with the
(10) invention of the movable type printing press. Although the separate elements of printing (the type, the ink, the press, and the paper) were not Gutenberg's own invention, his contribution was that he printed a large quantity of work of high quality.

(15)    Born in Mainz, Germany, in about 1397, Gutenberg was trained as a goldsmith, but he became a partner in a printing office in about 1436. It was in his home town of Mainz that he began the project he is most famous for: the printing of the Mazarin Bible. To
(20) finance this great project, he borrowed money from a lawyer named Johann Fust and from a printer. He was unable to pay back the money, however, and as a result lost both his printing press and the types to Fust, who carried on Gutenberg's work.

(25)    Gutenberg's method dominated the printing industry for almost 400 years. It required hand-setting particular pieces of type, locking them into place, and then printing on wooden flatbed handpresses. The rate was slow compared to modern printing; 300
(30) to 500 sheets a day printed on a single side was considered a good rate of production. Though not much is known about Gutenberg's life, his name lives on as a person who contributed significantly to the technology of human communication.

## MAIN IDEA

Almost every passage begins with a main idea question. The main idea is the main message that the passage conveys. The beginning and the end of a passage often give clues to the main idea.

> What is the main topic of this passage?
>
> (A)   A history of early printing
>
> (B)   Gutenberg's contribution to printing
>
> (C)   The printing of the Mazarin Bible
>
> (D)   Gutenberg's life in Germany

**The correct answer is (B).** Although this passage begins as though it might be a history of printing, the main focus is on Gutenberg's contributions to printing. This is evident in the last sentence of the first paragraph and the final sentence of the passage.

## INFERENCE

In inference questions, the answer is not stated directly in the text. Usually you must read several sentences to understand the inference.

**NOTE**

It is important to learn to focus on the main point of a passage. Most passages begin with a question about the main point. Practice by telling a friend the main point of a newspaper article you have read, or sections of a textbook or novel that you are studying.

**NOTE**

Read the first sentence of each passage carefully to see how the information is organized.

The author infers that the most significant aspect of Gutenberg's work in developing the art of printing is:

- (A)  The large number and quality of copies that he printed
- (B)  The printing of the Mazarin Bible
- (C)  The fact that he developed a new technique using known elements
- (D)  His inventive spirit and tenacious approach to his work

**The correct answer is (A).** Though all of the above are significant in some ways, the author states that Gutenberg's contribution to printing was that he printed a large quantity of work of high quality (lines 12–14). From this, we can infer that the author considers this the most significant aspect of Gutenberg's work.

## RESTATEMENT

In restatement questions, the answer might be found directly in the text, or it might use synonyms or a restructuring of the grammar in the text.

Why did Gutenberg borrow money from Fust?

- (A)  In order to fund his printing of the Bible
- (B)  In order to pay back loans for buying movable type
- (C)  In order to expand his printing ability
- (D)  In order to go into partnership with another printer

**The correct answer is (A).** Often a restatement question will use the exact words in the passage. In this restatement question, you must know that the phrase "this great project" (line 20) refers to the Mazarin Bible.

## VOCABULARY

Vocabulary questions test your ability to choose a synonym for a word or phrase as it is used in a passage.

The word "types" in line 23 could best be replaced by which of the following?

- (A)  Representative species
- (B)  Sets of equivalent forms
- (C)  Styles
- (D)  Metal pieces

**The correct answer is (D).** All of the above words could in some instances be used as synonyms for "types." In this passage, however, the word "types" refers to the metal pieces with raised letters or figures that were inked and then pressed against paper.

# NEGATIVE QUESTIONS

A negative question asks for something that is not in the passage. Three answers will be right, but you are to choose the one that is *wrong*.

> According to the author, which of the following did NOT precede Gutenberg in the use of movable type printing?
>
>   (A)   Fust
>
>   (B)   Koster
>
>   (C)   Castaldi
>
>   (D)   The Chinese

**The correct answer is (A).** The passage implies that Koster, Castaldi, and the Chinese preceded Gutenberg. It does not specifically state that Fust did not precede Gutenberg, but it states that Fust "carried on" Gutenberg's work. The phrase "carried on" implies that his work followed Gutenberg's.

# REFERENT

The word "referent" comes from the verb "to refer." For this type of question, you must decide which word or phrase a pronoun is referring to. Usually you look to the previous noun or phrase for the answer.

> In line 26, what does the word "it" refer to?
>
>   (A)   Pieces of type
>
>   (B)   400 years
>
>   (C)   The printing industry
>
>   (D)   Gutenberg's method

**The correct answer is (D).** For a referent question, you must look for the closest preceding (or sometimes following) phrase that means the same as the referring pronoun. In this case, the word "it" refers to whatever "required hand-setting particular pieces of type." It is Gutenberg's method that required the hand-setting of particular pieces of type.

# AUTHOR'S ATTITUDE/OPINION/PURPOSE

In this type of question, you are not looking for a specific answer in the passage. Instead, you read to find what the author might be implying. How does the author seem to feel about the topic. Why did the author write the passage or include particular pieces of info?

> Why does the author mention Koster and Costaldi?
>
>   (A)   To bring out the superiority of previous inventors
>
>   (B)   To show that Gutenberg had rivals
>
>   (C)   To demonstrate that historians disagree
>
>   (D)   To broaden the scope of this discussion

**NOTE**
When you are answering questions about information that is directly stated in the passage, look for an answer that paraphrases the information (uses different words to say the same thing).

**The correct answer is (D).** There is no evidence in this passage that the author wanted to discuss the superiority of previous inventors or that these inventors were rivals who were competing with Gutenberg. Choice (C) is possible, but there is no emphasis on whether historians agree or disagree on the facts. The best answer is that the addition of the names of previous inventors adds a broader perspective to the discussion of Gutenberg's work.

*Reading Passage 2*

Scarce diamonds are more valuable than the clusters of smaller crystals known as bort and carbonado. These diamonds are large single crystals of genuine crystalline carbon.

(5) Diamonds are found in diamantiferous earth that is located in both open-air pits and underground mines. To retrieve the diamonds, the earth is crushed and concentrated. The concentrated material is then sorted by passing it over streams of water on greased tables. (10) Because diamonds are water-repellent, they will stick to the grease, while the other minerals will absorb water and pass over the grease. The diamonds are then removed from the grease and cleaned, examined, (15) sorted, and graded. The best diamonds are noted for their cleavage, their translucence, and their color.

All diamonds have a natural line of cleavage along which they may be split, and it is essential to split them before they are cut and polished. Before they are cut (20) and polished, they look like tiny blue-grey stones; they do not twinkle or shine yet. A perfectly cut and polished diamond has 58 faces arranged regularly over its surface. It will be translucent and colorless, blue, white, green, or yellow. The value of a jewel (25) diamond depends largely on its color, or "water," as it is called professionally. A stone of the finest water is blue-white.

## PRECEDING/FOLLOWING TOPIC

For this type of question, you must infer what might have come just before the passage or what might come after the passage. Use the clues in the beginning or end of the passage to help you guess the topic.

> Which of the following most probably was the subject of the paragraph preceding the passage?
>
> (A) A discussion of scarce diamonds
>
> (B) A discussion of bort and carbonado
>
> (C) A discussion of the various colors of diamonds
>
> (D) A discussion of means of mining diamonds

**The correct answer is (B).** Because the first sentence compares scarce diamonds to bort and carbonado without defining either bort or carbonado, it is most likely that the preceding paragraph described these other types of diamond material.

## SENTENCE INSERTION

For this type of question, you must decide the best place in the passage to add a sentence.

**TIP**

Think of the topic as a one- or two-word answer to a question such as, "In general what is the passage about?" Think of the main idea (or what the passage mainly concerns) as a more detailed answer to the question "More specifically, what is the author saying about the topic?"

Where is the best place in the passage to add the following sentence?

If this step is omitted, the diamond may crack or split apart after it has been fully prepared for sale.

    (A)   In line 8 after the word "concentrated"

    (B)   In line 14 after the word "graded"

    (C)   In line 19 after the word "polished"

    (D)   In line 23 after the word "surface"

**The correct answer is (C).** Line 19 tells the reader that it is important to split diamonds along their natural cleavage line before they are cut and polished. It is best to add the new sentence after the word "polished" because it gives a specific explanation for the statement in line 19. Diamonds must be split before cutting and polishing to prevent them from cracking or splitting afterward.

> **NOTE**
> Sentence insertion questions are not found on the PBT; they are only on the CBT. Even if you are taking the PBT, however, this type of question is good to practice because it improves your critical reading skills.

## PARAGRAPH FOCUS

In this type of question, you must determine the central idea a paragraph.

What is the second paragraph mainly concerned with?

    (A)   The scarcity of large single diamonds

    (B)   The process used for extracting diamonds from their earth matrix

    (C)   The use of grease and water to clean and polish diamonds

    (D)   How diamonds are categorized by their "water"

**The correct answer is (B).** The second paragraph describes the process of getting diamonds out of the earth and separating them from their earth matrix or surrounding material.

## LINE FOCUS

This type of question asks you to find where in the passage a particular part of the topic is summarized or explained.

Where in the passage is a description of how cut and polished diamonds are valued?

    (A)   Lines 1–4

    (B)   Lines 8–12

    (C)   Lines 14–16

    (D)   Lines 24–27

**The correct answer is (D).** In lines 24–27, you learn that a main factor in determining the value of a diamond is its color. Choice (A) mentions the value of uncut and unpolished diamonds in their natural, raw state, but the question asks about cut and polished diamonds.

# Summary: What You Need to Know About the TOEFL Reading Section

- The Reading section tests your ability to understand short passages that American university students might read. The passages are similar in the CBT and PBT, although the CBT has a few types of questions that are not on the PBT.

- Both the CBT and the PBT give you several passages that are each followed by several questions.

- If you are taking the CBT, practice using a computer to read so that you are comfortable with this format. You can read anything; the point is to get used to reading from a computer screen.

- For both the CBT and the PBT, you can answer the questions in any order, and you can go back to reread or change answers of previous questions. In the CBT, however, it might be difficult to scroll back to look for omitted questions. It is better to answer each question when it is given.

- When you first see a reading passage on the CBT, you must scroll through the whole passage before you can begin answering the questions.

- For both the CBT and the PBT, it is a good idea to read the first few sentences carefully and then skim through the rest of the passage, noting the main ideas and locations of details. Then, as you read the questions, you can refer back to the passage for the answers.

- The Reading section is not testing you on your knowledge of subject matter. All the answers to the questions are in the passage. It helps you to read, however, if you have some general knowledge about a topic. Some common topics are general science, natural history, human physiology, North American history and government, geography, art, literature, music, and biographies of famous people.

- The common types of questions are main idea, inference, restatement, vocabulary, negative question, referent, author's attitude/opinion/ purpose, preceding/following topic, sentence insertion (CBT only), paragraph focus, and line focus.

- One way to help you learn new words is to study prefixes and root words.

# Writing Section and TWE

The Writing section is the last section of the CBT and can be either completed on the computer or handwritten on paper. If you take a paper-based test, you will also take the Test of Written English (TWE), which is the same as the Writing section of the CBT. The TWE test can only be written by hand. Both the CBT Writing section and the TWE require that you plan and write an essay on a given topic in 30 minutes. You may use scratch paper to organize your ideas before you begin writing. A list of essay topics is listed in the TOEFL Information Bulletins.

## SAMPLE WRITING FORMAT FOR THE CBT

When you take the CBT, you can choose whether to write the essay on the computer or by hand. If you do not want to write on the computer, you will be given essay paper to use.

If you choose to write on the computer, you need to learn a few commands, such as Cut, Paste, and Undo. The essay topic and the directions for writing the essay will appear at the top of your computer screen. You can learn and practice the commands during the Writing section tutorial that precedes the writing test.

When you are ready to begin writing, start at the blinking cursor. The screen will automatically scroll up as you type to give you more writing space. The following is an example of an essay topic as ot would appear on a computer screen.

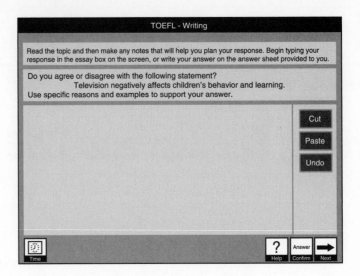

To end the writing section, click Next and Confirm at any time. After 30 minutes, the computer will automatically end this section of the test.

## SAMPLE ESSAY QUESTIONS

The list that follows contains sample essay questions that are similar to questions found in the CBT Writing section and on the TWE. See the CBT Information Bulletin for a complete list of the actual questions.

1.  There are advantages and disadvantages to different seasons of the year, such as rainy or dry weather. Pick any two seasons that you are familiar with and compare the two. Describe what makes you prefer one over the other. What activities do you engage in? What feelings do you have during this season?

2.  There are both advantages and disadvantages to going to school in another country.  Describe the good points and bad points about going to school in another country, and come to a conclusion about whether it is better to study abroad or stay home.  Give support for your opinion.

3.  Some families have many children, while others have only one child. Think about the positive and negative aspects of being in a family with several children. What size of family seems best? Why?

4.  We can be educated in many ways. Although much education happens in a classroom, we also are educated in our daily lives through doing activities and listening to our friends and our family members. Which is a better way to learn: in a classroom with a teacher or outside a classroom by doing things? Support your answer with examples and details.

5.  Some people usually cook and eat their meals in their homes, while others often eat their meals in restaurants, stores, or sidewalk cafes. What are some differences between these two ways of getting food? Which is better? Why? Give reasons to support your opinion.

6.  People have different ways of relaxing. Some people like to go out walking. Others like to read, sleep, eat, listen to music, or watch television. Some people

play sports or watch sports, while others dance and sing. What are some good ways to relax when you are not working? Describe some ways to relax that you are familiar with. Why are they good ways to relax? Explain your answer by giving examples.

# ESSAY-WRITING STRATEGIES FOR THE CBT AND TWE

To prepare for the essay writing, use the sample topics previously listed or the actual questions listed in the Information Bulletin. Practice writing an essay in 30 minutes. This is the amount of time you will have to read the question, think about the topic, plan what you will say, and write your essay.

Follow this plan-of-attack:

1. Read the question very carefully.

    a. Put a line under the main topic, or note it on the screen.

    b. Put a line under (or notice) the main words that tell you what you need to write. The following verbs are important: discuss, explain, state, describe, support, compare, and contrast.

    c. Put a mark or number by each part of the question that you must address in your essay. There could be as many as six parts to a question. For example, note the following question:

> Some people believe that it is better to attend a large university or college. Others prefer a smaller campus. Discuss the advantages and disadvantages of each. Which do you prefer, and why?

This question has six parts. To fully answer this question, your essay must include:

- Advantages of a large university
- Disadvantages of a large university
- Advantages of a smaller campus
- Disadvantages of a smaller campus
- Your preference
- Why (reasons for your preference)

In addition, always support your ideas with specific examples, even if the essay question doesn't specifically ask you to do so.

2. Make brief notes of the examples you want to write about or the opinions you are giving.

3. Look at your notes and organize them. What should you say first, what next? How will you conclude?

4. Check back to the words you underlined in the topic. Do you have an answer, example, or opinion for each part of the question?

5. Begin writing. Begin with a clear statement that answers the main question.

**NOTE**
When you begin the writing test, be sure to read the question thoroughly. Answer all parts of it, and make your perspective clear.

**TIP**

To create an organized essay, answer each part of the question in the same order that it appears in the question.

Give details and specific examples to support your opinion. Write clearly so that your paper can be read easily. End with a summary statement that reinforces your point of view. Remember that the readers do not know what you are thinking. You must make everything clear to them.

6. Check over your writing briefly to be sure that it is clear and that it answers the question. For some people, it helps to read the essay out loud (very quietly) to check the sentences.

## ESSAY-WRITING TESTING POINTS

The essay is scored by readers who read the whole essay and judge it according to the description that follows: The best essay receives a 6. Scores of 4, 5, and 6 are considered passing by many schools.

## ESSAY SCORES

**NOTE**

You have a limited amount of time to finish your essay. Watch the clock, and plan your time. As you practice, try the following suggested time plan, and adjust it to your own way of writing.

- **6–8 minutes—** Read the question and take notes to organize your answer

- **18–20 minutes—** Write your essay

- **2–4 minutes—** Check your writing

**6: Clearly competent**—An essay in this category is clear and well organized, has many details, and uses a wide variety of vocabulary words.

**5: Competent**—An essay in this category is well-organized but does not have as many details as a level-6 essay. The vocabulary is not as varied, and it might have a few grammatical errors.

**4: Minimal competence**—An essay in this category is adequately organized but might not answer all parts of the question. There might be grammatical errors that confuse the reader.

**3: Developing competence**—An essay in this category is poorly organized so that it is difficult for the reader to understand. It might have few details supporting the statements. There might be many grammatical errors and incorrect words.

**2: Possibly incompetent**—An essay in this category is not well-organized. There is no detail, and it is not focused on the question.

**1: Incompetent**—An essay in this category has serious errors in organization and sentence structure.

## TRANSITION WORDS

From the scoring description, you can see that it is very important for you to organize your essay carefully so that the reader can understand it. The following words and phrases might help you state your ideas clearly.

1.  To indicate a time or frequency or amount:

| | | | |
|---|---|---|---|
| in general | every | some | after |
| on the whole | usually | most | at other times |
| in most cases | frequently | main | finally |
| as a rule | rarely | before | meanwhile |

2.  To indicate an addition:

| | | |
|---|---|---|
| in addition | as well as | just as |
| again | along with | also |
| further | furthermore | likewise |
| in the same manner | in the same way | in addition to |

3.  To introduce an example:

| | | |
|---|---|---|
| for example | namely | for instance |
| as an example | that is | |

4.  To indicate a contrast or difference:

| | | |
|---|---|---|
| although | instead | rather than |
| but | nevertheless | though |
| however | on the other hand | otherwise |

5.  To indicate a conclusion:

| | | |
|---|---|---|
| all in all | in consequence | in brief |
| as a result | the point is | in conclusion |
| therefore | hence | in sum |

**NOTE**
For many institutions, you do not have to get the highest essay score. Many will consider that you have passed the test if you get a score of 4 or above. However, you must check with the institution in which you are interested to find out what minimum score is desired.

## SAMPLE ESSAYS

This section provides examples of student essays. These essays probably would receive high scores on the CBT writing section or the TWE. Next to each essay are notes indicating the organization of the essay. Use these notes as guidelines to practice your own essays.

**TIP**
Using transition words greatly enhances your writing. However, be careful to use each phrase in the right sentence structure.

## Sample Student Essay 1

**Question:** Some people prefer work or activities that mainly involve working with people. Others choose work or activities that mainly involve working with objects or machines. Compare these types of activities. Which of them do you prefer? Give reasons to support your answer.

Opinion — Of these two ways of working, either with people or with objects or machines, I prefer working with people.

**TIP**

Be sure to support or explain any general statement that you make. A general statement can be supported with an example, facts, specific details, or reasons.

**TIP**

Some test takers prefer to write a quick outline of the topic first. In this outline, organize your response using short words or phrases for the ideas you will develop in your essay.

Support for Opinion

When I work with people, I can work more efficiently than when I work with machines or objects. My work then becomes interesting and productive. The reason, in my opinion, is that working with people gives us power and competition. Rivalry is a very effective motive in improving one's ability. In addition, when we talk and have conferences, we can get better ideas than we can with only one person's idea.

Contrast Statement

On the other hand, working with machines or objects makes me bored, and it takes a lot of time to complete the work I am given. You can become inhuman if you spend most of your time only handling machines. Though they are very accurate, they don't have hearts. In other words, it is hard to feel love toward machines.

Conclusion/ Repeat Statement

The reason I like working with people is because of companionship. We can learn something from everybody, even if we don't like them. If there is companionship, people will love working with people, and we can expect progress in our lives.

## Sample Student Essay 2

**Question:** There are advantages and disadvantages to different seasons of the year, such as rainy or dry. Pick any two seasons that you are familiar with and compare the two. Describe what it is that makes you prefer one over the other. What activities do you engage in? What feelings do you have during this season?

Introduction with Opinion

Summer and winter are two seasons that I like the most among the four seasons. I like diversity in my life, and these two seasons provide me with just that.

Descriptions and Examples #1

In the hot summer season, the world is full of life. Flowers are blooming, birds are singing, and I feel energetic about different kinds of outdoor activities, such as jogging, bicycling, and swimming. Swimming is one of my favorite sports. In the water, both body and mind have to work together either to move forward or simply to float. It is good stress reduction for the intensive modern life that many of us have. Summer also enables us to have more fresh fruits and vegetables. I like to go to the farmers' market, where I can enjoy the good prices, the availability of fresh produce, and the farmers' smiles.

Description
and
Examples #2

In winter, on the other hand, the world is quiet. Many animals stay inside, and some of them even sleep inside. There is a nice warmth inside the house, while outside the world is beautiful with a white covering of snow. It's fun to watch children play in the snow. It's also fun to meet friends and relatives during winter holidays to exchange experiences and joy.

Conclusion/
Repeat
Opinion

Summer and winter are so different; they offer us good feelings and a variety of opportunities to do all kinds of activities. I like all seasons, but I like summer and winter the best.

## Sample Student Essay 3

**Question:** Public transportation includes buses, subways, trains, and taxis. Private transportation usually refers to private cars, bicycles, or motorcycles. Compare these two kinds of transportation, and discuss the advantages of each. Decide which is better, giving details to support your decision.

Introduction
and
Opinion

In many places, people have the freedom to choose whether they want to commute to work by public transportation or by private transportation. Both ways of commuting have advantages and disadvantages. In comparing the two, I prefer to use as much public transportation as possible. I use my car only when excessive inconvenience exists.

Support for
Opinion and
Examples

I like public transportation because I feel relaxed on the bus or subway. I don't have to concentrate on my driving. I can even get some reading and studying done during the commute time. Moreover, I don't have to worry about finding a parking place. In addition, when we use public transportation, we help lessen air pollution and traffic jams. A problem, however, is that the bus system in my town does not provide frequent enough stops, and the location of the bus stops is not very convenient. These two problems prevent people from using public transportation.

Contrast
Examples

Private cars, on the other hand, are a more convenient way to get any place at any time. But, unfortunately, cars have many disadvantages. They produce pollution. It is hard to find a parking place in the city. They produce traffic jams, and it takes energy to drive.

Conclusion/
Repeat
Opinion
— If more and more people used public transportation, air pollution would be better controlled and expenses would be reduced. That, in turn, would attract more people to use it. The more people that used it, the more money transportation businesses would get to improve their facilities and provide more locations and frequencies. I hope some day that the public transportation system will be able to provide the convenience that a private car provides.

# Summary: What You Need to Know About the TOEFL Writing Section

- Both the CBT and the PBT require a 30-minute essay. When you take the Supplemental version (PBT), the essay is called the Test of Written English (TWE).

- The essay requires you to organize your ideas, give your opinion, give examples, and support your statements.

- Questions used for the CBT Writing section and the TWE are listed in the TOEFL Information Bulletins.

- If you are taking the CBT, you can choose to write the essay by hand or on the computer.

- Read the question carefully, and underline the major parts of it. Be sure that you answer all parts of the question.

- The 30-minute essay is scored from 1 to 6, with 6 being the highest score. Often a score of 4 is considered to be passing, but you must check this with your institution. You receive the TWE score as a separate score on your TOEFL score report. For the CBT, the Writing score is combined with your Structure section score.

- For good writing, it is important to use clear transition words, such as *in general, for example, furthermore, on the other hand,* or *as a result.*

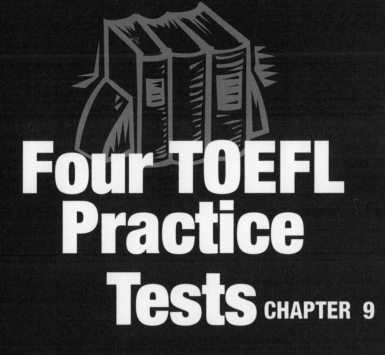

# Four TOEFL Practice Tests

# PART 3

## PREVIEW

# How to Score Your Practice Tests

In this book, there are four practice tests. The first two, Tests 1 and 2, are written in a format that is similar to the CBT. The next two, Tests 3 and 4, are written in a style that is similar to the PBT. See Part 1 of this book for a comparison of the two types of tests.

After you take the practice tests in this book, you can compute your score, but please note that this is only an approximation of an actual TOEFL test score. To compute your approximate score, you first need to convert your raw score (the number correct) to a converted score range. Look at the following tables for your converted score range. There is a different conversion table for each style of test.

## SCORE CONVERSION TABLE FOR THE CBT

Use the following score conversion table for Practice Tests 1 and 2.

Note: The following table is only an approximation of an actual score.

| Converted Score Range (Approximate) | | | |
|---|---|---|---|
| Raw Score (Number Correct) | Section 1 Listening | Section 2 Structure | Section 3 Reading |
| 55 | | | 28-30 |
| 50-54 | 27-30 | | 25-27 |
| 42-49 | 24-26 | | 21-24 |
| 35-41 | 20-23 | 27-30 | 16-20 |
| 27-34 | 15-19 | 25-27 | 13-16 |
| 20-26 | 10-14 | 21-24 | 9-12 |
| 15-19 | 8-9 | 17-20 | 7-9 |
| 12-14 | 6-8 | 7-9 | 5-6 |
| 6-11 | 2-6 | 6-7 | |

# SCORE CONVERSION TABLE FOR THE PBT

Use the following score conversion table for Practice Tests 3 and 4.

Note: The following table is only an approximation of an actual score.

| Raw Score (Number Correct) | Converted Score Range | | |
| --- | --- | --- | --- |
| | Section 1 | Section 2 | Section 3 |
| 60 | | | 68 |
| 57–59 | | | 66–67 |
| 54–56 | | | 62–64 |
| 51–53 | | | 60–61 |
| 48–50 | 65–68 | | 57–59 |
| 45–47 | 62–64 | | 55–56 |
| 42–44 | 59–61 | | 53–54 |
| 39–41 | 56–58 | | 51–53 |
| 36–38 | 54–55 | 62–68 | 50–51 |
| 33–35 | 52–53 | 57–60 | 48–49 |
| 30–32 | 50–51 | 54–56 | 46–47 |
| 27–29 | 48–50 | 51–53 | 44–45 |
| 24–26 | 47–48 | 48–50 | 42–43 |
| 21–23 | 45–46 | 45–47 | 40–41 |
| 18–20 | 43–44 | 42–44 | 37–39 |
| 15–17 | 41–43 | 38–41 | 35–36 |
| 12–14 | 39–40 | 36–38 | 31–33 |
| 9–11 | 35–38 | 33–35 | 28–30 |
| 6–8 | 31–34 | 29–32 | 26–27 |
| 3–5 | 28–30 | 25–28 | 23–25 |
| 0–2 | 25–27 | 21–24 | 21–22 |

# SCORE CALCULATION

To calculate your approximate score for the practice tests in this book, follow this procedure:

Count the total number correct for each section. This is your raw score.

Find your score range for the raw score of each section by using either the Score Conversion Table for the CBT or the Score Conversion Table for the PBT in this chapter.

Look across the column to find the converted score range for each section.

Multiply each of the converted score-range numbers by 10.

Divide each of the converted score numbers by 3.

Add the columns of numbers to get your total approximate Practice Test score.

## EXAMPLE OF SCORE COMPUTATION (PBT)

**Example (Using the Short Form Conversion Table):**

| | Number Correct | Raw Score Range | Converted Score Range | Approximate Score |
|---|---|---|---|---|
| Listening Comprehension | <u>30</u> | <u>30–32</u> | $50\text{–}51 \times 10 = 500\text{–}510 \div 3 = \underline{166\text{–}170}$ | |
| Structure and Written Expression | <u>25</u> | <u>24–26</u> | $48\text{–}50 \times 10 = 480\text{–}500 \div 3 = \underline{160\text{–}166}$ | |
| Reading Comprehension | <u>25</u> | <u>24–26</u> | $42\text{–}43 \times 10 = 420\text{–}430 \div 3 = \underline{140\text{–}143}$ | |

Total Approximate Score Range = <u>466–479</u>

# 10

# Practice Test 1 (CBT Style)

The Listening section measures your ability to understand spoken English. When you take the CBT, you will see pictures of the speakers and you will see and hear the test questions. On the CBT version, you will have about 15–25 minutes for this section. The time you spend listening to the talks is not counted. Also, since the CBT does not have a separate answer sheet, Tests 1 and 2 in this book do not have an answer sheet. You may mark you answer choices directly on this test or on a piece of scrap paper, if you prefer.

You can simulate actual TOEFL testing conditions by using the recordings that accompany this book. If you do not have the recordings, ask a friend to read the transcript for the Listening section of Practice Test 1 in Part 3 of this book, "Transcripts for Practice Tests."

**Now begin the recordings that accompany this book.**

**If you have the CD version, this test can be found on disc 1.**

## ROAD MAP

- *Section 1*
- *Section 2*
- *Section 3*
- *Answer Key*
- *Explanatory Answers*

# SECTION 1

## LISTENING (CBT STYLE)

## Time—Approximately 25 minutes

This test is written to represent the CBT in terms of the numbers of questions, types of questions, and length of time for each section. As on the CBT, the directions for both Parts A and B are given at the beginning of the test.

The Listening section includes two parts. In Part A, you hear conversations between two people. Sometimes the people speak only once, and at other times, they speak more than once. Each conversation is followed by one question. In Part B, you hear longer conversations and talks. Sometimes the talks are by professors in a classroom; for these, you might hear students in the classroom asking questions, answering questions, or giving comments. Each of the longer conversations and talks is followed by several questions.

**Now, listen to the directions for each part.**

## Part A

**Directions:** In the first part of the Listening section, Part A, you will hear conversations between two people. You will hear the conversation only one time, so you must listen carefully to what is said. After each conversation, a third person will ask a question. On the computer test, you will see pictures of the speakers and see the questions on your screen. Next, you will see the answer choices. Decide which is the correct choice, and select your answer. Answer all questions based on what is stated or implied by the speakers. On the computer test, you will not be able to return to a question once you have confirmed your answer.

\* *Note to test taker: In order to practice your listening skills for the TOEFL, do not stop the recording or replay it while you are taking this practice test. To simulate the CBT, cover the questions and answer choices below as you listen to the recording, and do not look ahead at the next questions.*

**Now listen to an example.**

\* *Note to test taker: On the CBT, at this point you would see a picture of a man and woman talking outside on a university campus.*

1. What does the man mean?

   Choose an answer in your book.

   (A)    He will call Pete before he goes home.

   (B)    He will call Pete after he gets home.

   (C)    He called Pete at home.

   (D)    He will call Pete tomorrow.

You learn from the conversation that the man will call Pete as soon as he gets home. The best answer to the question "What does the man mean?" is choice (B), "He will call Pete after he gets home."

**Now listen to the directions for Part B.**

# Part B

Directions: In the second part of the Listening section, Part B, you will hear longer conversations and talks. You will hear the conversation or talk only once, so listen carefully to what is said. After each conversation or talk, you will be asked several questions. Answer all questions based on what is stated or implied by the speakers. On the computer test, you will see pictures of the speakers and see the questions on your screen. Next, you will see the answer choices. Decide which is the correct choice, and select your answer. On the computer test, you will not be able to return to a question once you have confirmed your answer.

**Listen to the first example talk. There are two questions for this example.**

**Example talk 1**. Listen to a conversation between two friends at school.

* *Note to test taker: On the CBT at this point, you would see a picture of a man and woman talking outside on a university campus. Now, to simulate the CBT, cover the questions and answer choices below as you listen to the recording, and do not look ahead at the next questions.*

**Now listen to example question number one.**

1.  Where is the woman going?

    Choose an answer.

    (A)    To the cafeteria

    (B)    To the movie theater

    (C)    To her dorm room

    (D)    To the library

    The correct answer to the question "Where is the woman going?" is choice (D), "To the library."

**Now Listen to example question number two.**

2.  Which best describes the man's feelings about his classes?

    Choose an answer.

    (A)    Term papers are easy for him.

    (B)    He has a lot of essay exams.

    (C)    He finds lab experiments easier than writing term papers.

    (D)    He is busier this semester than last semester.

    The best answer to the question "Which best describes the man's feelings about his classes?" is choice (C), "He finds lab experiments easier than writing term papers."

**Now listen to the second example talk. There are two questions for this talk.**

**Example Talk 2. Listen to an announcement at a university.**

\* *Note to test taker: At this point on the CBT, you will see a picture of a woman speaking to a group of people. Now, to simulate the computer-based test, cover the questions and answer choices below as you listen to the recording, and do not look ahead at the next questions.*

**Now listen to example question number one.**

1.  What is the purpose of this announcement?

    Choose an answer.

    (A)    To demonstrate tutoring techniques

    (B)    To explain school policies

    (C)    To recruit child-care workers

    (D)    To explain a service

    The best answer to the question "What is the purpose of this announcement?" is choice (D), "To explain a service."

**Now listen to example question number two.**

2.  What does the speaker recommend?

    Choose an answer.

    (A)    Give your child extra tutoring.

    (B)    Take your child to the program today.

    (C)    Apply as soon as you can.

    (D)    Pay next month.

    The correct answer to the question "What does the speaker recommend?" is choice (C), "Apply as soon as you can."

**This is the end of the example questions for the Listening Section. Now begin the test with Part A. Get ready to listen.**

\* *Note to test taker: To simulate the CBT, cover the questions and answer choices below as you listen to each talk or conversation, and do not read ahead.*

# PART A

1. What does the man imply to the woman?

   (A)   She should study for the test.

   (B)   She should get some exercise.

   (C)   She should finish all her work before exercising.

   (D)   She should stay home and relax.

2. What does the woman mean?

   (A)   She spent almost all of her money on the books.

   (B)   She didn't have enough money to buy the books.

   (C)   She doesn't like the biology books.

   (D)   She rarely buys books.

3. What does the woman mean?

   (A)   She can't go on Wednesday.

   (B)   She thinks the man didn't hear her.

   (C)   The concert has been cancelled.

   (D)   The date of the concert has been changed.

4. What does the woman imply?

   (A)   She would rather have breakfast.

   (B)   She doesn't have time for lunch.

   (C)   She is also ready for lunch.

   (D)   She wants to eat lunch quickly.

5. What does the man imply?

   (A)   He will attend the conference.

   (B)   He isn't sure if he is free.

   (C)   He can't go to the conference.

   (D)   He has lost his calendar.

6. What does the woman say about Steve?

   (A)   He lost his term paper at the library.

   (B)   His paper got erased from the computer.

   (C)   He couldn't save his computer.

   (D)   He was able to save his whole paper.

7. What does the woman imply?

   (A)   Neither woman finished the article.

   (B)   Katy read the complete article.

   (C)   Both women found that the article wasn't difficult.

   (D)   The woman isn't sure if Katy finished the article.

8. What does the woman mean?

  (A)    Jason will have to work a little harder.

  (B)    She's certain he can work on something else.

  (C)    Jason can take the test on another day.

  (D)    Jason can disregard the test.

9. What does the woman mean?

  (A)    He'll be impressed with the new library.

  (B)    He'll have to wait to see the new library.

  (C)    The new library isn't very nice.

  (D)    The new library will be nicer by the time he sees it.

10. What does the woman mean?

  (A)    She must add an extra major before she can graduate.

  (B)    She thought she had already graduated.

  (C)    She found out that she doesn't need the extra requirement.

  (D)    She has to take another class before she can graduate.

11. What does the woman mean?

  (A)    She will not tell anyone.

  (B)    In time, the man will know if he and his roommate are compatible.

  (C)    The man and his roommate will be compatible soon.

  (D)    The man's roommate will learn to be neater in time.

12. What does the man imply?

  (A)    He stayed home by himself last night.

  (B)    The study group spent a lot of time analyzing the reading material.

  (C)    He should have studied alone last night.

  (D)    The study group should spend less time studying at home.

13. What does the man mean?

  (A)    He'll look at the lab manual early the next morning.

  (B)    He'll come as soon as it's bright to help his students.

  (C)    He's afraid that he won't be able to look at the lab manual.

  (D)    He'll be off campus all morning tomorrow.

14. What does the man mean?

  (A)    He'll give the woman a free meal.

  (B)    The woman should work in the dining hall too.

  (C)    Students working in the dining hall don't have to pay for food.

  (D)    The meals in the dining hall are so bad that he doesn't eat there.

15. What does the woman imply?

    (A)    The man shouldn't put off taking the exam.

    (B)    The man didn't give himself enough time to study for the exam.

    (C)    The man can postpone memorizing the formulas until the exam.

    (D)    The man should put off studying for the exam until Friday.

# PART B

Now go on to Part B. Remember, you are not allowed to take any notes or write in your test book. To simulate the CBT, do not read the answer choices while you listen to the recording. Do not read ahead, and do not return to a question once you have answered it.

16. What does the woman want to do after class?

    (A)    Go home

    (B)    Drink coffee

    (C)    Play the piano

    (D)    Study for an exam

17. How long has the man been playing the violin?

    (A)    Since he was 5

    (B)    For seven years

    (C)    Since he was in elementary school

    (D)    Since he was in high school

18. According to the discussion, what does the woman wish she had done?

    (A)    Continued to learn the piano

    (B)    Become a professional musician

    (C)    Had coffee before class

    (D)    Learned to play the violin, too.

19. What is the major issue that the professor is discussing?

    (A)    A difference of perspective between two groups of people

    (B)    Differing opinions on how to save the rain forest

    (C)    How words with the same root meaning change over time

    (D)    Why governments don't care about conservation

20. What does the Greek root word *eco-* mean?

    (A)    Progress

    (B)    Protection

    (C)    House

    (D)    Nature

21. According to the professor, what has been the result of an increasing human population?

    (A) Many plant and animal species have died or become endangered.

    (B) Scientists have spent more time studying plants and animals.

    (C) Governments have allocated more funds for endangered birds.

    (D) Only forty-five plant and animal species have been protected.

22. What is the main objective of the U.S. government's Endangered Species Act?

    (A) To stop land development

    (B) To protect the blue whale, the bald eagle, and the peregrine falcon

    (C) To stop farmers from planting more crops

    (D) To protect species that are in danger of extinction

23. What is the man's problem?

    (A) The man was unable to register for any of his classes.

    (B) The man had a bad dream about his classes.

    (C) The classes he needs for graduation are no longer open.

    (D) The man was unable to graduate last June.

24. How did the woman handle this problem in the past?

    (A) She attended the first class and talked to the professor.

    (B) She registered for the class anyway.

    (C) She preferred auditing classes to getting credit.

    (D) She asked some of the other students to drop the class so she could take their place.

25. What can we infer about the woman?

    (A) She is an undergraduate student.

    (B) She is no longer an undergraduate student.

    (C) She wants to graduate in June.

    (D) She graduated last June.

26. What will the man probably do?

    (A) Talk to the woman's professor

    (B) Drop some of his classes

    (C) Ask to join some of the woman's classes

    (D) Try the woman's suggestion

27. According to the first student's comment, what is the definition of sociology?

    (A) The study of groups and individuals

    (B) The study of the mind and personality

    (C) The study of social research

    (D) The study of human society and social behavior

28. According to the discussion, what is the main focus of sociology?

  (A)   Religious practices

  (B)   Social interaction

  (C)   Personality studies

  (D)   Genetic background

29. Which of the following would be of most interest to sociologists?

  (A)   The molecular structure of proteins

  (B)   Copper mining technology

  (C)   Marriage practices in early Samoan society

  (D)   Food sharing in non-human primates

30. What does the man want to do?

  (A)   Take a bookkeeping course for business owners

  (B)   Apply for the Certificate Program

  (C)   Take an accounting course

  (D)   Take classes only during the day

31. How many days a week does each class meet?

  (A)   Once a week

  (B)   Four times a week

  (C)   Three times a week

  (D)   Twice a week

32. What will the man probably do next?

  (A)   Receive his certificate

  (B)   Attend the Advanced Accounting Course

  (C)   Pay for the certificate courses

  (D)   Read the brochure

33. What is the main purpose of the professor's lecture?

  (A)   To discuss the differences between various numeric systems

  (B)   To explain why people learned to read and write

  (C)   To give a short introduction to a new topic

  (D)   To generate discussion about the video on writing skills

34. What does the professor say about the use of pictures and symbols to convey information?

  (A)   We still use this form of communication in the modern world.

  (B)   Pictures and symbols have helped people stop smoking.

  (C)   This form of communication has been replaced by the Roman alphabet.

  (D)   Pictures and symbols are still the best way to express complex ideas.

35. According to the professor, what was one limitation of the "logograph" system of writing developed by the Sumarians?

    (A)  It could only be used to convey complicated ideas.

    (B)  It could only be used by people who were able to draw pictures.

    (C)  It was too abstract.

    (D)  It could only be used for words that could be represented by a picture.

36. According to the professor, how are Cuneiform and Hieroglyphics similar?

    (A)  They are both word-syllabic writing systems.

    (B)  They both use wedge-like symbols to represent ideas.

    (C)  They were both derived from the Roman alphabet.

    (D)  They both have approximately 50,000 characters.

37. What is the main purpose of this talk?

    (A)  To prepare students for an exam about the Yolo River

    (B)  To introduce the students to a local archaeologist

    (C)  To train students in field techniques

    (D)  To tell students about a project that they can volunteer for

38. What will the students do if they join the Yolo River Project?

    (A)  Walk and talk as they learn about the Yolo Indians

    (B)  Walk slowly over the site and record their observations

    (C)  Create maps of Yolo River

    (D)  Look for arrowheads and fossils

39. Why are the students planning to do fieldwork?

    (A)  It's part of their class requirements.

    (B)  It's required for their major.

    (C)  It's exciting and a high adventure.

    (D)  It's an easy way to earn extra money.

40. Based on information from the talk, what can be implied about the early inhabitants of the Yolo River area?

    (A)  They were skilled hunters.

    (B)  They lived in large social groups.

    (C)  They ate shellfish.

    (D)  They inhabited the area for thousands of years.

41. How might students learn more about the Yolo River archaeological site?

    (A)  Read the textbooks that the speaker brought.

    (B)  Volunteer for the project.

    (C)  Watch an "Indiana Jones" movie.

    (D)  Talk with the president of the State Historical Society.

42. What is the purpose of the speaker's talk?

   (A)   To congratulate the students for completing phase 1 of the program

   (B)   To explain the requirements for phase 2 of the program

   (C)   To set up the student teaching positions

   (D)   To answer the students' questions about student teaching

43. What courses can they choose for their two elective courses?

   (A)   Any courses related to teaching

   (B)   Any of the methodology courses

   (C)   Any courses that are approved by their adviser

   (D)   Any courses offered in the public schools

44. Based on the talk, what can we infer about the required courses for phase 2 of the Teacher Education Program?

   (A)   They are designed to help students teach reading.

   (B)   They are designed to prepare students for classroom teaching.

   (C)   They were designed by Deana Cantor.

   (D)   They will be a little bit easier than the requirements for phase 1.

45. Based on the talk, what can we assume about the students?

   (A) They will all become teachers.

   (B) They have already done some teaching in the public schools.

   (C) They always enjoy observing in the public schools.

   (D) They have already taken some education courses.

46. Why are students advised to reduce their observation hours in the public schools?

   (A)   They will need more time for their academic studies.

   (B)   They will need more time for their student teaching assignments.

   (C)   They will need extra time to do educational research.

   (D)   They do not need to do classroom observation during phase 2 of the program.

47. What is the main focus of this lecture?

   (A)   How basketry developed among the Indians of the Southeast

   (B)   Why baskets are the best technology of food procurement

   (C)   Why a rich basketry tradition developed among certain indigenous groups

   (D)   How a fishing and gathering lifestyle prevented the development of pottery

48. Why does the professor use the example of the California Indians?

    (A) Because California Indians were the only ones to develop basketry

    (B) To show how certain technologies developed in response to environment and lifestyle

    (C) To show how specific environments were affected by the development of technology

    (D) Because California Indian baskets are some of the finest ever made

49. According to the talk, what is true about the California Indians?

    (A) Each tribe spoke many different languages.

    (B) They didn't develop any pottery.

    (C) Each tribe member owned about 15–20 baskets

    (D) Many different languages were spoken among the various tribes.

50. According to the talk, why did California Indians make boats out of reeds?

    (A) Because reeds were plentiful, and reed boats were very reliable

    (B) Because reeds were the only available material for making boats

    (C) Because reed boats could be made quickly and cheaply

    (D) Because reed boats were lightweight and easily maneuverable

**This is the end of the Listening Comprehension section for Test 1. Turn off the recording and continue with Section 2, Structure.**

# SECTION 2

## STRUCTURE

## Time—20 minutes

In the Structure section, there are two types of questions: Sentence Completion and Error Identification. Both types measure your ability to recognize standard written English.

> **Directions:** In the Sentence Completion questions, one or more words are left out of each sentence. Under each sentence, you will see four words or phrases. Click on the one word or phrase that completes the sentence correctly. After you confirm your answer, you will not be allowed to return to that question.
>
> In the Error Identification questions, each sentence has four underlined words or phrases. Click on the one word or phrase that must be changed in order for the sentence to be correct. On the CBT, after you confirm your answer, you are not allowed to return to that question.

### Sentence Completion Example Questions

1.  Birds make nests in trees _____ hide their young in the leaves and branches.

    (A)   can where they

    (B)   where they can

    (C)   where can they

    (D)   where can

    The sentence should read, "Birds make nests in trees *where they can* hide their young in the leaves and branches." Therefore, you should select choice (B).

2.  Sleeping, resting, and _____ are the best ways to care for a cold.

    (A)   to drink fluids

    (B)   drank fluids

    (C)   one drink fluids

    (D)   drinking fluids

    The sentence should read, "Sleeping, resting, and *drinking fluids* are the best ways to care for a cold." Therefore, you should select choice (D).

### Error Identification Example Questions

1.  Aspirin is <u>recommend</u> to <u>many</u> people for <u>its</u> ability <u>to thin</u> the blood.
                        (A)              (B)                    (C)                (D)

    The sentence should read, "Aspirin is *recommended* to many people for its ability to thin the blood." Therefore, you should choose answer (A).

2. Some people <u>believe that</u> human beings will never <u>use away</u> all <u>the</u>
             (A)                                       (B)    (C)

natural resources <u>on earth</u>.
             (D)

The sentence should read, "Some people believe that human beings will never *use up* all the natural resources on earth." Therefore, you should choose answer (B).

**Now go on to the Structure section of Test 1.**

1. About 75 percent of the nation's two- and four-year universities offer online courses _____ to continue their education at home.

   (A) give people the opportunity

   (B) who give people the opportunity

   (C) that give people the opportunity

   (D) have given people the opportunity

2. To adequately <u>discuss</u> literacy in the United States, <u>one</u> must <u>looks at</u>
                    (A)                           (B)    (C)

the common attitudes and <u>beliefs about</u> language diversity.
                                (D)

3. Mono Lake, _____ in the Inyo National Forest, is at least 760,000 years old, making it one of the oldest lakes in North America.

   (A) it is located

   (B) located

   (C) is located

   (D) which located

4. <u>A typical</u> weather pattern for Coastal California <u>consisting of</u> morning
    (A)                                         (B)

fog, <u>bright</u> afternoon sunshine, and <u>chilly</u> evenings.
       (C)                   (D)

5. In ancient Greek mythology, _____ as the sender of thunder and lightning, rain, and wind.

   (A) Zeus was regarded

   (B) was regarded Zeus

   (C) regarded Zeus

   (D) Zeus regarded

6. Specimens <u>of</u> ancient coiled and plaited basketwork <u>has been found</u> in
            (A)                                   (B)

the Nile Delta, <u>some</u> as old as 8000 <u>years</u>.
                   (C)           (D)

7. <u>Of the many</u> cranial nerves, the olfactory nerve, <u>which</u> transmits our
      (A)                                        (B)
  sense of <u>smell</u>, is the <u>shorter.</u>
            (C)        (D)

8. The versatility of modern cross-country skiing equipment allows
  skiers _____ techniques to diverse terrain.

  (A)    if they applied both  downhill and cross-country

  (B)    to apply both downhill and cross-country

  (C)    apply both downhill and cross-country

  (D)    to be applied to downhill and cross-country

9. During the Ice Age, many of the <u>earth's</u> most <u>spectacularly</u> landforms
                           (A)           (B)
  <u>were created</u> <u>by</u> glaciers.
      (C)      (D)

10. The world travels of Ernest Hemingway, an American novelist and
   short-story writer, _____ the background for much of his writing.

  (A)    formed

  (B)    he formed

  (C)    while forming

  (D)    was formed

11. In a critical review of an experiment, a researcher should <u>question</u> the
                                                            (A)

  <u>validity,</u> the <u>reliable,</u> and the <u>importance</u> of any test results.
    (B)         (C)           (D)

12. Despite the fact _____ over a century ago, Hans Christian
   Anderson's fairy tales are still popular with children around the
   world today.

  (A)    when they first appeared

  (B)    that first appeared

  (C)    appearing first

  (D)    that they first appeared

13. The continued efforts of the organization, Mothers Against Drunk
   Driving, or MADD, _____ alcohol related deaths by 43 percent
   since 1980.

  (A)    which helped reduce

  (B)    is helping reduce

  (C)    helps to reduce

  (D)    have helped reduce

14. Digital hearing aids produce clearer sounds by changing the sounds to a computer code before _____ .

   (A)    amplifying them

   (B)    amplified them

   (C)    them amplified

   (D)    to amplify them

15. <u>Legendary</u> singer/songwriter Woody Guthrie wrote <u>over 1,000</u> folk

     (A)                                      (B)

songs <u>including</u> the <u>populous</u> "This Land Is Your Land."

           (C)         (D)

16. _____ to use natural light for photography is usually just before, during, and after sunrise or sunset.

   (A)    The most best time

   (B)    The best time

   (C)    The time is best

   (D)    It is best

17. Olive oils can range <u>in color</u> from deep green to <u>buttery</u> yellow

                       (A)                  (B)

<u>depend</u> on <u>the age of</u> the olives at harvest time.

   (C)       (D)

18. <u>It is estimated</u> that <u>approximately</u> 2.65 <u>billions of</u> Christmas cards

                (A)        (B)        (C)

<u>are</u> <u>sold</u> in the United States each year.

   (D)

19. Elephant seals, _____ for their large hooked noses, are found along the Northern California coast.

   (A)    naming

   (B)    named

   (C)    are named

   (D)    which name

20. Today, global warming <u>is occurring</u> at <u>a faster</u> rate than <u>has ever</u>

                        (A)      (B)       (C)

<u>before</u>.

   (D)

21. _____ a yo-yo dating to 500 BC dispelled the common notion that yo-yos are a twentieth-century invention.

   (A)    After discovering

   (B)    Of the discovery

   (C)    Discovering it

   (D)    The discovery of

22. Bicycle courier services <u>operates</u> in many <u>traffic-clogged</u> cities for
                            (A)                     (B)

    <u>speedy</u> <u>delivery</u> of documents and small packages.
     (C)    (D)

23. <u>Each year</u> the Academy of Motion Picture Arts and Sciences <u>hosts</u> its
      (A)                                                (B)

    <u>spectacular</u> academy awards <u>presentments.</u>
       (C)                     (D)

24. Dairy farming _____ in the lush valley grasslands of the Pacific Northwest.

    (A)    that flourished

    (B)    flourished

    (C)    flourish

    (D)    flourishing

25. Called "Gateway Cities," places such as New York City, San Francisco, and Miami continue _____ as entry points for many immigrants.

    (A)    serve

    (B)    which have served

    (C)    to serve

    (D)    to be served

# SECTION 3

# READING

# Time—55 minutes

This section tests your ability to read and understand short passages.

> **Directions:** In this section, you will read several passages. Each passage is followed by questions about it. Choose the best answer for each question. Answer all questions based on what is stated or implied in the passage.

## Reading comprehension example questions

### Read the following passage:

A new hearing device is now available for some hearing-impaired people. This device uses a magnet to hold the detachable sound-processing portion in place. Like other aids, it converts sound into vibrations. But it is unique in that it can transmit the vibrations directly to the magnet and then to the
(5) inner ear. This produces a clearer sound. The new device will not help all hearing-impaired people only those with a hearing loss caused by infection or some other problem in the middle ear. It will probably help no more than 20 percent of all people, with hearing problems. Those people who have persistent ear infections, however, should experience restored hearing
(10) with the new device.

What is the author's main purpose?

(A)    To describe a new cure for ear infections

(B)    To inform the reader of a new device

(C)    To urge doctors to use a new device

(D)    To explain the use of a magnet

The author's main purpose is to inform the reader of a new device for hearing-impaired people. Therefore, you should choose answer (B).

The word "restored" in the last sentence could best be replaced by which of the following words.

(A)    Renewed

(B)    Diminished

(C)    Distorted

(D)    Refurbished

The word "renewed" is similar in meaning to "restored" in this sentence. Therefore, you should choose answer (A).

## Now begin with the questions.

### Questions 1–11 are based on the following passage.

One of the most interesting authors of the twentieth century, J.R.R. Tolkien, achieved fame through his highly inventive trilogy, *The Lord of the Rings*. Born in 1892, Tolkien received his education from Oxford and then served in World War I. After the war, he became a professor of Anglo-Saxon and
(5) English language and literature at Oxford University.

Although published in 1965, the three books that comprise *The Lord of the Rings* were written in intervals from 1936 to 1949. This was mainly due to Tolkien's responsibilities as a professor and the outbreak of World War II. By the late 1960s, this fascinating trilogy had become a sociological
(10) phenomenon as young people intently studied the mythology and legends created by Tolkien.

The trilogy is remarkable not only for its highly developed account of historical fiction but also its success as a modern heroic epic. The main plot chronicles the struggle between good and evil kingdoms as they try to
(15) acquire a magic ring that has the power to rule the world. The novels, which are set in a time called Middle Earth, describe a detailed fantasy world. Established before humans populated the Earth, Middle Earth was inhabited by good and evil creatures such as hobbits, dwarves, elves, monsters, wizards, and some humans. The characters and the setting of Middle Earth
(20) were modeled after mythological stories from Greece and Northern Europe.

Although readers have scrutinized the texts for inner meaning and have tried to connect the trilogy with Tolkien's real life experiences in England during World War II, he denies the connection. He claims that the story began in his years as an undergraduate student and grew out of his desire to
(25) create mythology and legends about elves and their language.

Tolkien was a masterful fantasy novelist who used his extensive knowledge of folklore to create a body of work that is still read and enjoyed throughout the world today.

1. What does this passage mainly discuss?
    - (A)   J.R.R. Tolkien's work as a professor
    - (B)   All of J.R.R. Tolkien's fantasy books
    - (C)   The popularity of J.R.R. Tolkien
    - (D)   J.R.R. Tolkien and his trilogy, *The Lord of the Rings*

2. What does the word "trilogy" mean in line 2?
    - (A)   A group of three related literary works
    - (B)   A specific type of fantasy novel
    - (C)   A book on mythology
    - (D)   A long epic novel

3. What is one of the reasons it took Tolkien thirteen years to complete the trilogy?

    (A)   His military service in World War II

    (B)   His need to study more mythology

    (C)   His duties at the university

    (D)   His family responsibilities

4. According to the passage, when did *The Lord of the Rings* trilogy become popular with young people?

    (A)   During World War II

    (B)   Between 1936 and 1946

    (C)   In the late 1960s

    (D)   In 1892

5. What is the setting of Tolkien's trilogy?

    (A)   England in the 1800's

    (B)   Middle Earth

    (C)   Oxford University

    (D)   Greece and Northern Europe

6. What can we assume is NOT true about Middle Earth?

    (A)   People dominated Middle Earth.

    (B)   The good and evil kingdoms fought for power.

    (C)   Middle Earth was based on European folktales.

    (D)   Middle Earth was a fictional world.

7. The following sentence could be added to paragraph 2. Where would it best fit into this paragraph?

    "When the ring is found by a hobbit, a wizard appoints a group to take it to a volcano where it is to be destroyed."

    (A)   In line 13 after the sentence that ends with "heroic epic"

    (B)   In line 15 after the sentence that ends with "rule the world"

    (C)   In line 16 after the sentence that ends with "fantasy world"

    (D)   In line 19 after the sentence that ends with "monster, wizards, and some humans."

8. The word "modeled" in line 20 is closest in meaning to which of the following words?

    (A)   Patterned

    (B)   Known

    (C)   Misrepresented

    (D)   Distorted

9. The word "scrutinized" in line 21 could best be replaced by which of the following words?

    (A)   Criticized

    (B)   Examined

    (C)   Enjoyed

    (D)   Denied

10. When did Tolkien begin to create his trilogy?

    (A)    During World War II

    (B)    When he was a professor

    (C)    When he was a student

    (D)    During World War I

11. What can we assume is true about Tolkien?

    (A)    He enjoyed studying mythology and folklore.

    (B)    He wrote the trilogy about his real life experiences.

    (C)    He spent most of his life in the military.

    (D)    He lived in Greece.

**Questions 12–23 are based on the following passage.**

Another large group of Canada's indigenous population, the Coast Salish, was located on the West Coast in what is now Vancouver, British Columbia. The Coast Salish people thrived in this area because of its abundant natural resources; rich variety of sea life, such as beluga whales, salmon and seals;
*(5)* and its remarkably mild climate.

    A sedentary people, the Coast Salish lived in villages made up of red cedar longhouses, but they often camped on nearby island beaches or paddled their seagoing canoes across the straits of the Puget Sound in pursuit of food. Because of the abundance of natural resources in this area, there was
*(10)* time for leisure activities that led to the development of a dynamic culture.

    The Coast Salish had an artistic heritage rich in ceremonial traditions that were inspired by nature and strongly related to myth and spirituality. They were best known for their woodworking of carved animal figures and their yarn making for blankets. The canoes of the Coast Salish were also of
*(15)* exceptional craftsmanship. Made from a single log, the canoes were used for daily activities as well as intertribal racing, so speed was factored into the design.

    At the time of European contact in the early 1800s, the Coast Salish population was quite large and much denser than other Native American
*(20)* tribes in central and eastern Canada, where groups were more spread out. In 1820, there were approximately 25,000 Coast Salish. But by 1915, the plagues and epidemics brought about by contact with Europeans had reduced the population to only 4,120. Today, the Coast Salish are thriving with a steadily increasing population and a renewed interest in preserving
*(25)* their culture and traditions.

12. What is the main topic of the passage?

    (A)    The indigenous groups of Canada

    (B)    The decimation of the Coast Salish

    (C)    The migration of indigenous populations

    (D)    One indigenous group of the Vancouver area

13. The paragraph preceding this passage most likely discusses which of the following?

    (A)    A tribe from another part of Canada

    (B)    The European migration to Canada

    (C)    The ceremonies of the Coast Salish

    (D)    The history of Vancouver

14. According to the passage, how was the population of the Salish different from central and eastern Canadian tribes?

    (A)    The Salish lived farther away from one another.

    (B)    The Salish population was smaller.

    (C)    The Salish lived in close proximity to each other.

    (D)    The Salish didn't live in villages.

15.  In line 5, what does "its" refer to?

    (A)    The Coast Salish tribe

    (B)    The abundant sea life

    (C)    The Vancouver area

    (D)    Canada

16. Why did the population of the Coast Salish decrease in the early 1900s?

    (A)    The Europeans sent them to eastern and central Canada.

    (B)    The Europeans carried unusual diseases.

    (C)    The Europeans depleted their food supply.

    (D)    The Europeans brought unhealthy food.

17. The word "sedentary" in line 6 is closest in meaning to which of the following?

    (A)    Remaining in one area

    (B)    Living close to one another

    (C)    Enjoying the outdoors

    (D)    Living near the sea

18. According to the passage, why were the Salish able to develop such a dynamic culture?

    (A)    Because they lived in villages, they had a permanent place to create things.

    (B)    Because their population was large, they had people with many different skills.

    (C)    Because of European influence, they adopted many aspects of European culture.

    (D)    Because food and resources were abundant, they had spare time for other activities.

19. Which of the following is closest in meaning to the word "abundance" in line 9?

(A)  Large amount

(B)  Limited supply

(C)  Deficiency

(D)  Variety

20. According to the passage, what is NOT true about the Coast Salish?

(A)  They sea provided much of their food.

(B)  They lived in a harsh climate.

(C)  They lived in the region now called Vancouver.

(D)  They built homes made of wood.

21.  Where in the passage would be the best place to add the following sentence?

"Despite this near decimation, the Coast Salish people managed to survive."

(A)  In line 9 after the word "food"

(B)  In line 17 after the word "design"

(C)  In line 20 after the words "spread out"

(D)  In line 23 after the words "only 4,120"

22. The information in the passage implies which of the following?

(A)  Indigenous people began living in Canada around 1800.

(B)  Europeans contacted the Coast Salish for trade and cultural exchange.

(C)  Some indigenous groups still live in Canada.

(D)  The coastal tribes of Canada were wiped out as a result of European contact.

23. This passage would most likely be assigned reading in which course?

(A)  European History

(B)  U.S. History

(C)  Geography

(D)  Canadian History

**Questions 24–35 are based on the following passage.**

In this era of increased global warming and diminishing fossil fuel supplies, we must begin to put a greater priority on harnessing alternative energy sources. Fortunately, there are a number of readily available, renewable resources that are both cost-effective and earth-friendly. Two such re-
(5) sources are solar power and geothermal power.

Solar energy, which reaches the earth through sunlight, is so abundant that it could meet the needs of worldwide energy consumption 6,000 times over.

And solar energy is easily harnessed through the use of photovoltaic cells that convert sunlight into electricity. In the United States alone, more than
*(10)* 100,000 homes are equipped with solar electric systems in the form of solar panels or solar roof tiles. And in other parts of the world, including many developing countries, the use of solar systems is growing steadily.

Another alternative energy source, which is abundant in specific geographical areas, is geothermal power, which creates energy by tapping heat
*(15)* from below the surface of the earth. Hot water and steam that are trapped in underground pools are pumped to the surface and used to run generators, which produce electricity. Geothermal energy is 50,000 times more abundant than the entire known supply of fossil fuel resources. And as with solar power, the technology needed to utilize geothermal energy is fairly simple.
*(20)* A prime example of effective geothermal use is in Iceland, a region of high geothermal activity, where over 80 percent of private homes are heated by geothermal power.

Solar and geothermal energy are just two of a number of promising renewable alternatives to conventional energy sources. The time is long
*(25)* overdue to invest in the development and use of alternative energy on a global scale.

24. What is the main topic of this passage?

(A)  The benefits of solar and wind power over conventional energy sources

(B)  How energy resources are tapped from nature

(C)  Two types of alternative energy sources that should be further utilized

(D)  Examples of the use of energy resources worldwide

25. According to the passage, why should we consider using alternative energy sources?

(A)  Because fossil fuels are no longer available

(B)  Because global warming has increased the amount of sunlight that reaches the earth

(C)  Because they are free and available worldwide

(D)  Because conventional energy sources are being depleted, and they cause environmental damage.

26. Which of the following words could best replace the word "harnessing" in line 2?

(A)  Capturing

(B)  Harassing

(C)  Depleting

(D)  Exporting

27. According to the passage, what can be inferred about solar roof tiles?

    (A)    They are being used in many undeveloped countries.

    (B)    They can convert geothermal power to electricity.

    (C)    They are more expensive than solar panels.

    (D)    They contain photovoltaic cells.

28. According to the passage, how is solar energy production similar to geothermal energy production?

    (A)    They both require the use of a generator.

    (B)    They both use heat from the earth's surface.

    (C)    They both require fairly simple technology.

    (D)    They are both conventional and costly.

29. Where is the best place in the passage to add the following sentence:

"Although the United States is not yet utilizing geothermal resources to this extent, the western part of the United States has a similar capacity to generate geothermal power."

    (A)    In line 4 after the phrase "earth-friendly"

    (B)    In line 12 after the phrase "growing steadily"

    (C)    In line 22 after the phrase "geothermal power"

    (D)    In line 26 after the phrase "global scale"

30. According to the passage, which of the following is true about solar power?

    (A)    There is very little of it available in Iceland.

    (B)    It is being used in 100,000 private homes worldwide.

    (C)    It is 6,000 times more powerful than energy from fossil fuels.

    (D)    There is enough of it to far exceed the energy needs of the world.

31. The word "renewable" in line 24 of the passage could best be replaced by which of the following words?

    (A)    Replaceable

    (B)    Unconventional

    (C)    Alternate

    (D)    Revolutionary

32. Where in the passage does the author discuss how geothermal energy is harnessed?

    (A)    In lines 3–5

    (B)    In lines 8–9

    (C)    In lines 15–17

    (D)    In lines 18–22

33. What can be inferred about the use of geothermal energy in Iceland?

    (A)    It is a widely used form of energy for heating homes.

    (B)    Twenty percent of the geothermal energy created is used to heat businesses.

    (C)    It is not cost effective for use in private homes.

    (D)    It is 80 times more efficient than traditional forms of energy.

34. What does the author imply about alternative energy sources?

    (A)    Solar and geothermal energy are the only effective forms of alternative power.

    (B)    Most alternative energy sources are too impractical for private use.

    (C)    Alternative energy is too expensive for developing countries to produce.

    (D)    Many different types of alternative energy sources exist.

35. What best describes the author's purpose in writing the passage?

    (A)    To warn people about the hazards of fossil fuel use

    (B)    To describe the advantages and disadvantages of alternate energy use

    (C)    To convince people of the benefits of developing alternative energy sources

    (D)    To outline the problems and solutions connected with global warming

**Questions 36–45 are based on the following passage.**

Once the home of the nation's most dangerous criminals, Alcatraz Island in the San Francisco Bay is now host to a less fearsome population—various large colonies of sea birds. Today, as a national park and wildlife sanctuary, Alcatraz provides a welcome nesting site for western gulls and cormorants,
(5) as well as several species of herons, egrets, and pigeons that thrive on the lush overgrown vegetation from abandoned prison gardens and on the trees and shrubs planted in earlier days.

At one time, Alcatraz was a bleak and barren outcropping of rock in the middle of San Francisco Bay—earning its name, "The Rock." Considered
(10) uninhabitable, it became the site of the first West Coast lighthouse in 1854. Later, a military fort and military prison were built on the island. Then, in 1934, during a crime wave that was sweeping the nation, the first maximum security federal penitentiary was established on the island to house the country's most incorrigible criminals, like the notorious gangsters Al
(15) Capone and "Machine Gun" Kelly. Alcatraz was an appropriate place for these criminals. Rising 130 feet above the rough and chilly waters of the bay and often windy and shrouded in fog, it offered no easy escape for the prisoners. In fact, in the history of Alcatraz prison, few inmates even attempted escape, and of those who did, all but three died in the attempt or
(20) were recaptured.

Alcatraz remained a federal prison until 1963. And by 1972, when the island became part of Golden Gate National Recreational Area, the bird population was already well established.  With few other animals and no feral cats on the island to prey on the birds, the colonies have remained

(25) relatively stable. Though the island is visited by as many as 4,000 people each day, park biologists have managed to further protect and maintain the bird population by barring visitors from certain areas of the island during breeding and nesting seasons. Thus, Alcatraz's current population of feathered inhabitants is thriving, and enjoying a more carefree life than that of

(30) most previous human residents on "The Rock."

36. What is the topic of this passage?

   (A)    The  maximum security prison on Alcatraz Island

   (B)    The bird species of Alcatraz Island

   (C)    The changing face and function of Alcatraz Island

   (D)    The infamous criminals of Alcatraz Prison

37. The word "shrouded" in line 17 of the passage could best be replaced by which of the following?

   (A)    Packaged

   (B)    Hidden

   (C)    Revealed

   (D)    Destroyed

38. Which of the following is NOT mentioned in the passage as a former use of Alcatraz Island?

   (A)    A military prison

   (B)    A lighthouse station

   (C)    A stable

   (D)    A fort

39. Where in the passage would be the best place to add the following sentence?

   "Norway rats, recently discovered on the island, could pose a serious threat to the birds, but measures are being taken to quickly eradicate them."

   (A)    In line 3 after the word "birds"

   (B)    In line 15 after the word "Kelly"

   (C)    In line 20 after the word "recaptured"

   (D)    In line 25 after the word "stable"

40. Which of the following is mentioned in the passage as a nickname for Alcatraz Island?

   (A)    Bird Island

   (B)    Gangster Island

   (C)    The Fort

   (D)    The Rock

41. What are two reasons that the bird colonies have been able to thrive on Alcatraz Island?

    (A)    The abundance of rich vegetation and few predators

    (B)    The concern of visitors and former inmates

    (C)    The remaining prison gardeners and park rangers

    (D)    The absence of other animals and the barring of visitors.

42. What can be inferred from the passage?

    (A)    That feral cats used to lived on the island

    (B)    That the island was not a wildlife sanctuary during the prison era

    (C)    That no birds inhabited the island until 1973

    (D)    That the birds are not able to nest during tourist season

43. Which of the following could best replace the word "feral" in line 24?

    (A)    Wild

    (B)    Large

    (C)    Domesticated

    (D)    Nocturnal

44. Where in the passage does the author discuss the use of Alcatraz before it was a federal penitentiary?

    (A)    In lines 3–7

    (B)    In lines 10–13

    (C)    In lines 15–17

    (D)    In lines 21–23

45. This passage might be read in which of the following courses?

    (A)    North America Birds

    (B)    Introduction to Law

    (C)    Oceanography

    (D)    California History

**Questions 46–55 are based on the following passage.**

Ranked as the number one beverage consumed worldwide, tea takes the lead over coffee in both popularity and production with more than 5 million metric tons of tea produced annually. Although much of this tea is consumed in Asian, European and African countries, the United States drinks its fair
(5) share. According to estimates by the Tea Council of the United States, tea is enjoyed by no less than half of the U.S. population on any given day. Black tea or green tea—iced, spiced, or instant—tea drinking has spurred a billion-dollar business with major tea producers in Africa, South America, and throughout Asia.

*(10)*     Tea is made from the leaves of an evergreen plant, *camellia sinensis,* that grows tall and lush in tropical regions. On tea plantations, the plant is kept trimmed to approximately four feet tall, and as new buds, called flush, appear they are plucked off by hand. Even in today's world of modern agricultural machinery, hand harvesting continues to be the preferred
*(15)* method. Ideally, only the top two leaves and a bud should be picked. This new growth produces the highest quality tea.

    After being harvested, tea leaves are laid out on long drying racks, called withering racks, for 18 to 20 hours. During this process, the tea softens and becomes limp. Next, depending on the type of tea being produced, the leaves
*(20)* may be crushed or chopped to release flavor, and then fermented under controlled conditions of heat and humidity. For green tea, the whole leaves are often steamed to retain their green color, and the fermentation process is bypassed. Producing black tea requires fermentation during which the tea leaves begin to darken. After fermentation, black tea is dried in vats to
*(25)* produce its rich brown or black color.

    No one knows when or how tea first became popular, but legend has it that tea as a beverage was discovered in 2737 B.C. by Emperor Shen Nung of China when leaves from a Camellia plant dropped into his drinking water as it was boiling over a fire. As the story goes, Emperor Shen Nung drank the
*(30)* resulting liquid and proclaimed the drink to be most nourishing and fortifying. Though this account cannot be documented, it is thought that tea drinking probably originated in China and spread to other parts of Asia, then to Europe, and ultimately to the American colonies around 1650.

    With about half the caffeine content as coffee, tea is often chosen by those
*(35)* who want to reduce, but not necessarily eliminate, their caffeine intake. Some people find that tea is less acidic than coffee and therefore easier on the stomach. Others have become interested in tea drinking since the National Cancer Institute published its findings on the antioxidant proper-ties of tea. But whether tea is enjoyed for it perceived health benefits, its
*(40)* flavor, or as a social drink, teacups continue to be filled daily with the world's most popular beverage.

46. What best describes the topic of this passage?

     (A)    How tea is produced and brewed

     (B)    The two most popular types of tea

     (C)    The benefits of tea consumption worldwide

     (D)    Tea consumption and production

47. Based on the passage what is implied about tea harvesting?

     (A)    It has been facilitated by the use of modern agricultural machinery.

     (B)    It is no longer done in China.

     (C)    The method has remained unchanged for centuries.

     (D)    The method involves trimming the uppermost branches of the plant.

48. Why might the author include statistics on the amount of tea produced, sold, and consumed?

    (A)  To show the expense of processing such a large quantity of tea

    (B)  To explain why coffee is not the most popular beverage worldwide

    (C)  To demonstrate tea's popularity

    (D)  To impress the reader with factual sounding information

49. Which of the following is NOT true about the tea production process?

    (A)  Black tea develops its dark color during fermentation and final drying.

    (B)  Green tea requires a complex fermentation process.

    (C)  Green tea is often steamed to retain color.

    (D)  Black tea goes through two drying phases during production.

50. The word "documented" as used in line 31 could best be replaced by which of the following words?

    (A)  Verified

    (B)  Ignored

    (C)  Filed

    (D)  Discounted

51. Where in the passage would be the best place to add the following sentence?

    "Recent studies with laboratory animals suggest that both black and green teas may have an effect on reducing the formation or growth of tumors."

    (A)  In line 9 after the phrase "throughout Asia"

    (B)  In line 24 after the phrase "to darken"

    (C)  In line 31 after the phrase "and fortifying"

    (D)  In line 39 after the phrase "of teas"

52. What does the word "they" in line 13 of the passage refer to?

    (A)  Tea pickers

    (B)  New buds

    (C)  Evergreen plants

    (D)  Tropical regions

53. According to the passage, what is true about tea drinking?

    (A)  Its orgin can be traced to the Shen Nung dynasty.

    (B)  It's orgin has been documented in China.

    (C)  It is unknown when tea first became popular.

    (D)  It predated coffee drinking in most countries.

54. According to the passage, what may be a reason that someone would choose to drink tea instead of coffee?

    (A) It's easier to digest than coffee

    (B) It has a higher nutritional content than coffee

    (C) It prevents cancer

    (D) It has more caffeine than coffee

55. Where in the passage does the author mention research conducted on the beneficial affects of tea drinking?

    (A) In paragraph 1

    (B) In paragraph 2

    (C) In paragraph 4

    (D) In paragraph 5

# ANSWER KEY

## SECTION 1—LISTENING

### Part A

| | | | |
|---|---|---|---|
| 1. B | 5. B | 9. A | 13. A |
| 2. A | 6. B | 10. D | 14. C |
| 3. D | 7. A | 11. B | 15. B |
| 4. C | 8. C | 12. C | |

### Part B

| | | | | | | |
|---|---|---|---|---|---|---|
| 16. B | 21. A | 26. D | 31. A | 36. A | 41. B | 46. A |
| 17. C | 22. D | 27. D | 32. D | 37. D | 42. B | 47. C |
| 18. A | 23. C | 28. B | 33. C | 38. B | 43. C | 48. B |
| 19. A | 24. A | 29. C | 34. A | 39. A | 44. B | 49. D |
| 20. C | 25. B | 30. C | 35. D | 40. C | 45. D | 50. A |

## SECTION 2—STRUCTURE

| | | | | |
|---|---|---|---|---|
| 1. C | 6. B | 11. C | 16. B | 21. D |
| 2. C | 7. D | 12. D | 17. C | 22. A |
| 3. B | 8. B | 13. D | 18. C | 23. D |
| 4. B | 9. B | 14. A | 19. B | 24. B |
| 5. A | 10. A | 15. D | 20. C | 25. C |

## SECTION 3—READING

| | | | | |
|---|---|---|---|---|
| 1. D | 12. D | 23. D | 34. D | 45. D |
| 2. A | 13. A | 24. C | 35. C | 46. D |
| 3. C | 14. C | 25. D | 36. C | 47. C |
| 4. C | 15. C | 26. A | 37. B | 48. C |
| 5. B | 16. B | 27. D | 38. C | 49. B |
| 6. A | 17. A | 28. C | 39. D | 50. A |
| 7. B | 18. D | 29. C | 40. D | 51. D |
| 8. A | 19. A | 30. D | 41. A | 52. B |
| 9. B | 20. B | 31. A | 42. B | 53. C |
| 10. C | 21. D | 32. C | 43. A | 54. A |
| 11. A | 22. C | 33. A | 44. B | 55. D |

# EXPLANATORY ANSWERS

## SECTION 1—LISTENING

## Part A

1. **The correct answer is (B).** The man is encouraging the woman to work out, which means "to exercise," because he believes it will help her relax before she studies for the test.

2. **The correct answer is (A).** When the woman says she barely had enough money, she means that she has just enough to buy the books, but no more.

3. **The correct answer is (D).** If something has been rescheduled, it means that the date or time of the event has been changed.

4. **The correct answer is (C).** By saying, "Me, too!" the woman is agreeing with the man. She is also hungry and would like to eat lunch.

5. **The correct answer is (B).** The man doesn't know if he has time available, so he needs to look at his schedule before he can agree to attend the conference.

6. **The correct answer is (B).** To *lose* a term paper on the computer means that it got *erased* from the computer.

7. **The correct answer is (A).** When the woman says, "Neither could I," she means that she also could not finish the article. So neither Katy nor the woman finished the article.

8. **The correct answer is (C).** The professor says, "We can work something out," which implies that she can arrange another time for the student to take the exam, as he has requested.

9. **The correct answer is (A).** The woman's expression, "Wow, wait until you see it," means that the man will be surprised when he sees the new library. And her enthusiastic tone of voice suggests that he will have a very positive reaction to the library.

10. **The correct answer is (D).** The woman's comment that "they've added an extra course requirement" means that she now must take an extra course in order to fulfill her graduation requirements. She says that she thought that she was ready to graduate until she learned that a new requirement had been added.

11. **The correct answer is (B).** The expression "time will tell" means that in time or after a while, it will be obvious. In this case, after living together for a while, it will be easier for the man to know if he and his roommate are compatible.

12. **The correct answer is (C).** The man's comment that he "might as well have stayed home..." implies that he didn't receive any benefit from going to the study group and could have studied better at home by himself.

13. **The correct answer is (A).** The man says that he'll come in bright and early, which means that he'll arrive *early in the morning* to take a look at the lab manual.

14. **The correct answer is (C).** The man says that free meals are one of the advantages, or positive aspects, of working in the dining hall. He doesn't say that he can give the woman a free meal, nor does he suggest that she should work there. He does not make any mention of the quality of the food.

15. **The correct answer is (B).** The idiom "put off" in this example means to postpone or avoid doing something. The woman's question "why did you put off studying for the exam until now?" tells us that the man has just now begun to study for the upcoming exam, and the woman wonders why he waited so long to begin studying. She implies that he didn't give himself enough time to memorize the formulas before the exam.

# Part B

16. **The correct answer is (B).** This is a restatement question. The woman asks the man if he'd like to go get a cup of coffee after class.

17. **The correct answer is (C).** This is a restatement question. The man began playing the violin at the age of 7 when he was in elementary school.

18. **The correct answer is (A).** This is an inference question. When the woman says she wishes she "hadn't given up on the piano," she means she wishes she hadn't *quit playing* the piano. Therefore, we can infer that she wishes she had continued to learn the piano.

19. **The correct answer is (A).** This is an inference/main idea question. The general issue is the conflict between factions that are most interested in preserving the environment and those whose main interest is achieving economic progress. At one point, the professor says, "And it is this issue—development versus environmental protection—that is the basis of the clash."

20. **The correct answer is (C).** This is a restatement question. The professor asks a question and a student answers, saying that "eco-" means "house."

21. **The correct answer is (A).** This is a restatement question. The professor says that human progress has been accompanied by a mass extinction of plants and animals. Whereas choices (B) and (C) may also be true, they are not stated in the talk. Choice (D) is incorrect, because the professor says that forty-five plant and animal species die in one day.

22. **The correct answer is (D).** This is a restatement question. The professor states that the Endangered Species Act was established to protect animals and plant life that are in danger of extinction.

23.  **The correct answer is (C).** This is a restatement question. The man says that a number of the classes he wanted are already full. This implies that, although he was able to register for some classes, the classes he needs for graduation had closed. Choice (B) is incorrect because, when the man refers to his experience as a "nightmare," he is not talking about a bad dream, but a terrible experience. Choices (A) and (D) are untrue.

24.  **The correct answer is (A).** This is a restatement question. The woman says that she would go to the first class and then talk to the instructor if the class she wanted was full. Choice (B) is wrong because she would not be able to register for the class if it were closed. Choice (C) is wrong because the woman never says she preferred auditing classes. Choice (D) is wrong because, although some students would drop the course, she did not ask them to do so.

25.  **The correct answer is (B).** This is an inference question. The woman tells the man about the method she used "when she was an undergraduate." By saying this, she tells us that she used to be an undergraduate student, but isn't any longer. She says nothing about wanting to graduate in June, and though she implies that she has already graduated, she does not mention *when* she graduated.

26.  **The correct answer is (D).** This is an inference question. When the man says, "…it's worth a try," he implies that he is willing to try her suggestion.

27.  **The correct answer is (D).** This is a restatement question. The student says that sociology is the study of human society and social behavior.

28.  **The correct answer is (B).** This is a restatement question. The professor states that sociologists are mainly interested in social interaction, therefore, we can assume that social interaction is the focus of sociology.

29.  **The correct answer is (C).** This is an inference question. Sociologists would most likely be interested in marriage practices in early Samoan society because they involve human social interaction within a particular group. Sociologists would be less interested in molecular science and technology that is not directly related to social interaction and behavior. Also, they do not tend to study non-human primates such as monkeys and apes.

30.  **The correct answer is (C).** This is a restatement question. The man says that he would like to take an accounting course. He does not say he wants to take a bookkeeping course for business owners, although the woman mentions that the Certificate Program is useful for business owners. The man doesn't mention a preference for day courses and says he might be interested in the Certificate Program.

31.  **The correct answer is (A).** This is a restatement question. The woman says that each class meets one night a week.

32. **The correct answer is (D).** This is an inference question. The man wants to take a brochure and application, so we can assume that he'll read the brochure next and fill out the application. He must complete the application before he pays for the class. He cannot take the advanced class or receive a certificate until he's taken the other accounting courses.

33. **The correct answer is (C).** This is a main idea question. The professor indicates that she is introducing a new topic by saying that she has written this week's topic on the board. She then gives a brief introduction to the topic Choices (A), (B), and (D) all contain an error.

34. **The correct answer is (A).** This is a restatement question. The professor states that people continue to use pictures and symbols as an effective form of communication, but that pictures and symbols are limited in their ability to express complex ideas. Choice (B) is incorrect because the "no smoking" symbol to which the professor refers does not help people quit smoking—it only prohibits them from smoking in certain areas.

35. **The correct answer is (D).** This is a restatement question. The professor states that the "logograph" system of writing, in which one picture represented one word, could not be used to express complex or abstract ideas. It could only be used if the word could be shown as a picture. Choices (A) and (C) are the opposite of what is true. In choice (B), it may be true that only people capable of creating the pictures could write with this system, but the professor doesn't mention this as one of the system's limitations.

36. **The correct answer is (A).** This is a restatement question. The professor describes cuneiform and hieroglyphics as word-syllabic systems, where pictures and symbols represent words or syllables. Only cuneiform uses wedge-like symbols. The Roman alphabet was developed much later, and Chinese is the writing system with 50,000 characters. The number of pictures or syllables in cuneiform and hieroglyphics was not mentioned.

37. **The correct answer is (D).** This is a main idea/purpose question. The main purpose of the speaker's visit is to explain one of the volunteer projects that the students can get involved in. The students are not preparing for an exam or learning any field techniques during this presentation. And although they do meet a local archaeologist, that is not the main purpose of the presentation.

38. **The correct answer is (B).** This is a restatement question. The speaker says that the work involves walking slowly over the entire site and recording what they see on a grid. The speaker does not mention Yolo Indians, fossils, or anything about the river itself. She also tells one of the students that he probably will not see any arrowheads.

39. **The correct answer is (A).** This is a restatement question. The professor states that the speaker will be talking about a fieldwork project that meets the requirement for the class. We don't know what the students' majors are or what the specific requirements their students' majors are. The speaker clarifies that, in general, archaeological work can be tedious and is not the high adventure portrayed in movies. This is not a way for students to earn money because they will be volunteers, which means that they will not be paid for their work.

40. **The correct answer is (C).** This is an inference question. The speaker tells the students that they might see pieces of shellfish at the site as evidence of early human habitation. Therefore, we can assume that shellfish were part of the early inhabitants' diet. Regarding evidence of hunting, the speaker says that tools such as arrowheads would probably not be found. In addition, the speaker does not say anything about the size of their social groups of how long they inhabited the area.

41. **The correct answer is (B).** This is a restatement question. The students can learn more about the project if they volunteer for it. Choice (A) is incorrect because the speaker did not bring textbooks—she brought fact sheets. The students will learn nothing about the site by watching an "Indiana Jones" movie, and the president of the State Historical Society, who will speak the next day, will be talking about a different project.

42. **The correct answer is (B).** This is a main idea/purpose question. Though the speaker begins by congratulating the students, she says that she's there to discuss phase 2 of the program and explain the requirements for that phase.

43. **The correct answer is (C).** This is a restatement question. The speaker says that they can choose their elective courses from any discipline but the courses must be approved by their adviser.

44. **The correct answer is (B).** This is an inference question. We can assume that the required courses for phase 2 of the program are designed to prepare students for classroom teaching because of the titles and content of the courses. Also, when students finish taking the courses, they will begin teaching in public schools as student teachers. Only one of the courses includes instruction on teaching reading. There is no mention that the courses were designed by Deana Cantor, and she states that the coursework will be heavier in phase 2, which means it will be more difficult than the coursework in phase 1.

45. **The correct answer is (D).** This is an inference question. Because the students have finished phase 1 of the Teacher Education Program, we can assume that they already took some education courses during phase 1. Although they are all in the Teacher Education Program, we do not know if all of them will eventually become teachers. According to the speaker, the students have been observing in the public schools but will not actually teach until they finish phase 2. Then, they will be teaching for the first time as student teachers. And although we can assume that the students want to become teachers and usually enjoy observing in the public schools, we cannot assume that they always enjoy it.

46. **The correct answer is (A).** This is an inference question. The speaker advises the students to reduce their observation hours because their phase 2 coursework will be heavier, meaning more difficult. Thus, we can infer that they will need more time for academic studies during this phase. They will not be starting their student teaching assignment until they finish phase 2. In addition, there is no mention that extra time will be needed for educational research. The speaker states that they must continue their observations during phase 2, but reduce the hours.

47. **The correct answer is (C).** This is a main idea question. The professor mainly discusses how the environment and lifestyle encouraged the development of a highly refined basketry tradition among California Indians. He does not talk about Southwest Indian groups. Though baskets served the California Indians well in procuring food, the professor does not say that this is the best food procurement technology overall. The development of pottery was not prevented by fishing and gathering. The California Indians simply found a different technology that was very efficient.

48. **The correct answer is (B).** This is a restatement question. The main theme of the professor's presentation is how environment and lifestyle shaped the development of certain technologies. He states that the basketry tradition of the California Indians is a specific example used to demonstrate the main topic. The professor never says or implies that California Indians were the only ones to develop basketry. Choice (C) is opposite in meaning to the correct answer. And, though it is mentioned that California Indian baskets are some of the finest ever made, this is not the reason why the professor is discussing them.

49. **The correct answer is (D).** This is a restatement question. The professor says that there were as many as eighty different language groups, meaning that among the Native Californian tribes, many different languages were spoken. Each tribe spoke only one of these languages. The professor clarifies that some tribes or groups did make some pottery, but most daily items were made of plant materials. The professor states that some women knew 15–20 basketry designs.

50. **The correct answer is (A).** This is a restatement question. The professor mentions that reeds were readily available, which means that they were plentiful. He also states that the boats made of reeds were unsinkable, meaning that they floated well, and thus, they were reliable. Although reeds were used for boats, it is not mentioned that they were the only material available for that purpose. Also, the professor does not mention how quickly the boats could be made, how lightweight they were, or if they were maneuverable.

# SECTION 2—STRUCTURE

In the following explanations, the correct answer is followed by the part of speech that the question is testing.

1. **The correct answer is (C).** Adjective clause. The word "that" introduces the clause that describes the noun "courses."

2. **The correct answer is (C).** Verb. Modals, such as *must*, must be followed by the simple form of the verb, so "looks at" is incorrect and should read "look at."

3. **The correct answer is (B).** Reduced adjective clause. Adjective clauses can appear in reduced form. This means that the adjective clause connector (that) and the "to be"-verb that follows are omitted.

4. **The correct answer is (B).** Subject/verb. The correct answer is "consists of," which is the present tense form of the main verb, which agrees with the main subject word "pattern." The original sentence is missing a main verb.

5. **The correct answer is (A).** Subject/verb. The sentence needs a subject and a verb in the passive form.

6. **The correct answer is (B).** Subject/verb agreement. The subject of the sentence is "specimens," so the verb must be "have been found" to match the plural subject.

7. **The correct answer is (D).** Superlative. Since it is stated that there are many nerves, "shortest" must be used to indicate "the most."

8. **The correct answer is (B).** Infinitive. In this sentence, the verb "allows" must be followed by an infinitive in the active voice.

9. **The correct answer is (B).** Adjective/adverb. "Spectacularly" is an adverb, but the sentence requires the adjective "spectacular" before the noun "land-form."

10. **The correct answer is (A).** Verb. Since "travels" is the plural subject, the correct choice is "formed," which is a main verb that agrees with the plural subject.

11. **The correct answer is (C).** Parallel construction/word form. The correct word is "reliability," a noun that is parallel to "validity" and "importance."

12. **The correct answer is (D).** Noun clause. A "that" clause is frequently used with "despite the fact" to introduce a noun clause.

13. **The correct answer is (D).** Verb .The present perfect tense of the verb is needed here, because the sentence refers to efforts that began in 1980 and continue today. "Have helped reduce" is the verb for the subject "efforts."

14. **The correct answer is (A).** Gerund. The gerund form of the verb is required after the word "before."

15. **The correct answer is (D).** Word form. The correct adjective form is "popular," not "populous."

16. **The correct answer is (B).** Superlative/word order. "The best time" is the subject of the sentence and agrees with the main verb "is." In choice (A), the word "most" is incorrect. Choices (C) and (D) are wrong because they include an additional main verb "is" for the subject "time."

17. **The correct answer is (C).** Adverb clause. The correct form of the verb is "depending." This word introduces an adverb clause "which depends on…" but the clause is in the reduced form, therefore, the verb becomes "depending."

18. **The correct answer is (C).** Plural. The correct answer is "billion," the singular form without the word "of." "Billions of" can only be used correctly when no specific number amount is given, for example "Billions of Christmas cards…"

19. **The correct answer is (B).** Reduced adjective clause. The word "named" introduces a reduced adjective clause that is in the passive form and describes the seals. The full clause would be "…which are named for…"

20. **The correct answer is (C).** Preposition. The correct answer is "than ever before." In this sentence, the expression "ever before" should not be preceded by the verb "has."

21. **The correct answer is (D).** Noun. The sentence requires a subject "discovery" to agree with the main verb "dispelled." Choices (A) and (B) do not give the sentence a subject, and choice (C) gives the sentence two subjects "it" and "yo-yo."

22. **The correct answer is (A).** Verb. The correct form of the verb is "operate," which agrees with the main subject "services."

23. **The correct answer is (D).** Word form. The correct form of the noun is "presentations," not "presentments."

24. **The correct answer is (B).** Verb. "Flourished" is the only verb form among the answer choices that agrees with the main subject "farming." Choices (A) and (D) introduce clauses and do not give the sentence a verb. Choice (C) does not agree with the subject "farming"

25. **The correct answer is (C).** Infinitive. The verb "continue" is followed by an infinitive, in this case, "to serve." Choice (D) is also in infinitive form, but it is passive, and the verb "to serve" must be in the active form here.

## SECTION 3—READING

1. **The correct answer is (D).** This is a main idea question. The passage mainly talks about Tolkien and one of his works, *The Lord of the Rings*. It doesn't talk about his other books.

2. **The correct answer is (A).** This is a line focus question. The root word "tri-" means three, so trilogy in this case means a group of three things. The passage mentions "the three books of *The Lord of the Rings.*"

3. **The correct answer is (C).** This is a restatement question. The passage states that his responsibilities as a professor and the outbreak of World War II were the reasons it took him thirteen years to write the books.

4. **The correct answer is (C).** This is a restatement question. The passage states that young people "intently studied" the books in the late 1960s. The other answers refer to all time periods before the books were published.

5. **The correct answer is (B).** This is a restatement question. The books were set in Middle Earth.

6. **The correct answer is (A).** This is an inference question. The passage states that "some humans" lived in Middle Earth along with Hobbits, Elves, and others creatures. There is no mention that people dominated Middle Earth, and from the passage, we can assume that other types of beings were present in greater abundance than humans in Middle Earth.

7. **The correct answer is (B).** This is a line focus question. The sentence that ends "rule the world" is describing the plot of the books. Therefore, the new sentence would fit best after this because it is a continuation of the description of the plot.

8. **The correct answer is (A).** This is a line focus question. If the characters and setting were "modeled" after Greek and Northern European stories, they were similar to the original stories and patterned after them.

9. **The correct answer is (B).** This is a line focus question. "Scrutinize" means to look at closely, so the best choice is choice (B), "examined."

10. **The correct answer is (C).** This is a restatement question. Although he wrote most of the books when he was a professor, the passage states that "the stories began in his years as an undergraduate student." So, the stories were created when he was a student.

11. **The correct answer is (A).** This is an inference question. Choice (A) is the only possible choice. Although Tolkien served in World War I , the passage does not imply that he spent most of his life in the military. Tolkien claimed that his books are not about his real life experiences, and the passage does not mention if he ever lived in Greece.

12. **The correct answer is (D).** This is a main topic question. The passage focuses on one native group, the Coast Salish, which continues to live in Canada in the Vancouver area. Choice (A) is too general, choice (B) is too specific, and choice (C) was not mentioned in the passage.

13. **The correct answer is (A).** This is a preceding paragraph question. The passage begins with "Another large group of Canada's indigenous population…was located on the West Coast…" So, we can assume that the preceding paragraph discussed an indigenous group from another part of Canada. Choices (B), (C), and (D) would not logically be followed by the topic sentence of this passage

14. **The correct answer is (C).** This is a restatement question. The passage states that at the time of European contact, the Coast Salish tribe was quite large and much denser than tribes of central and eastern Canada. "Denser" means that they lived closer together; they were not spread out like some other tribes.

15. **The correct answer is (C).** This is a line focus question. The word "its" refers to "this area" in which the Coast Salish lived, now the Vancouver area.

16. **The correct answer is (B).** This is a restatement question. The passage states that the Coast Salish population was drastically reduced because of plagues and epidemics brought on by contact with Europeans. Thus, we can assume that Europeans brought diseases for which the indigenous population had little immunity. Choices (A), (C), and (D) are not mentioned or inferred in the passage.

17. **The correct answer is (A).** This is a line focus question. The word "sedentary" as used in line 6 refers to a settled lifestyle in which people stay in one place as opposed to a nomadic lifestyle of people that constantly move from place to place. The context of the passage suggests that the Coast Salish basically lived a settled lifestyle in villages of permanent wood structures.

18. **The correct answer is (D).** This is a restatement question. The passage states that the abundance of resources allowed them time for leisure activities. Although choices (A) and (B) may be true, they were not mentioned in the passage as contributing to the development of a dynamic culture. Choice (C) is not mentioned in the passage.

19. **The correct answer is (A).** This is a line focus question. The word "abundance" means "plenty" or "more than enough," thus, a large amount. The words "limited supply" and "deficiency" refer to a lack of excess or not enough. "Variety" means many different kinds.

20. **The correct answer is (B).** The passage states that the Coast Salish lived in an area of "remarkably mild climate," so they did not live in a harsh climate. Choices (A), (C), and (D) were all mentioned in the passage as pertaining to the Salish.

21. **The correct answer is (D).** This is a line focus question. The only logical place for the added sentence is after the words "…only 4120." The added sentence with the transition words "Despite this…." Introduces a contrasting idea and provides a link between the discussion of the near destruction of the Salish and their increased numbers today.

22. **The correct answer is (C).** This is an inference question. The passage states that the Salish are thriving today, and it can be assumed that they are not the only Canadian tribe that still exists. There is no mention in the passage of the time that indigenous people began living in Canada, and there is no mention of why Europeans came to Canada. Choice (D) is incorrect because the Salish, a coastal tribe, were neither wiped out nor completely destroyed.

23. **The correct answer is (D).** This is an inference question. The passage focuses on the history of one group of indigenous Canadians, so the most likely course in which this reading would be assigned is Canadian history. The passage does not focus on European history. There is no mention of the United States in the passage, and there is little reference to the geography of the area.

24. **The correct answer is (C).** This is a main idea question. The passage focuses on two alternative energy sources, and the author urges their use on a global scale. Choice (A) contains an error; the passage doesn't mention wind power. Choice (B) is too specific: though the passage mentions how the two energy sources can be tapped, this is not the focus of the passage. Choice (D) is too general.

25. **The correct answer is (D).** This is a restatement question. The passage mentions that fossil fuels are diminishing, which means they are being reduced or depleted. Also, the author refers to alternative sources as "earth-friendly," thus, we can assume that conventional sources are not "friendly" or beneficial to the earth. Choice (A), (B), and (D) are all untrue. Fossil fuels are still available. There is no mention in the passage about an increase in sunlight due to global warming. And alternative energy sources are not free or available worldwide—"cost-effective" means they can be produced or utilized at a reasonable cost, and some resources, such as geothermal power, are only available in specific geographic regions.

26. **The correct answer is (A).** This is a line focus question. To "harness" means to capture and control something that is free, wild, or able to escape. To "harass" means to criticize, annoy, or attack someone repeatedly. To "deplete" means to reduce, diminish, or use up something. To "export" means to ship or send a product or resource produced in one country to another country.

27. **The correct answer is (D).** This is an inference question. The passage states that solar energy is harnessed through photovoltaic cells. Therefore, we can assume that both solar panels and solar roof tiles contain these types of cells. Choices (A), (B), and (C) all contain errors. Though some undeveloped countries are tapping solar power, there is no mention of solar roof tiles being used there. Photovoltaic cells are not used to convert geothermal power. And there is no cost comparison mentioned between solar panels and solar roof tiles.

28. **The correct answer is (C).** This is a restatement question. The passage states that fairly simple technology is needed to produce both solar and geothermal energy. Choices (A), (B), and (D) all contain errors. Of the two energy sources, only geothermal power requires a generator to produce energy and uses heat from the earth's surface—or more specifically, just below the earth's surface. Neither energy source is considered conventional. And both energy sources are described as "cost-effective" which is the opposite of "costly."

29. **The correct answer is (C).** This is a line focus question. This sentence fits best after the discussion of geothermal power usage in Iceland. In the added sentence, the phrase "to this extent" refers to a previously mentioned amount— 80 percent of private homes in Iceland. Also, in the added sentence, the word "similar" refers to a previously mentioned capacity to generate geothermal power, specifically Iceland's ability.

30. **The correct answer is (D).** This is a restatement question. The passage states that there is enough solar energy reaching the earth to meet worldwide energy needs 6,000 times over. This means that there is 6,000 times more solar energy available than is needed for the energy consumption of the entire world. Choices (A), (B), and (C) all contain errors. There is no mention of how much solar energy is available in Iceland. Solar power systems are being used in 100,000 homes in the United States, not worldwide. And there is no discussion of how much more or less powerful solar power is than power generated from fossil fuel.

31. **The correct answer is (A).** This is a line focus question. The word "renewable" means that something can be constantly replenished, or replaced.

32. **The correct answer is (C).** This is a line focus question. This is an organization question. Lines 14–17 in paragraph 3 discuss how geothermal sources are tapped, or harnessed, and turned into usable power.

33. **The correct answer is (A).** This is an inference question. According to the passage, 80 percent of private homes in Iceland are heated by geothermal energy, so we can infer that geothermal energy is widely used or used by a large number of people. Choices (B), (C), and (D) cannot be inferred from the information in the passage.

34. **The correct answer is (D).** This is an inference question. The only choice that is implied in the passage is choice (D), because the author mentions that solar and geothermal power are just two of a number of alternative sources that exist. Choices (A), (B), and (C) are not correct. The author mentions that a number of effective sources exist, and that these sources are cost-effective (therefore, practical for private use) and that some developing countries are using various forms of alternative energy.

35. **The correct answer is (C).** This is an author purpose question. The author discusses the advantages of using alternative energy sources such as solar and geothermal power and uses persuasive language. For example, the statement in the first line of the passage, "…we must begin to put greater priority…." and in the last line, "The time is long overdue…" reveal that the author is hoping to convince the reader of the need and urgency of the situation.

36. **The correct answer is (C).** This is a main idea question. The passage discusses the various uses of Alcatraz Island and how the island itself changed over time. Choices (A) and (D) are too specific, and choice (B) is too general, as only a few seabird species are mentioned.

37. **The correct answer is (B).** This is a line focus question. The word "shrouded" means "covered" or "hidden." From the context, it can be inferred that the island may be "hidden" in fog since fog can be dense and can obstruct one's view.

38. **The correct answer is (C).** There is no mention of Alcatraz ever serving as a stable or a place to keep horses.

39. **The correct answer is (D).** This is a line focus question. The added sentence mentions a possible threat to the bird population, so it best fits after the sentence that discusses the lack of feral cats on the island.

40. **The correct answer is (D).** This is a restatement question. Only "The Rock" is mentioned as a nickname that was given to Alcatraz. Choices (A), (B), and (C) are not mentioned in the passage.

41. **The correct answer is (A).** This is a restatement question. The passage mentions that an abundance of vegetation and lack of major predators is a factor in maintaining a steady and thriving population of nesting seabirds. Choice (B) is incorrect because there is no mention of visitors' concern or concern of former inmates. Choices (C) and (D) both contain errors.

42. **The correct answer is (B).** This is an inference question. The island did not become a national park and a protected area until 1972, and the prison closed in 1963, so we can infer that the island was not a wildlife sanctuary during the time that the prison was in operation. Choices (A) and (C) cannot be inferred from the passage. Choice (D) is incorrect because the passage states that areas of the island where birds are nesting are prohibited to human visitors.

43. **The correct answer is (A).** This is a line focus question. The word "feral" means "wild" or "not domesticated." The word "domesticated" means tame, such as a house pet or farm animal. The word "nocturnal" refers to an animal that is active during the night rather than during the day.

44. **The correct answer is (B).** This is a line focus question. This is an organization question. Lines 10–13 discuss Alcatraz as a lighthouse and then a military fort and prison before it became a federal penitentiary.

45. **The correct answer is (D).** This is an inference question. A course in California History is the most likely place in which the passage would be read. It discusses one historical site in California. The courses mentioned in choices (A), (B), and (C) are too general for a reading on the various functions of Alcatraz Island over the years.

46. **The correct answer is (D).** This is a main idea question. The passage discusses the tea production process and gives facts and general information on tea consumption today and in the past. Choice (A) is incorrect because there is no mention of how tea is brewed. Choices (B) and (C) are too specific.

47. **The correct answer is (C).** This is an inference question. The passage states that despite the fact that modern agricultural machinery is available, tea is still picked by hand. Since tea has been enjoyed for hundreds or thousands of years, it can be assumed that hand picking is a very old method. Choices (A), (B), and (D) all contain errors.

48. **The correct answer is (C).** This is an inference question. We can assume that the author includes statistics to substantiate or support the comment that tea is the number one beverage in the world. The figures serve to demonstrate how widely popular tea is today. The author doesn't state or imply that tea production is an expensive process, and the statistics do not reveal anything about the popularity of coffee. Though the reader may be impressed with the figures on how much tea is produced and consumed in the world, this is not the reason that the author includes the statistics.

49. **The correct answer is (B).** This is a restatement question. Although green tea is steamed, it is not fermented. The passage states that the fermentation process is "bypassed," which means that it is "not done". All of the other answers are true according to the passage.

50. **The correct answer is (A).** This is a line focus question. In this line, the word "documented" means "verified" or "proven to be true." "Discounted" means "thought to be false" or "of no importance."

51. **The correct answer is (D).** This is a line focus question. The added sentence fits most logically after the sentence on the findings of the National Cancer Institute. Only in that part of the passage is there a discussion on the possible health benefits of tea and research on its beneficial properties.

52. **The correct answer is (B).** This is a line focus question. "They" refers to the closest plural noun, which in this case is "new buds."

53. **The correct answer is (C).** This is a restatement question. The passage states that no one knows when or how tea drinking became popular. Choices (A), (B), and (D) all contain errors. There was no mention of a Shen Nung dynasty, nor has it ever been confirmed that tea drinking began in China.

54. **The correct answer is (A).** This is a restatement question. The passage states that some people drink tea instead of coffee because tea is less acidic and is easier on the stomach. This means that the person can digest tea better than coffee. There is no mention of the nutritional content of either tea or coffee in the passage. Although it is known that tea contains antioxidants, and the National Cancer Institute has seen some positive results in studies with laboratory animals, it is not proven, or even implied that tea prevents cancer. Choice (D) is the opposite of what is true. Tea has less, not more caffeine than coffee.

55. **The correct answer is (D).** This is a paragraph focus question. Paragraph 5 mentions "published findings" of the National Cancer Institute on the possible benefits of tea drinking. "Published findings" refer to the published results of scientific or academic research.

# Practice Test 2 (CBT Style)

The Listening section measures your ability to understand spoken English. When you take the CBT, you will see pictures of the speakers and you will see and hear the test questions. On the CBT version, you will have about 15–25 minutes for this section. The time you spend listening to the talks is not counted. Also, since the CBT does not have a separate answer sheet, Tests 1 and 2 in this book do not have an answer sheet. You may mark you answer choices directly on this test or on a piece of scrap paper, if you prefer.

You can simulate actual TOEFL testing conditions by using the recordings that accompany this book. If you do not have the recordings, ask a friend to read the transcript for the Listening section of Practice Test 1 in Part 3 of this book, "Transcripts for Practice Tests."

**Now begin the recordings that accompany this book.**

**If you have the CD version, this test can be found on disc 2.**

## ROAD MAP

- *Section 1*
- *Section 2*
- *Section 3*
- *Answer Key*
- *Explanatory Answers*

# SECTION 1

## LISTENING (CBT STYLE)

## Time—Approximately 25 minutes

This test is written to represent the CBT in terms of the numbers of questions, types of questions, and length of time for each section. As on the CBT, the directions for both Parts A and B are given at the beginning of the test.

The Listening section includes two parts. In Part A, you hear conversations between two people. Sometimes the people speak only once, and at other times, they speak more than once. Each conversation is followed by one question. In Part B, you hear longer conversations and talks. Sometimes the talks are by professors in a classroom; for these, you might hear students in the classroom asking questions, answering questions, or giving comments. Each of the longer conversations and talks is followed by several questions.

**Now, listen to the directions for each part.**

## Part A

**Directions:** In the first part of the Listening section, Part A, you will hear conversations between two people. You will hear the conversation only one time, so you must listen carefully to what is said. After each conversation, a third person will ask a question. On the computer test, you will see pictures of the speakers and see the questions on your screen. Next, you will see the answer choices. Decide which is the correct choice, and select your answer. Answer all questions based on what is stated or implied by the speakers. On the computer test, you will not be able to return to a question once you have confirmed your answer.

\* *Note to test taker: In order to practice your listening skills for the TOEFL, do not stop the recording or replay it while you are taking this practice test. To simulate the CBT, cover the questions and answer choices below as you listen to the recording and do not look ahead at the next questions.*

**Now listen to an example.**

*Note to test taker: On the CBT, at this point you would see a picture of a man and woman talking outside on a university campus.*

1. What does the man mean?

   Choose an answer in your book.

   (A)   He will call Pete before he goes home.

   (B)   He will call Pete after he gets home.

   (C)   He called Pete at home.

   (D)   He will call Pete tomorrow.

You learn from the conversation that the man will call Pete as soon as he gets home. The best answer to the question "What does the man mean?" is choice (B), "He will call Pete after he gets home."

**Now listen to the directions for Part B.**

# Part B

**Directions:** In the second part of the Listening section, Part B, you will hear longer conversations and talks. You will hear the conversation or talk only once, so listen carefully to what is said. After each conversation or talk, you will be asked several questions. Answer all questions based on what is stated or implied by the speakers. On the computer test, you will see pictures of the speakers and see the questions on your screen. Next, you will see the answer choices. Decide which is the correct choice, and select your answer. On the computer test, you will not be able to return to a question once you have confirmed your answer.

**Listen to the first example talk. There are two questions for this example.**

**Example talk 1.**    **Listen to a conversation between two friends at school.**

*Note to test taker: On the CBT at this point, you would see a picture of a man and woman talking outside on a university campus. Now, to simulate the CBT, cover the questions and answer choices below as you listen to the recording, and do not look ahead at the next questions.*

**Now listen to example question number one.**

1.  Where is the woman going?

    Choose an answer.

    (A)    To the cafeteria

    (B)    To the movie theater

    (C)    To her dorm room

    (D)    To the library

    The correct answer to the question "Where is the woman going?" is choice (D), "To the library."

**Now Listen to example question number two.**

2.  Which best describes the man's feelings about his classes?

    Choose an answer.

    (A)    Term papers are easy for him.

    (B)    He has a lot of essay exams.

    (C)    He finds lab experiments easier than writing term papers.

    (D)    He is busier this semester than last semester.

    The best answer to the question "Which best describes the man's feelings about his classes?" is choice (C), "He finds lab experiments easier than writing term papers."

**Now listen to the second example talk. There are two questions for this talk.**

**Example Talk 2. Listen to an announcement at a university.**

*\* Note to test taker: At this point on the CBT, you will see a picture of a woman speaking to a group of people. Now, to simulate the computer-based test, cover the questions and answer choices below as you listen to the recording, and do not look ahead at the next questions.*

**Now listen to example question number one.**

1. What is the purpose of this announcement?

   Choose an answer.

   (A)   To demonstrate tutoring techniques

   (B)   To explain school policies

   (C)   To recruit child-care workers

   (D)   To explain a service

   The best answer to the question "What is the purpose of this announcement?" is choice (D), "To explain a service."

**Now listen to example question number two.**

2. What does the speaker recommend?

   Choose an answer.

   (A)   Give your child extra tutoring.

   (B)   Take your child to the program today.

   (C)   Apply as soon as you can.

   (D)   Pay next month.

   The correct answer to the question "What does the speaker recommend?" is choice (C), "Apply as soon as you can."

**This is the end of the example questions for Listening Comprehension. Now begin the test with Part A. Get ready to listen.**

*\* Note to test taker: To simulate the CBT, cover the questions and answer choices below as you listen to each talk or conversation, and do not read ahead.*

1. What do the speakers mean?

   (A)   Sylvia lost her job.

   (B)   Sylvia got burned.

   (C)   Jim and Sylvia got divorced.

   (D)   Sylvia got angry at Jim.

2. What is the man's situation?

   (A)    He is finished with school.

   (B)    He has a lot of schoolwork to do.

   (C)    He is going away for two weeks.

   (D)    His papers are overdue.

3. What will the man probably do?

   (A)    Read his book more carefully.

   (B)    Go to the library to study.

   (C)    Go talk to the professor.

   (D)    Read the woman's notes.

4. What will the man do?

   (A)    He will change the time of the study group.

   (B)    He will ask the mechanics to look at her car.

   (C)    He will tell the group members that she will be late.

   (D)    He will pick her up at the bus stop.

5. What does the woman mean?

   (A)    She's interested in going to the class.

   (B)    She can't go every day.

   (C)    She wants to go at noon.

   (D)    She would prefer another type of exercise.

6. What does the woman mean?

   (A)    She hopes that Laura will come back alone.

   (B)    She wants Laura to return.

   (C)    She doesn't want Laura to come back.

   (D)    She knows Laura is thinking about coming back.

7. What does the woman mean?

   (A)    Why did Barbara mail the letter so early?

   (B)    Why is Barbara late in mailing the check?

   (C)    Why didn't Barbara call?

   (D)    Why did Barbara mail the check a week ago?

8. What does the man mean?

   (A)    The new position is just as good as his old one.

   (B)    He's going to resign his position.

   (C)    He'll probably continue with his old job for now.

   (D)    He doesn't agree with the woman.

9. What do the man and woman think?

   (A)    Peter should have gone home.

   (B)    Peter should have rested for a longer time.

   (C)    Peter was forced to stay away from his classes.

   (D)    Peter went on vacation.

10. What does the man mean?

    (A)    He doesn't know when it's open.

    (B)    He doesn't want to go.

    (C)    He thinks it is open in the evening.

    (D)    He agrees with the woman.

11. What does the woman mean?

    (A)    She's here permanently.

    (B)    She hopes the change will be for the best.

    (C)    She's currently looking for a good job.

    (D)    She'll stay as long as she can.

12. What does the woman mean?

    (A)    They don't have time to get there.

    (B)    This way should take less time.

    (C)    They are lost on the path.

    (D)    They are on the cutting edge.

13. What does the man mean?

    (A)    The test wasn't as easy as he thought it would be.

    (B)    The final exam room was farther away than he thought.

    (C)    He doesn't think he gave the appropriate compliments.

    (D)    He thought the test would be a lot harder.

14. What do the man and woman imply?

    (A)    Their friends were lucky that the phone was near.

    (B)    They should not have been afraid.

    (C)    There was a robbery, and the man was close to them.

    (D)    Something dangerous almost happened but didn't.

15. What does the woman mean?

    (A)    She bought them last year.

    (B)    She's using last year's books.

    (C)    She hasn't bought it yet.

    (D)    She's going to ask other students.

# Part B

Now go on to Part B. Remember, you are not allowed to take any notes or write in your test book. To simulate the CBT, do not read the answer choices while you listen to the tape. Do not read ahead, and do not return to a question once you have answered it.

16. Which of the following most clearly reflects Jimmy Carter's childhood?

    (A)    His family lived in severe poverty.

    (B)    The ideals of hard work and a simple life were important.

    (C)    As a youth, he was hired as a farm worker.

    (D)    Working on the farm was easy for him.

17. According to the speaker, which two of the following did Carter do with his father for recreation?

    1. Go fishing

    2. Go sailing

    3. Go hunting

    4. Go hiking

    >(A) 1 and 3

    >(B) 2 and 4

    >(C) 1 and 2

    >(D) 3 and 4

18, After his term of presidency ended, what activity did he get involved in?

    (A)    Modernizing policies in the U.S. Navy

    (B)    Working with blacks to grow cotton

    (C)    Increasing sales of peanuts

    (D)    Assisting poor people to get homes

19. When did Carter begin his term as President?

    (A)    1946

    (B)    1953

    (C)    1977

    (D)    1984

20. What is it that the man does not understand?

    (A)    The professor's lecture

    (B)    The TA's comments

    (C)    The professor's response

    (D)    The friend's suggestion

21. Why does the man feel bad?

    (A)    Because he doesn't like the topic

    (B)    Because he almost always needs help

    (C)    Because he didn't understand the lecture

    (D)    Because he worked hard on the paper

22. What will the man probably do?

    (A)    Contact the TA

    (B)    Make an appointment with the professor

    (C)    Begin a new paper

    (D)    Do more research

23. How does the man seem to feel after this interview?

    (A)    Nervous

    (B)    Scared

    (C)    Excited

    (D)    Hopeful

24. How many people have been asked for a second interview?

    (A)  1
    (B)  4
    (C)  8
    (D)  16

25. What does the man's girlfriend want?

    (A)  She wants to continue her study.
    (B)  She hopes to find a job near Ed.
    (C)  She hopes Ed is offered the job.
    (D)  She hopes Ed finds a job near her.

26. How does the woman feel at the beginning of the conversation?

    (A)  Relieved
    (B)  Angry
    (C)  Frustrated
    (D)  Excited

27. What was the woman's first response to the man's suggestion?

    (A)  She thought it was a good idea.
    (B)  She wanted to read about art first.
    (C)  She didn't want to go.
    (D)  She said she was too tired.

28. Which city will the art exhibit go to next?

    (A)  Los Angeles
    (B)  Chicago
    (C)  San Francisco
    (D)  New York

29. What does the man suggest they do after going to the art museum?

    (A)  Study again
    (B)  Visit another museum
    (C)  Walk in a park
    (D)  Go to a restaurant

30. What is the woman trying to do?

    (A)  Enroll in classes
    (B)  Get a new phone
    (C)  Convince her friend to register
    (D)  Contact her counselor

31. What does the man suggest?

    (A)  That she should wait until later
    (B)  That she should change her schedule
    (C)  That she should enroll in classes
    (D)  That she should see a counselor

32. How does the man seem to feel?

   (A)   Relaxed

   (B)   Worried

   (C)   Scared

   (D)   Excited

33. What is the main purpose of this lecture?

   (A)   To explain why it is difficult to study ancient music

   (B)   To emphasize the importance of Roman and Greek traditions of Western music

   (C)   To give particulars about Greek and Roman musical theory and practice

   (D)   To justify the actions of early Church leaders

34. Why does the professor say it is easier to study ancient architecture and sculpture than ancient music?

   (A)   Because buildings and statues were protected by the Church

   (B)   Because there is physical evidence of ancient buildings and statues

   (C)   Because there are many paintings of ancient buildings

   (D)   Because festival and rituals occurred in ancient buildings

35. What two of the following indicate the connection between ancient Roman festivals and the destruction of music?

   1. Music was banned in the church, so it didn't survive.

   2. Music was destroyed since it was associated with pagan festivals.

   3. Music flourished at festivals, so it died out when festivals were banned.

   4. Music was not religious, so the early church leaders did not keep records of it.

   (A) 1 and 2

   (B) 3 and 4

   (C) 2 and 3

   (D) 1 and 4

36. Which of the following will the professor talk about next?

   (A)   Medieval Christian church music

   (B)   The connection between musical theory and practice

   (C)   Music in Roman pagan festivals

   (D)   Ancient Greek music

37. What is the main topic of this lecture?

   (A)   Uses of the rooms of the White House

   (B)   Gilded furniture in the White House

   (C)   Controversy over White House changes

   (D)   Changes in decorations in the White House

38. What did Abigail Adams use the East Room for?

    (A)    Giving receptions

    (B)    Drying her clothes

    (C)    Cleaning carpets

    (D)    Playing billiards

39. What is the argument that the professor mentions?

    (A)    Whether money should be spent on foreign objects to decorate the White House

    (B)    Whether the British actually were the ones who burned down the White House

    (C)    Whether billiards should be played in the White House

    (D)    Whether the Congress should approve ways money is spent on decorations and objects

40. Which of the following is true according to the professor?

    (A)    Most of the objects in the White House were made in America.

    (B)    The portrait of George Washington was hung in the White House when it was rebuilt in 1814.

    (C)    Martin Van Buren and James Monroe furnished the White House with objects from abroad.

    (D)    George Washington and his wife were the first family to decorate the White House.

41. What does the speaker say is the common misconception about crocodile mothers?

    (A)    That they leave the water

    (B)    That they dig a hole in the sand

    (C)    That they rip open their nests

    (D)    That they eat their babies

42. Where do the young hatch?

    (A)    In a hole

    (B)    In the water

    (C)    Under the mother's tail

    (D)    In the mother's mouth

43. Why does the crocodile put her babies in her mouth?

    (A)    To keep them warm

    (B)    To protect them from harm

    (C)    To transport them to the water

    (D)    To clean them

44. How long does the mother wait for the young to hatch?

    (A)    5 weeks

    (B)    10 weeks

    (C)    12 weeks

    (D)    15 weeks

45. Which of the following was Borlaug's goal?

    (A)    To improve low-yielding varieties of wheat

    (B)    To receive the Nobel Peace prize

    (C)    To take over his father's farm

    (D)    To be the Father of the Green Revolution

46. What helped finance Borlaug's trip abroad?

    (A)    The Nobel Prize

    (B)    The Rockefeller Foundation

    (C)    His family farm

    (D)    The Green Revolution

47. What did Borlaug do when he left the United States?

    (A)    Introduced new technology

    (B)    Became a plant pathologist

    (C)    Worked for peace

    (D)    Got a doctorate degree

48. What can you best infer about the speaker's attitude toward the St. Lawrence River?

    (A)    The coal has polluted the river.

    (B)    It's a beautiful place to visit.

    (C)    The water is too cold for swimming.

    (D)    It is an unusual border between two countries.

49. What happened in 1959?

    (A)    Detroit and Duluth were established.

    (B)    The Great Lakes were linked with the Atlantic Ocean.

    (C)    Cargo boats began carrying grain on the river.

    (D)    Canals and locks were built on the river.

50. Which of the following best describes the Thousand Islands?

    (A)    An area of tree-covered islands

    (B)    A series of castles near the river

    (C)    A place where cargo ships carry coal

    (D)    A destination of ocean-going vessels

# SECTION 2

## STRUCTURE

## Time—20 minutes

In the Structure section, there are two types of questions: Sentence Completion and Error Identification. Both types measure your ability to recognize standard written English.

**Directions:** In the Sentence Completion questions, one or more words are left out of each sentence. Under each sentence, you will see four words or phrases. Click on the one word or phrase that completes the sentence correctly. After you confirm your answer, you will not be allowed to return to that question.

In the Error Identification questions, each sentence has four underlined words or phrases. Click on the one word or phrase that must be changed in order for the sentence to be correct. On the CBT, after you confirm your answer, you are not allowed to return to that question.

### Sentence Completion Example Questions

1. Birds make nests in trees _____ hide their young in the leaves and branches.

   (A)   can where they

   (B)   where they can

   (C)   where can they

   (D)   where can

   The sentence should read, "Birds make nests in trees *where they can* hide their young in the leaves and branches." Therefore, you should select choice (B).

2. Sleeping, resting, and _____ are the best ways to care for a cold.

   (A)   to drink fluids

   (B)   drank fluids

   (C)   one drink fluids

   (D)   drinking fluids

   The sentence should read, "Sleeping, resting, and *drinking fluids* are the best ways to care for a cold." Therefore, you should select choice (D).

### Error Identification Example Questions

1. Aspirin is <u>recommend</u> to <u>many</u> people for <u>its</u> ability <u>to thin</u> the blood.

                (A)       (B)       (C)       (D)

   The sentence should read, "Aspirin is *recommended* to many people for its ability to thin the blood." Therefore, you should choose answer (A).

2.  Some people <u>believe that</u> human beings will never <u>use away</u> all <u>the</u>
               (A)                                         (B)     (C)

    natural resources <u>on earth</u>.
                   (D)

    The sentence should read, "Some people believe that human beings will never *use up* all the natural resources on earth." Therefore, you should choose answer (B).

**Now go on to the Structure section of Test 2.**

1.  In <u>the</u> national parks of East Africa, <u>lions</u> and elephants generally
         (A)                               (B)

    keep <u>their</u> distance <u>to</u>  each other.
          (C)       (D)

2.  In <u>the early</u> days <u>of flying</u>, pilots sometimes <u>wear</u> leather helmets,
           (A)      (B)                   (C)

    goggles, and <u>neck</u> scarves.
                (D)

3.  <u>When</u> volcanoes <u>explode</u> they <u>give away</u> gases and ash that can be
        (A)         (B)       (C)

    <u>damaging</u> to the surrounding area.
      (D)

4.  The tides of the Atlantic and Pacific <u>Oceans</u> vary <u>considerable</u>,
                                       (A)      (B)

    though <u>surprisingly</u> their mean sea levels <u>are</u> almost the same.
            (C)                     (D)

5.  <u>Every</u> baby birds, called nestlings, eat <u>a</u> variety of <u>food</u> including
        (A)                            (B)     (C)

    spiders, beetles, moths, and <u>mosquitoes</u>.
                  (D)

6.  Kitchen appliances called blenders began _____ in the 1930s, when Stephen J. Poplawski developed a machine that excelled at making his favorite drink.

    (A)  using

    (B)  to use

    (C)  to be used

    (D)  which used

7.  Built at the beginning of the century, the Library of Congress houses one of the largest _____ collections of books in the world.

    (A)  and fine

    (B)  and finest

    (C)  or finest

    (D)  yet fine

8. In the preparation of fibrous material for production uses, stiff woody fibers from plants _____ fibers from animal sources.

    (A)    the most heat the

    (B)    need more heat than

    (C)    than more heat needed

    (D)    need the more heat than

9. A partnership is an association of two or more individuals who _____ together to develop a business.

    (A)    worked

    (B)    they work

    (C)    work

    (D)    working

10. Chosen as the nation's capital at the end of the American Civil War, _____ a city of over a million people.

    (A)    Washington, D.C., is now

    (B)    for Washington, D.C.,

    (C)    to Washington, D.C.,

    (D)    now in Washington, D.C.,

11. Within an area of only 100 miles, Death Valley sinks to 282 feet below sea level, while Mount Whitney _____ to a height of 14,494 feet.

    (A)    soaring

    (B)    soar

    (C)    soared

    (D)    soars

12. The cosmopolitan flavor of San Francisco is enhanced by _____ shops and restaurants.

    (A)    an ethnic

    (B)    its many ethnic

    (C)    its ethnicity

    (D)    ethnicity

13. _____ that increasing numbers of compact-disc players will be bought by consumers in the years to come.

    (A)    They are anticipated

    (B)    In anticipation

    (C)    Anticipating

    (D)    It is anticipated

14. It took eight years <u>to complete</u> the Erie Canal, <u>the 365-mile</u> waterway

                            (A)                   (B)

<u>which it</u> <u>connects</u> Albany and Buffalo in New York State.

    (C)    (D)

15. Every candidate <u>under</u> <u>considering</u> for a federal job must <u>undergo</u> a

                     (A)      (B)                          (C)

    thorough <u>medical</u> examination.

              (D)

16. <u>The</u> masterpiece *A Christmas Carol* <u>wrote</u> <u>by</u> Charles Dickens <u>in</u>

  (A)                           (B)  (C)          (D)

    1843.

17. Species <u>like</u> snakes, lizards, coyotes, squirrels, and jack rabbits

      (A)

    <u>seems</u> <u>to</u> exist <u>quite happily</u> in <u>the</u> desert.

    (B)            (C)      (D)

18. The disposable camera, <u>a</u> single-use camera <u>preloaded with</u> print film,

                     (A)                  (B)

    <u>has appeared</u> in the late 1980s and <u>is still</u> popular today.

    (C)                   (D)

19. <u>Until</u> recently, photocopy machines <u>were regarded</u> <u>strict as</u> business and

  (A)                        (B)     (C)

    professional office equipment <u>that required</u> a lot of expensive servicing.

                          (D)

20. Before <u>bridges</u> <u>were built</u>, all transport across major rivers in the

            (A)    (B)

    United States <u>were</u> <u>by</u> ferryboat.

             (C) (D)

21. Public health experts say that <u>the</u> money one spends <u>avoiding</u> illness

                       (A)            (B)

    is <u>less</u> than the cost <u>of be</u> sick.

    (C)         (D)

22. People in the world <u>differ</u> in <u>his</u> beliefs <u>about</u> the cause of sickness

                (A)    (B)      (C)

    <u>and</u> health.

    (D)

23. <u>In the</u> 1840s, <u>hundreds</u> of <u>families pioneer</u> moved west in <u>their</u>

  (A)       (B)        (C)          (D)

    covered wagons.

24. <u>When</u> children get their first <u>pair</u> of glasses, they are often <u>surprise</u> to

  (A)               (B)                 (C)

    see that trees and flowers <u>have</u> sharp clear outlines.

               (D)

25. The indiscriminate and continual <u>use of</u> any drug <u>without</u> <u>medical</u>

                              (A)           (B)    (C)

supervision can be <u>danger</u>.

                (D)

# SECTION 3

# READING

## Time—55 minutes

This section tests your ability to read and understand short passages.

> **Directions:** In this section, you will read several passages. Each passage is followed by questions about it. Choose the best answer for each question. Answer all questions based on what is stated or implied in the passage.

**Reading comprehension example questions**

**Read the following passage:**

A new hearing device is now available for some hearing-impaired people. This device uses a magnet to hold the detachable sound-processing portion in place. Like other aids, it converts sound into vibrations. But it is unique in that it can transmit the vibrations directly to the magnet and then to the
(5) inner ear. This produces a clearer sound. The new device will not help all hearing-impaired people, only those with a hearing loss caused by infection or some other problem in the middle ear. It will probably help no more than 20 percent of all people with hearing problems. Those people who have had persistent ear infections, however, should experience restored hearing with
(10) the new device.

What is the author's main purpose?

(A)     To describe a new cure for ear infections

(B)     To inform the reader of a new device

(C)     To urge doctors to use a new device

(D)     To explain the use of a magnet

The author's main purpose is to inform the reader of a new device for hearing-impaired people. Therefore, you should select choice (B).

The word "restored" in the last sentence could best be replaced by which of the following words?

(A)     Renewed

(B)     Diminished

(C)     Distorted

(D)     Refurbished

The word "renewed" is similar in meaning to "restored" in this sentence. Therefore, you should select choice (A).

**Now begin with the questions.**

**Questions 1–10 are based on the following passage.**

It's hard to find artifacts that are genuinely American, but the present day banjo may be one of them. Even though its ancestry is African, the modern banjo is nothing like the early instruments first brought by Africans to the southern plantations. In the nineteenth century, the banjo was a standard
(5) instrument in minstrel shows, and, as it continued to be used, it was changed in various ways. Machined pegs were added for precise tuning, frets were added for better intonation, and vellum heads were added to improve the tension. The number of strings also continued to change. Early banjos had four strings, while later models had as many as nine. In the late 1800s, the
(10) five-string banjo was developed, a model that had a small, unfretted drone string that was played with the thumb. This was the instrument that country singer Earl Scruggs played and was the type used to produce that great style of music known as American bluegrass.

In the 1920s, the four-string tenor banjo made a remarkable comeback, as
(15) banjo bands became popular in schools and clubs from coast to coast. Again in the 1960s, there was a renewed interest in folk and country music that brought the banjo back into the forefront of American music. It's an American instrument that continues to live on.

1. What does this passage mainly discuss?

   (A)   The lasting effects of bluegrass music

   (B)   The development of an American instrument

   (C)   The life of a banjo

   (D)   Changes in music in the nineteenth and twentieth centuries

2. According to the passage, where did the banjo originally come from?

   (A)   Southern plantations

   (B)   Folk and country music

   (C)   Minstrel shows

   (D)   Africa

3. The word "plantations" in line 4 most probably refers to which of the following?

   (A)   Types of farms in the South

   (B)   Southern states

   (C)   Southern musical theaters

   (D)   Bands common in the South

4. Which of the following words is most similar to the word "pegs" in line 6?

   (A)   Holes

   (B)   Bars

   (C)   Pins

   (D)   Strings

5. The word "precise" in line 6 could best be replaced by which of the following?

    (A) Accurate

    (B) Confirmed

    (C) Processed

    (D) Forthcoming

6. According to the passage, all of the following are true of the five-string banjo EXCEPT which of the following?

    (A) It was used by Earl Scruggs.

    (B) It was famous in the production of bluegrass music.

    (C) It had an unfretted string.

    (D) It was a tenor banjo.

7. Which of the following is most similar to the meaning of "comeback" in line 14?

    (A) Performance

    (B) Reappearance

    (C) Gain

    (D) Achievement

8. The word "renewed" in line 16 could be best replaced by which of the following?

    (A) Rescued

    (B) Remarkable

    (C) Revived

    (D) Renowned

9. Which of the following means most nearly the same as the word "forefront" as used in line 17?

    (A) Forecast

    (B) Spotlight

    (C) Footnote

    (D) Record

10. Which of the following best indicates the author's attitude toward the banjo?

    (A) It is a unique instrument.

    (B) It should be in a museum.

    (C) It should be used more.

    (D) It must be kept alive.

**Questions 11–20 are based on the following passage.**

Franklin D. Roosevelt, the thirty-second president of the United States, was from a wealthy, well-known family. As a child, he attended private school, had private tutors, and traveled with his parents to Europe. He attended

Harvard University and afterward studied law. At age 39, Roosevelt
(5) suddenly developed polio, a disease that left him without the full use of his legs for the rest of his life. Even through the worst of his illness, however, he continued his life in politics. In 1924, he appeared at the Democratic National Convention to nominate Al Smith for president, and eight years after that he himself was nominated for the same office. Roosevelt was
(10) elected to the presidency during the Great Depression of the 1930s, at a time when more than 5,000 banks had failed and thousands of people were out of work. Roosevelt took action. First he declared a bank holiday that closed all the banks so that no more could fail; then he reopened the banks little by little with government support. Roosevelt believed in using the full power
(15) of government to help what he called the "forgotten people." And it was these workers, the wage earners, who felt the strongest affection toward Roosevelt. There were others, however, who felt that Roosevelt's policies were destroying the American system of government, and they opposed him in the same intense way that others admired him.

(20)   In 1940, the Democrats nominated Roosevelt for an unprecedented third term. No president in American history had ever served three terms, but Roosevelt felt an obligation not to quit while the United States' entry into World War II was looming in the future. He accepted the nomination and went on to an easy victory.

11. What does the passage mainly discuss?

   (A)   Political aspects of Roosevelt's life

   (B)   Problems during the Great Depression

   (C)   Roosevelt's upbringing

   (D)   Criticisms of Roosevelt's actions

12. Which one of the following statements is NOT mentioned in the passage?

   (A)   Roosevelt was elected during the Great Depression.

   (B)   Roosevelt voted for Al Smith.

   (C)   Roosevelt had difficulty walking during his presidency.

   (D)   Roosevelt supported strong government powers.

13. The phrase "took action" in line 12 could best be replaced by which of the following?

   (A)   Performed admirably

   (B)   Exerted himself physically

   (C)   Responded immediately

   (D)   Got assistance

14. As used in lines 13–14, what does the phrase "little by little" imply about Roosevelt's reopening of the banks?

   (A)   That he opened the smaller banks first.

   (B)   That he opened the banks for minimal services.

   (C)   That he opened the banks a few at a time.

   (D)   That he opened the bank for a short time.

15. The word "full" in line 14 could best be replaced by which of the following?

    (A)  Packed

    (B)  Loaded

    (C)  Overflowing

    (D)  Complete

16. Where in the passage does the author discuss Roosevelt's response to the Great Depression?

    (A)  Line 1–14

    (B)  Lines 14–23

    (C)  Lines 12–15

    (D)  Lines 3–7

17. The word "affection" as used in line 16 could best be replaced by which of the following?

    (A)  Fascination

    (B)  Fondness

    (C)  Lure

    (D)  Appeal

18. The word "unprecedented" in line 20 could best be replaced by which of the following?

    (A)  Unimportant

    (B)  Unheard of

    (C)  Unjustified

    (D)  Unhampered

19. It can be inferred from the passage that the people who liked Roosevelt best were

    (A)  poor people.

    (B)  bankers.

    (C)  rich people.

    (D)  average workers.

20. In line 23, the word "looming" is closest in meaning to which of the following?

    (A)  Reservation

    (B)  Determination

    (C)  Regret

    (D)  Threat

**Questions 21–30 are based on the following passage.**

Our eyes and ears might be called transformers because they not only sense light and sound but also turn these sensations into electrical impulses that the brain can interpret. These electrical impulses that have been transformed by the eyes and ears reach the brain and are turned into messages that we can

(5) interpret. For the eye, the process begins as the eye admits light waves, bends them at the cornea and lens, and then focuses them on the retina. At the back of each eye, nerve fibers bundle together to form optic nerves, which join and then split into two optic tracts. Some of the fibers cross so that part of the input from the right visual field goes into the left side of the brain, and vice
(10) versa. The process in the ear is carried out through sensory cells that are carried in fluid-filled canals and that are extremely sensitive to vibration. Sound that is transformed into electricity travels along nerve fibers in the auditory nerve. These fibers form a synapse with neurons that carry the messages to the auditory cortex on each side of the brain.

21. According to the author, why might we call our eyes and ears "transformers"?

    (A)    Because they sense light and sound.

    (B)    Because they create electrical impulses.

    (C)    Because the brain can interpret the input.

    (D)    Because the messages travel in the brain.

22. Which of the following is closest in meaning to the word "admits" in line 5?

    (A)    Selects

    (B)    Interprets

    (C)    Lets in

    (D)    Focuses on

23. In line 5, to what does the word "them" refer?

    (A)    Light waves

    (B)    Processes

    (C)    Eyes

    (D)    Messages

24. The word "bundle" in line 7 could best be replaced by which of the following?

    (A)    Group

    (B)    Grow

    (C)    Branch

    (D)    Settle

25. The word "split" as used in line 8 is closest in meaning to which of the following?

    (A)    Tear

    (B)    Fracture

    (C)    Separate

    (D)    Crack

26. Which part of the passage best describes the first step in transforming light into electrical impulses?

(A) Lines 5–6

(B) Lines 12–13

(C) Lines 1–3

(D) Lines 9–10

27. According to the passage, when input from the right visual field goes into the left side of the brain, what happens?

(A) The nerve fibers bundle together.

(B) The optic nerves split.

(C) The retina receives light waves.

(D) Input from the left field goes to the right side.

28. The phrase "carried out" in line 10 could best be replaced by which of the following?

(A) Brought over

(B) Taken away

(C) Accomplished

(D) Maintained

29. Which of the following is most similar to the word "vibration" as used in line 11?

(A) Sound

(B) Movement

(C) Light

(D) Heat

30. According to the passage, optic nerves eventually

(A) bend.

(B) split.

(C) admit light waves.

(D) become messages.

**Questions 31–42 are based on the following passage.**

Like many neighborhoods in large cities, Harlem has undergone a multitude of changes. One of the most significant in this part of New York City occurred during the early part of the twentieth century. At that time, there was a large increase in the number of African Americans who migrated there
(5) from the American south. They came looking for better jobs and better lives for their families. This influx of people, combined with a general movement toward artistic experimentation that occurred in the 1920s, formed the basis for a creative outburst of activity in all areas of the arts, a period known as the Harlem Renaissance. The period lasted from about 1919-1929, and
(10) during this time, a host of artists became celebrated. Among these were the poet Langston Hughes, jazz singers Bessie Smith and Billie Holiday, and author and civil rights leader, W.E.B. Du Bois. These artists, and many

others, led the way to a revival of artistic energy among blacks and a redefinition of artistic expression.

*(15)*   Along with a celebration of arts and artistic talents, the Harlem Renaissance was intimately associated with a new expression among Blacks, one that exalted their African heritage. They were known as the "New Negroes," a term coined by the sociologist Alain Leroy Locke in 1925. This new atmosphere laid the groundwork for future civil rights activism, though it *(20)* was some time before that came to the fore. In the meantime, the economic depression of the 1930s and World War II affected Harlem and were associated with a decline in this exciting period of artistic activity.

31. What is the main idea of this passage?

   (A)   The American South

   (B)   A major movement in Harlem

   (C)   The lives of Harlem artists

   (D)   An exaltation of African-American heritage

32. Which of the following does the word "there" refer to in the first paragraph, line 5, in the phrase "who migrated there?"

   (A)   The neighborhood of Harlem

   (B)   The state of New York

   (C)   The American South

   (D)   The continent of Africa

33. Which word is closest in meaning to the word "influx" in line 6?

   (A)   Increase

   (B)   Migration

   (C)   Arrival

   (D)   Occurrence

34. Which phrase is closest in meaning to the phrase "a host" in line 10?

   (A)   An educated elite

   (B)   A select group

   (C)   A group of entertainers

   (D)   A large number

35. The major period of artistic movement in Harlem was during what period of time?

   (A)   Around 1919

   (B)   The decade after 1919

   (C)   The 1930s and 1940s

   (D)   The last century

36. What period of time does "in the meantime" refer to in line 19?

   (A)   Around 1925

   (B)   Between 1919 and 1929

   (C)   From about 1925 until sometime after World War II

   (D)   From after the economic depression to the present

37. Where in the first paragraph is the best place for the following sentence?

   "At that time, Harlem became an important center of artistic talent for African Americans."

   (A)   In line 2 after the word "changes"

   (B)   In line 9 after the phrase "Harlem Renaissance"

   (C)   In line 10 after the word "celebrated"

   (D)   In line 14 after the phrase "artistic expression"

38. According to the passage, which of the following people was most likely a performer?

   (A)   Bessie Smith

   (B)   Langston Hughes

   (C)   Alan Locke

   (D)   W.E.B. Dubois

39. According to the passage, what were two factors that led to the Harlem Renaissance?

   (A)   A revival of African energy and a redefinition of self

   (B)   A large city district and an artistic atmosphere

   (C)   An increase in people and a general movement toward artistic creativity

   (D)   Civil rights activism and a new atmosphere of creativity

40. According to the passage, who were the "New Negroes?"

   (A)   Blacks who celebrated their African heritage

   (B)   Blacks who were future civil rights leaders

   (C)   Blacks who became community economic leaders

   (D)   Blacks who fought in World War II

41. In which part of the passage does the author identify the source of the creative energy of Harlem?

   (A)   Lines 1-2

   (B)   Lines 3-4

   (C)   Lines 5-6

   (D)   Lines 9-10

42. Why does the author mention that Harlem has been through "a multitude of changes" in lines 1–2?

   (A)   To emphasize the importance of the migration from the South

   (B)   To introduce the topic of the Harlem Renaissance

   (C)   To focus attention on economic conditions leading to the depression

   (D)   To set the time period in the early twentieth century

**Questions 43–55 are based on the following passage.**

In the early 1800s, the western part of what is now the United States was unknown to most Americans. There were a few trappers and explorers in the area, however, and some of them sent stories of incredible sights back to their friends in the eastern part of the U.S. One of the stories was about
(5) seeing boiling springs, steamy vapors, and bubbling mud pots in the region called Yellowstone. More than 50 years after the first of these stories appeared, and after seeing photographs of the area from a scientific expedition, the United States Congress voted to set the area aside as a national park. This was the first U.S. national park and is, for many, the most loved. It
(10) comprises 2,219,791 acres (308,317 hectares) and is located in an area that overlaps three states: Wyoming, Idaho, and Montana. Though Yellowstone hosts impressive canyons, waterfalls, lakes, and abundant wildlife, the most spectacular features are the geysers, which spew hot water high into the air at regular intervals. Other geothermal attractions, such as boiling mud pots
(15) and steaming hot pools, are equally impressive.

Years of research into the geologic forces of Yellowstone Park have revealed that the area beneath the park contains chambers of hot magma that are connected to the surface by faults in the earth's crust. Groundwater from the earth seeps into these faults and travels 2 or 3 kilometers downward into
(20) the magma chamber. It may take the water a year to sink into the chambers, but eventually it reaches the magma in which water simmers at three times the boiling point. The heat lowers the density of the water, and this superheated water begins to rise. How this water appears on the surface depends on the constrictions of the channels the water is in. If they are very
(25) narrow, the water and steam come spewing out as geysers into the air. If the cracks are wide, a pool of clear boiling water may develop on the earth. And if only a tiny trickle of water can reach the surface, strong acids may turn the water and steam into pots of bubbling mud.

43. What is the main purpose of this passage?

   (A)   To explain the establishment of Yellowstone

   (B)   To justify the support of the U. S. Park System

   (C)   To describe features of Yellowstone Park

   (D)   To discuss the system of U.S. national parks

44. According to the author, who first told people in the eastern part of the U.S. about Yellowstone?

   (A)   Travelers

   (B)   Journalists

   (C)   Pilgrims

   (D)   Artists

45. When was the Yellowstone National Park Service established?

    (A)    About 1750

    (B)    In the early 1800s

    (C)    In the mid-1800s

    (D)    About 100 years ago

46. Which of the following phrases is most similar to the word "incredible" in line 3?

    (A)    Hard to believe

    (B)    Possibly dangerous

    (C)    Quite unusual

    (D)    Difficult to understand

47. Which of the following words are closest in meaning to the word "spew" in line 13?

    (A)    Shake

    (B)    Spin

    (C)    Shoot

    (D)    Spill

48. Which of the following is closest in meaning to the word "faults" in line 19?

    (A)    Mistakes

    (B)    Cracks

    (C)    Problems

    (D)    Tubes

49. What does the author say about magma?

    (A) It causes water to be much hotter than the boiling point.

    (B) It may take a year to seep through the faults.

    (C) It begins to rise when it is heated enough.

    (D) It has a lower density than water.

50. Where in the passage is the best place for the following sentence?

    "Most people were astonished that such sights actually existed."

    (A)    In line 2 after the word "Americans"

    (B)    In line 6 after the word  "Yellowstone"

    (C)    In line 9 after the word "park"

    (D)    In line 14 after the word "intervals"

51. Look at the word "it" in line 21. To which of the following words from the paragraph does the word "it" refer?

    (A)    Chamber

    (B)    Fault

    (C)    Water

    (D)    Area

52. What does the author imply about the scientific expedition to Yellowstone mentioned in the first paragraph?

    (A)   Fifty years of experiments led to a scientific understanding of the geologic formations.

    (B)   The photographs were published in a scientific magazine.

    (C)   The U.S. Congress gave money to fund the scientists' expedition.

    (D)   The trip led to the establishment of Yellowstone National Park.

53. Why does the author mention "canyons, waterfalls, lakes, and abundant wildlife" in paragraph 1?

    (A)   To emphasize the natural monuments in Yellowstone

    (B)   To warn the reader of danger in Yellowstone

    (C)   To identify the most spectacular attractions of Yellowstone

    (D)   To indicate that Yellowstone has a natural beauty

54. According to the passage, which of the following processes is correct?

    (A)   Water seeps down, causing constrictions of the channels

    (B)   Water simmers, causing it to reach the magma chamber

    (C)   Density of water is lowered, causing water temperature to rise

    (D)   Water rises, causing it to seep toward the magma

55. In which lines does the author explain the difference between the formation of geysers, pools, and mud pots?

    (A)   Lines 4–6

    (B)   Lines 12–15

    (C)   Lines 16–18

    (D)   Lines 25-28

# ANSWER KEY

## SECTION 1—LISTENING

### Part A

| | | | |
|---|---|---|---|
| 1. A | 5. A | 9. B | 13. A |
| 2. B | 6. B | 10. A | 14. D |
| 3. D | 7. B | 11. A | 15. C |
| 4. C | 8. C | 12. B | |

### Part B

| | | | | | | |
|---|---|---|---|---|---|---|
| 16. B | 21. D | 26. A | 31. D | 36. D | 41. D | 46. B |
| 17. A | 22. A | 27. C | 32. A | 37. D | 42. A | 47. A |
| 18. D | 23. D | 28. A | 33. A | 38. B | 43. C | 48. B |
| 19. C | 24. B | 29. B | 34. B | 39. A | 44. C | 49. D |
| 20. C | 25. D | 30. A | 35. C | 40. C | 45. A | 50. A |

## SECTION 2—STRUCTURE

| | | | | |
|---|---|---|---|---|
| 1. D | 6. C | 11. D | 16. B | 21. D |
| 2. C | 7. B | 12. B | 17. B | 22. B |
| 3. C | 8. B | 13. D | 18. C | 23. C |
| 4. B | 9. C | 14. C | 19. C | 24.C |
| 5. A | 10. A | 15. B | 20. C | 26.D |

## SECTION 3—READING

| | | | | |
|---|---|---|---|---|
| 1. B | 12. B | 23. A | 34. D | 45. C |
| 2. D | 13. C | 24. A | 35. B | 46. A |
| 3. A | 14. C | 25. C | 36. C | 47. C |
| 4. C | 15. D | 26. A | 37. B | 48. B |
| 5. A | 16. C | 27. D | 38. A | 49. A |
| 6. D | 17. B | 28. C | 39. C | 50. B |
| 7. B | 18. B | 29. B | 40. A | 51. C |
| 8. C | 19. D | 30. B | 41. C | 52. D |
| 9. B | 20. D | 31. B | 42. B | 53. D |
| 10. A | 21. B | 32. A | 43. C | 54. C |
| 11. A | 22. C | 33. C | 44. A | 55. D |

# EXPLANATORY ANSWERS

## SECTION 1—LISTENING

## Part A

1. **The correct answer is (A).** The phrase "to be fired" means that a person loses his or her job because the boss or the manager tells him or her to leave. It implies a negative reaction from the manager, though a person could also get fired if the company or workplace is reducing their personnel.

2. **The correct answer is (B).** The man is complaining that he has a lot to do: a midterm test and two papers to write. The woman's response of "perk up" means that she is telling him to be happy because the school term will be ending soon.

3. **The correct answer is (D).** The woman says that the man can borrow her notes, so he will probably take her notebook and read over what she wrote. The phrase "to catch what someone says" means "to understand" or "to hear clearly."

4. **The correct answer is (C).** The man will tell the others in the study group that the woman will be late. She is telling the man about her car in order to explain why she will be late.

5. **The correct answer is (A).** When the woman says, "I'll look into it," she means that she will find out more about it. Therefore, we can infer that she is interested in going to the class.

6. **The correct answer is (B).** The expression "come back" means the same as "return." The structure "if only" means the same as "I wish that…" Choice (A) is incorrect because the woman does not say that she wants Laura to be alone when she comes back.

7. **The correct answer is (B).** When the man says, "She should have mailed the check a week ago," he implies that Barbara did not mail the check at the expected (or required) time – a week ago. The woman then assumes that there was some problem with mailing the check and she wonders what the problem is.

8. **The correct answer is (C).** When the woman says, "hang on to the job," she means that he should continue to work at his current job. He agrees with this when he says, "At least for a while," implying that he may not stay for a very long time at his current job.

9. **The correct answer is (B).** The man and woman imply that Peter was sick and that he stayed home for a while but then went back to his classes sooner than they thought he should. The woman's statement is in the past conditional and also implies that Peter may have gotten sick again, or continued to be sick, since he did not stay home to rest long enough.

10. **The correct answer is (A).** Because the man says, "Let's find out," we can assume that he does not know the answer to the woman's question.

11. **The correct answer is (A).** The expression "for good" means that something is permanent, that it will last a long time, or that there are no plans to change it.

12. **The correct answer is (B).** The expression "in no time" means "very quickly." A shortcut refers to an alternate route somewhere that is shorter than the regular route.

13. **The correct answer is (A).** The answer restates the man's comment in the opposite form. The man says that he didn't think the test would be so complicated, which means that it was more complicated than he thought. Therefore, it was not easy.

14. **The correct answer is (D).** The term "close call" means that something bad almost happened but didn't actually happen. Or it might mean that a minor problem didn't become a major problem. It has nothing to do with a telephone and does not necessarily mean that something was physically near.

15. **The correct answer is (C).** When the woman says she is waiting, we can assume that she hasn't bought them yet. Choice (B) is wrong because she is not using last year's books now. Choice (D) is wrong because we don't know how she will get the books. Maybe she will buy them from the students themselves, but maybe the bookstore will resell the used books.

## Part B

16. **The correct answer is (B).** This is a restatement question. The speaker says that the Carter family, "followed ideals of simplicity, frugality, and hard work." Choice (C) is incorrect because the phrase "to be hired" implies getting paid for a job. In Jimmy's case, he was a child doing work around the farm with his family. We don't know if he was paid.

17. **The correct answer is (A).** This is a restatement question. The speaker says, "For fun, he and his father used to go fishing and hunting."

18. **The correct answer is (D).** This is a restatement question. The speakers says that Carter got involved in projects such as building homes for working-class people through the organization, Habitat for Humanity.

19. **The correct answer is (C).** This is a restatement question. In the beginning, the speaker says that Carter's term was from 1977 to 1981. At the end of his talk, the speaker says that he ran for president, and won, in 1976 (which would mean that he would begin his term the next year.)

20. **The correct answer is (C).** This is an inference question. The man says, "I really don't understand why she didn't like it" after he says, "Professor Adams wrote comments all over it." He is referring to the written comments from the professor on his paper.

21. **The correct answer is (D).** This is an inference question. The man says, "I feel pretty bad" and after that he says, "I worked like crazy on that paper." The phrase "to work like crazy" means "to work very hard." We know that he worked hard, and we know that he still got negative comments from the professor. Therefore, we can infer that he feels bad because he worked hard and still did not do well.

22. **The correct answer is (A).** This is a restatement question. The woman suggests that he see the TA (teaching assistant), and he says, "I'll give it a try." This means that he plans to see the TA at least once to see if it helps him. A teaching assistant (TA) is often hired in universities to help a professor by meeting with students to assist them with understanding lectures and doing assignments.

23. **The correct answer is (D).** This is a restatement question. At the beginning of the conversation, the man says that he is "pretty hopeful this time."

24. **The correct answer is (B).** This is a restatement question. The man says that they interviewed 16 the first time but that only 4 of them were asked to return this time.

25. **The correct answer is (D).** This is a restatement question. The man says that his girlfriend doesn't want to leave her family and that she hopes he finds a job close to home.

26. **The correct answer is (A).** This is a restatement question. The woman says that she finished her two term papers and can now "see the light." The idiomatic expression "see the light" refers to finally being able to understand something or being free from a load of work or problems.

27. **The correct answer is (C).** This is an inference question. When the man asks her to go to the art exhibit, her first response is, "Oh, I don't know." This implies that she doesn't want to go or can't go.

28. **The correct answer is (A).** This is a restatement question. The man says, "Next week, it will go to Los Angeles."

29. **The correct answer is (B).** This is a restatement question. The man says, "We could hit both of them." The idiomatic expression "hit" in this case means "go to."

30. **The correct answer is (A).** This is a restatement. In the beginning, the woman says she just finished trying the new telephone system to enroll in classes.

31. **The correct answer is (D).** This is a restatement question. The man says, "Maybe you should see a counselor."

32. **The correct answer is (A).** This is a restatement question. The man says, "I don't think I'll have any trouble . . . last semester, it was easy."

33. **The correct answer is (A).** This is an inference question. The speaker begins by saying that he will discuss one of the main problems that researchers and historians run into when they study ancient music. He goes on to say that the major problem is that there is often nothing tangible to examine. The word "tangible" means "real" and often refers to something that you can see or touch.

34. **The correct answer is (B).** This is a restatement question. The professor says that one can find remnants of old buildings and statues around to examine. This means that there is physical evidence of them. The word "remnants" means "pieces" or "small amounts of a larger original object."

35. **The correct answer is (C).** This is a restatement question. The professor states that music died out since it occurred mostly during festivals and pagan rituals. He also states that early church leaders thought that pagan festivals and theater should be exterminated. The verb "died out" infers that something disappeared by itself over time. The verb "exterminated" means "destroyed."

36. **The correct answer is (D).** This is in inference question. The speaker ends by saying that he will go on to talk about particular aspects of Greek musical practice and theory. Choice (D) is the choice that relates best to this statement. Choice (A) is wrong because it is not medieval music that will be talked about next. He says that they will study medieval music later. Choice (B) is too general. Choice (C) is about the Romans instead of the Greeks.

37. **The correct answer is (D).** This is a restatement question. The professor states that she will talk about some of the changes in décor that have occurred over the years, then continues to describe some of the differences in objects that have been brought in.

38. **The correct answer is (B).** This is a restatement question. The professor says that Abigail used the East Room for hanging out her washing.

39. **The correct answer is (A).** This is an inference question. The professor says that some Americans have argued that the objects used in White House décor should only be American.

40. **The correct answer is (C).** This is a restatement question. The professor says that Martin Van Buren bought carpets from abroad and that James Monroe bought furniture from France.

41. **The correct answer is (D).** This is a restatement question. The speaker says, "Many people have heard that crocodiles eat their babies . . . in fact, they don't."

42. **The correct answer is (A).** This is a restatement question. The speaker says that the crocodile digs a hole and then lays her eggs in it.

43. **The correct answer is (C).** This is a restatement question. The speaker says that the mother "takes the young into a pouch of skin in her lower jaw and carries them to the safety of the water." Choice (B) is close, because of course she is also protecting the young, but the main reason to put them into her mouth is to transport them.

44. **The correct answer is (C).** This is a restatement question. The speaker says she guards her nest for 12 weeks.

45. **The correct answer is (A).** This is a restatement question. The speaker says Borlaug's goal was to improve low-yielding wheat.

46. **The correct answer is (B).** This is an inference question. The speaker says that Borlaug was chosen by the Rockefeller Foundation to go abroad. This happened before the Nobel Peace Prize was given to him.

47. **The correct answer is (A).** This is a restatement question. The speaker says that Borlaug went abroad to introduce new agricultural technology to farmers.

48. **The correct answer is (B).** This is an inference question. The speaker refers to the beauty of the homes and castles on the islands in the river. The other choices are not mentioned at all.

49. **The correct answer is (D).** This is a restatement question. The speaker says that "it's only been since 1959 that a series of canals, locks, and dams have made the river navigable."

50. **The correct answer is (A).** This is a restatement question. The speaker says that the Thousand Islands is an area dotted with tree-covered islands.

## SECTION 2—STRUCTURE

1. **The correct answer is (D).** Preposition. The answer should be "from," or "keep their distance from each other."

2. **The correct answer is (C).** Verb. The verb should be in the past tense, "wore," since it refers to "the early days" of flying. The phrase "in the early days" refers to a time when something is new or still being developed. Therefore, "the early days of flying" refers to the early 1900s when airplanes were a new type of transportation.

3. **The correct answer is (C).** Preposition. The answer should be" give out" or "give off" gases.  It means "to produce."

4. **The correct answer is (B).** Word form.  The answer should be "considerably."  It is an adverb that modifies "vary."

5. **The correct answer is (A).** Wrong word.  The word should be "some." The sentence is plural and specific, referring to "some particular baby birds." These baby birds are called nestlings.

6. **The correct answer is (C).** Verb. This is a passive construction.

7. **The correct answer is (B).** Conjunction. The two words that are connected are "largest" and "finest."

8. **The correct answer is (B).** Comparison. The correct phrase includes the main verb "need" plus the comparison "more heat than fibers from animal sources."

9. **The correct answer is (C).** Verb. The sentence is all in the present tense, as shown by the first verb, "is."

10. **The correct answer is (A).** Subject + verb. Choice (A) is the only choice that includes a verb.

11. **The correct answer is (D).** Verb/parallel construction. The two verbs that must be parallel are "sinks" and "soars." "Sinks" means to go down, while "soars" means to rise up.

12. **The correct answer is (B).** Adjective. The answer is part of the noun phrase "its many ethnic shops and restaurants." The word "ethnicity" is a noun and would not fit here. Choice (A) is incorrect because the word "shops" is plural.

13. **The correct answer is (D).** Pronoun. This is also called "empty it." The word "it" has no meaning and is put in the sentence to fill the subject position.

14. **The correct answer is (C).** Unnecessary word. The word "it" is not necessary in this phrase. It is correct to say that the waterway connects Albany and Buffalo.

15. **The correct answer is (B).** Word form. The correct phrase is "under consideration."

16. **The correct answer is (B).** Verb. The verb should be the passive form "was written."

17. **The correct answer is (B).** Verb. The correct verb is the plural form, "seem to," to go with the plural noun "species."

18. **The correct answer is (C).** Verb. The correct verb is in the simple past tense, "appeared," because a specific date is given from a past time.

19. **The correct answer is (C).** Adverb. The correct word is "strictly." This means the same as "only" or "inflexibly."

20. **The correct answer is (C).** Verb. The verb should be singular, "was," in order to go with the main noun "transport."

21. **The correct answer is (D).** Infinitive/gerund. The correct phrase is "the cost of being sick."

22. **The correct answer is (B).** Pronoun. The word "his" cannot be the pronoun that carries the meaning of "people" because "people" is plural and "his" is singular. The correct pronoun is "their."

23. **The correct answer is (C).** Reversed words. The correct phrase is "pioneer families." The word "pioneer" describes the type of families.

24. **The correct answer is (C).** Verb/word form. The correct answer is "surprised." It is the passive form of the verb.

25. **The correct answer is (D).** Word form. The correct word is "dangerous," an adjective that describes that rest of the sentence: "the indiscriminate and continual use of any drug without medical supervision."

# SECTION 3—READING

1. **The correct answer is (B).** This is a main idea question. Choice (A) can be inferred but is not the main subject. Choice (C) is too specific, and choice (D) is too broad.

2. **The correct answer is (D).** This is a restatement question. The passage states that the "ancestry [of the banjo] is African."

3. **The correct answer is (A).** This is a vocabulary question. A "plantation" is an area that consists of fields for planting crops and homes for the landowners and field workers.

4. **The correct answer is (C).** This is a vocabulary question. A "peg" is a type of small pin, often made of wood.

5. **The correct answer is (A).** This is a vocabulary question. The words "precise" and "accurate" both mean "exact."

6. **The correct answer is (D).** Choices (A), (B), and (C) are all stated in the passage.

7. **The correct answer is (B).** This is a vocabulary question. A "comeback" means a "reappearance." In this sense, it means to return and become famous or popular again.

8. **The correct answer is (C).** This is a vocabulary question. The words "renewed" and "revived" both mean to become important again, "to be brought to life" again.

9. **The correct answer is (B).** This is a vocabulary question. To be in the "forefront" means to be in the extreme front or "the position of most importance." To be in the "spotlight" means to be in a place of prominence.

10. **The correct answer is (A).** This is an author's attitude question. We can infer that the author thinks that the banjo is unique in part from the first sentence, which says that it is hard to find artifacts that are genuinely American.

11. **The correct answer is (A).** This is a main idea question. Although all of the answers are mentioned, choice (A) is the most comprehensive.

12. **The correct answer is (B).** We know that Roosevelt nominated Al Smith, but the passage does not say that Roosevelt voted for him.

13. **The correct answer is (C).** This is a vocabulary question. The phrase "to take action" means to take charge of something, usually a task that needs to be done. In this case, the action was that Roosevelt responded to the problem of bank failure. We can assume from the sentence that he acted quickly to solve the problem.

14. **The correct answer is (C).** This is a vocabulary question. The phrase "little by little" means doing something in small doses.

15. **The correct answer is (D).** This is a vocabulary question. All of these choices might mean "full" in some situations, but only "complete" is appropriate in this sentence. The "full power" of the government means all the power of the government.

16. **The correct answer is (C).** This is a line focus question. Lines 12–15 say that Roosevelt "took action" by closing the banks.

17. **The correct answer is (B).** This is a vocabulary question. The words "affection" and "fondness" indicate a warm emotional feeling or attachment toward someone or something.

18. **The correct answer is (B).** This is a vocabulary question. The words "Unprecedented" and "unheard of" both mean something that is unusual and may not have happened before.

19. **The correct answer is (D).** This is an inference question. The passage refers to "forgotten people," "workers," and "wage earners" as those who felt the strongest attraction to Roosevelt. Choice (A) is not correct because poor people may not be earning regular wages. It would probably not be referring to bankers or rich people because we might infer that these people would not be called "forgotten people." The term "wage earners" usually refers to people who are earning regular wages but are not rich.

20. **The correct answer is (D).** This is a vocabulary question. The word "looming" refers to something that appears or rises before us. This word often gives the idea that the thing appearing may be large and possibly threatening.

21. **The correct answer is (B).** This is a restatement question. The first sentence says that our eyes and ears turn light and sound into electrical impulses. The "transformation," then, is the making of electrical impulses.

22. **The correct answer is (C).** This is a vocabulary question. The verbs "to admit" and "to let in" both refer to allowing something to enter.

23. **The correct answer is (A).** This is a referent question. The word "them" refers back to the previous noun, "light waves."

24. **The correct answer is (A).** This is a vocabulary question. The word "bundle" is a verb in this sentence, referring to an assortment of things that come together, possibly being wrapped or tied together. The word "group" is the closest of these words.

25. **The correct answer is (C).** This is a vocabulary question. All of the answer choices can mean "split" in some contexts. In this sentence, "split" means "to divide" or "to separate." The words "tear," "fracture," and "crack" all connote something negative. "Crack" and "fracture" refer to the breaking of something that is hard and brittle, while "tear" means to pull apart something by force.

26. **The correct answer is (A).** This is a line focus question. The beginning step in the process of transforming light into electrical impulses is described in lines 5–6, which state that "the process begins as the eye admits light."

27. **The correct answer is (D).** This is a restatement question. In line 9, the phrase "vice versa" means that the opposite happens.

28. **The correct answer is (C).** This is a vocabulary question. The verbs "to carry out" and "to accomplish" both refer to getting something done or achieving some purpose.

29. **The correct answer is (B).** This is a vocabulary question. A vibration is a movement like a tremble, a flutter, or a quiver.

30. **The correct answer is (B).** This is a restatement question. Lines 7–8 say that optic nerves join and split into two optic tracts.

31. **The correct answer is (B).** This is a main purpose question. Choice (B) is the most inclusive of the choices. Choice (A) is only mentioned as a place that several people came from. Choice (C) is too general. Some artists are mentioned, but their lives are not discussed. Choice (D) is too general since the passage is focused on Harlem.

32. **The correct answer is (A).** This is a referent question. Harlem is a neighborhood or area in New York City and is referred to as "part of New York City." Choice (B) is not correct since the migration refers to people moving specifically to this part of New York city, not to the whole state.

33. **The correct answer is (C).** This is a vocabulary question. The word "influx" refers to the arrival of a large number of people or things to a place. The answer choices are close. An influx results in an increase, and a migration (movement from one place to another) can lead to an influx of people. The best choice, however, is choice (C), since the increase is a result of the influx and a migration might not be large enough to be called an influx. In addition, a migration might not result in people staying in one place; they might continue to move.

34. **The correct answer is (D).** This is a vocabulary question. The word "host" has many meanings. In this sentence, it refers to a large number of something. One can refer to "a host of flowers" as well as "a host of people." The word "host" can also refer to a person who introduces guests on a television or radio show or someone who entertains guests at his or her home. Choice (B) is close since the "host" may also be a select group of people, but it is too specific for this sentence.

35. **The correct answer is (B).** This is a restatement question. The passage states that the period of artistic movement lasted from 1919 to 1929. This is one decade (ten years).

36. **The correct answer is (C).** This is a vocabulary question. This is an inference question. The phrase "in the meantime" refers to a period of time between two points that are mentioned in the text. The first is "the new atmosphere" that accompanied the Harlem Renaissance and that was given a date of 1925. The second is "future civil rights activism." We don't know the date of future civil rights activism; we only know that it is "some time later." But we are told that an economic depression and World War II occur during that time, which is "in the meantime."

37. **The correct answer is (B).** The best place is after the phrase "Harlem Renaissance" because it adds information about the result of the migration of people to Harlem. Choice (A) is not good because it would break up the connection between "changes" and "one of the most significant" of the changes. Choice (C) is not good because the sentence that ends with "celebrated" should be followed by a description of artists. Choice (D) is not good because the sentence that ends in "artistic expression" is a summary sentence that does not lend itself to more description of Harlem at that time.

38. **The correct answer is (A).** This is an inference question. The passage states that Bessie Smith was a jazz singer. She is the most likely to be a stage performer. Of the others, the passage states that one is a poet, one a civil rights leaders, and one a sociologist.

39. **The correct answer is (C).** This is a restatement question. The passages states that the influx of people combined with a general movement toward artistic experimentation formed the basis of the Harlem Renaissance.

40. **The correct answer is (A).** This is a restatement question. The passage states that there was a new atmosphere of expression among Blacks in which they exalted their African heritage; these were known as the "New Negroes."

41. **The correct answer is (C).** This is a line focus question. The author states that the new arrivals and the general movement toward artistic expression formed the basis for a creative outburst of activity.

42. **The correct answer is (B).** This is an author's purpose question. The author follows the statement about changes with a comment that the most significant change is the one that occurred in the early part of the twentieth century, which is the period of the Harlem Renaissance.

43. **The correct answer is (C).** This is a main purpose question. Most of the passage describes various aspects of Yellowstone National Park, including its main attractions and its geological structure.

44. **The correct answer is (A).** This is restatement question that relates to vocabulary.  In the first paragraph, the author states that trappers and explorers sent stories to their friends in the eastern part of the U.S. Trappers are people who catch wild animals, often to sell their fur. Explorers are people who go on journeys to discover something. The best choice to describe these people is "travelers" since both trappers and explorers are people who move around. Journalists are people who write articles, usually for a magazine or newspaper.  Pilgrims are people who make a journey, usually for religious purposes.

45. **The correct answer is (C).** This is a restatement question. The passage states that Yellowstone National Park was established 50 years after sometime in the early 1800s. The closest to this period is the mid-1800s.

46. **The correct answer is (A).** This is a vocabulary question. The word "incredible" means "not believable" or "very difficult to believe."

47. **The correct answer is (C).** This is a vocabulary question. Both "spew" and "shoot" refer to something coming out, often quickly.

48. **The correct answer is (B).** This is a vocabulary question. In geology, a fault is a crack in the surface of the earth.  Earthquakes occur when two fault lines move in opposite ways.

49. **The correct answer is (A).** This is an inference question. The passage states that the groundwater seeps into the earth through faults, until it reaches the magma in which water simmers at three times the boiling point.  Choices (B), (C), and (D) refer to water, not magma.

50. **The correct answer is (B).** The added sentence expands on the comment about sights such as boiling springs, steamy vapors, and bubbling mud pots. In the other places, the added sentence breaks up the connection between the existing sentences or does not relate directly to the sights of Yellowstone. Choice (D) is not correct even though the sentence that ends in "intervals" relates to astonishing sights since the verb in the sentence is in the present instead of the past tense.

51. **The correct answer is (C).** This is a referent question. This is a referent question.  The main noun phrase prior to the word "it" is "water."

52. **The correct answer is (D).** This is an inference question. The author states that the U.S. Congress voted to make Yellowstone a national park after seeing the photographs. We can assume that the scientific expedition that resulted in photographs had more influence on the Congress people than the verbal stories of these unusual geologic features.

53. **The correct answer is (D).** This is an author's purpose question. The passage infers that the canyons, waterfalls, lakes, and wildlife in Yellowstone are impressive even though they are not as unusual as the spectacular geysers and mud pots.

54. **The correct answer is (C).** This is an inference question. The sentence states, "The heat lowers the density of the water, and this superheated water begins to rise." The sentence implies that the lowered density of the water causes the water to heat.

55. **The correct answer is (D).** This is a line focus question. The author explains that the way water appears on the surface depends on the constrictions of the channels. If they are very narrow, the result is geysers; if they are wide, the result is a pool; and if they are tiny, the result is bubbling mud.

# ANSWER SHEET FOR PRACTICE TEST 3

## Section 1: Listening Comprehension

| | 1 | 2 | 3 | 4 | 5 | 6 | 7 | 8 | 9 | 10 | 11 | 12 | 13 | 14 | 15 | 16 | 17 | 18 | 19 | 20 | 21 | 22 | 23 | 24 | 25 | 26 | 27 | 28 | 29 | 30 | 31 | 32 | 33 | 34 | 35 | 36 | 37 | 38 | 39 | 40 | 41 | 42 | 43 | 44 | 45 | 46 | 47 | 48 | 49 | 50 |
|---|---|---|---|---|---|---|---|---|---|---|---|---|---|---|---|---|---|---|---|---|---|---|---|---|---|---|---|---|---|---|---|---|---|---|---|---|---|---|---|---|---|---|---|---|---|---|---|---|---|---|
| | Ⓐ Ⓑ Ⓒ Ⓓ | Ⓐ Ⓑ Ⓒ Ⓓ | Ⓐ Ⓑ Ⓒ Ⓓ | Ⓐ Ⓑ Ⓒ Ⓓ | Ⓐ Ⓑ Ⓒ Ⓓ | Ⓐ Ⓑ Ⓒ Ⓓ | Ⓐ Ⓑ Ⓒ Ⓓ | Ⓐ Ⓑ Ⓒ Ⓓ | Ⓐ Ⓑ Ⓒ Ⓓ | Ⓐ Ⓑ Ⓒ Ⓓ | Ⓐ Ⓑ Ⓒ Ⓓ | Ⓐ Ⓑ Ⓒ Ⓓ | Ⓐ Ⓑ Ⓒ Ⓓ | Ⓐ Ⓑ Ⓒ Ⓓ | Ⓐ Ⓑ Ⓒ Ⓓ | Ⓐ Ⓑ Ⓒ Ⓓ | Ⓐ Ⓑ Ⓒ Ⓓ | Ⓐ Ⓑ Ⓒ Ⓓ | Ⓐ Ⓑ Ⓒ Ⓓ | Ⓐ Ⓑ Ⓒ Ⓓ | Ⓐ Ⓑ Ⓒ Ⓓ | Ⓐ Ⓑ Ⓒ Ⓓ | Ⓐ Ⓑ Ⓒ Ⓓ | Ⓐ Ⓑ Ⓒ Ⓓ | Ⓐ Ⓑ Ⓒ Ⓓ | Ⓐ Ⓑ Ⓒ Ⓓ | Ⓐ Ⓑ Ⓒ Ⓓ | Ⓐ Ⓑ Ⓒ Ⓓ | Ⓐ Ⓑ Ⓒ Ⓓ | Ⓐ Ⓑ Ⓒ Ⓓ | Ⓐ Ⓑ Ⓒ Ⓓ | Ⓐ Ⓑ Ⓒ Ⓓ | Ⓐ Ⓑ Ⓒ Ⓓ | Ⓐ Ⓑ Ⓒ Ⓓ | Ⓐ Ⓑ Ⓒ Ⓓ | Ⓐ Ⓑ Ⓒ Ⓓ | Ⓐ Ⓑ Ⓒ Ⓓ | Ⓐ Ⓑ Ⓒ Ⓓ | Ⓐ Ⓑ Ⓒ Ⓓ | Ⓐ Ⓑ Ⓒ Ⓓ | Ⓐ Ⓑ Ⓒ Ⓓ | Ⓐ Ⓑ Ⓒ Ⓓ | Ⓐ Ⓑ Ⓒ Ⓓ | Ⓐ Ⓑ Ⓒ Ⓓ | Ⓐ Ⓑ Ⓒ Ⓓ | Ⓐ Ⓑ Ⓒ Ⓓ | Ⓐ Ⓑ Ⓒ Ⓓ | Ⓐ Ⓑ Ⓒ Ⓓ | Ⓐ Ⓑ Ⓒ Ⓓ | Ⓐ Ⓑ Ⓒ Ⓓ |

## Section 2: Structure and Written Expression

| | 1 | 2 | 3 | 4 | 5 | 6 | 7 | 8 | 9 | 10 | 11 | 12 | 13 | 14 | 15 | 16 | 17 | 18 | 19 | 20 | 21 | 22 | 23 | 24 | 25 | 26 | 27 | 28 | 29 | 30 | 31 | 32 | 33 | 34 | 35 | 36 | 37 | 38 | 39 | 40 |
|---|---|---|---|---|---|---|---|---|---|---|---|---|---|---|---|---|---|---|---|---|---|---|---|---|---|---|---|---|---|---|---|---|---|---|---|---|---|---|---|---|
| | Ⓐ Ⓑ Ⓒ Ⓓ | Ⓐ Ⓑ Ⓒ Ⓓ | Ⓐ Ⓑ Ⓒ Ⓓ | Ⓐ Ⓑ Ⓒ Ⓓ | Ⓐ Ⓑ Ⓒ Ⓓ | Ⓐ Ⓑ Ⓒ Ⓓ | Ⓐ Ⓑ Ⓒ Ⓓ | Ⓐ Ⓑ Ⓒ Ⓓ | Ⓐ Ⓑ Ⓒ Ⓓ | Ⓐ Ⓑ Ⓒ Ⓓ | Ⓐ Ⓑ Ⓒ Ⓓ | Ⓐ Ⓑ Ⓒ Ⓓ | Ⓐ Ⓑ Ⓒ Ⓓ | Ⓐ Ⓑ Ⓒ Ⓓ | Ⓐ Ⓑ Ⓒ Ⓓ | Ⓐ Ⓑ Ⓒ Ⓓ | Ⓐ Ⓑ Ⓒ Ⓓ | Ⓐ Ⓑ Ⓒ Ⓓ | Ⓐ Ⓑ Ⓒ Ⓓ | Ⓐ Ⓑ Ⓒ Ⓓ | Ⓐ Ⓑ Ⓒ Ⓓ | Ⓐ Ⓑ Ⓒ Ⓓ | Ⓐ Ⓑ Ⓒ Ⓓ | Ⓐ Ⓑ Ⓒ Ⓓ | Ⓐ Ⓑ Ⓒ Ⓓ | Ⓐ Ⓑ Ⓒ Ⓓ | Ⓐ Ⓑ Ⓒ Ⓓ | Ⓐ Ⓑ Ⓒ Ⓓ | Ⓐ Ⓑ Ⓒ Ⓓ | Ⓐ Ⓑ Ⓒ Ⓓ | Ⓐ Ⓑ Ⓒ Ⓓ | Ⓐ Ⓑ Ⓒ Ⓓ | Ⓐ Ⓑ Ⓒ Ⓓ | Ⓐ Ⓑ Ⓒ Ⓓ | Ⓐ Ⓑ Ⓒ Ⓓ | Ⓐ Ⓑ Ⓒ Ⓓ | Ⓐ Ⓑ Ⓒ Ⓓ | Ⓐ Ⓑ Ⓒ Ⓓ | Ⓐ Ⓑ Ⓒ Ⓓ | Ⓐ Ⓑ Ⓒ Ⓓ |

## Section 3: Reading Comprehension

| | 1 | 2 | 3 | 4 | 5 | 6 | 7 | 8 | 9 | 10 | 11 | 12 | 13 | 14 | 15 | 16 | 17 | 18 | 19 | 20 | 21 | 22 | 23 | 24 | 25 | 26 | 27 | 28 | 29 | 30 | 31 | 32 | 33 | 34 | 35 | 36 | 37 | 38 | 39 | 40 | 41 | 42 | 43 | 44 | 45 | 46 | 47 | 48 | 49 | 50 | 51 | 52 | 53 | 54 | 55 | 56 | 57 | 58 | 59 | 60 |
|---|---|---|---|---|---|---|---|---|---|---|---|---|---|---|---|---|---|---|---|---|---|---|---|---|---|---|---|---|---|---|---|---|---|---|---|---|---|---|---|---|---|---|---|---|---|---|---|---|---|---|---|---|---|---|---|---|---|---|---|---|
| | Ⓐ Ⓑ Ⓒ Ⓓ | Ⓐ Ⓑ Ⓒ Ⓓ | Ⓐ Ⓑ Ⓒ Ⓓ | Ⓐ Ⓑ Ⓒ Ⓓ | Ⓐ Ⓑ Ⓒ Ⓓ | Ⓐ Ⓑ Ⓒ Ⓓ | Ⓐ Ⓑ Ⓒ Ⓓ | Ⓐ Ⓑ Ⓒ Ⓓ | Ⓐ Ⓑ Ⓒ Ⓓ | Ⓐ Ⓑ Ⓒ Ⓓ | Ⓐ Ⓑ Ⓒ Ⓓ | Ⓐ Ⓑ Ⓒ Ⓓ | Ⓐ Ⓑ Ⓒ Ⓓ | Ⓐ Ⓑ Ⓒ Ⓓ | Ⓐ Ⓑ Ⓒ Ⓓ | Ⓐ Ⓑ Ⓒ Ⓓ | Ⓐ Ⓑ Ⓒ Ⓓ | Ⓐ Ⓑ Ⓒ Ⓓ | Ⓐ Ⓑ Ⓒ Ⓓ | Ⓐ Ⓑ Ⓒ Ⓓ | Ⓐ Ⓑ Ⓒ Ⓓ | Ⓐ Ⓑ Ⓒ Ⓓ | Ⓐ Ⓑ Ⓒ Ⓓ | Ⓐ Ⓑ Ⓒ Ⓓ | Ⓐ Ⓑ Ⓒ Ⓓ | Ⓐ Ⓑ Ⓒ Ⓓ | Ⓐ Ⓑ Ⓒ Ⓓ | Ⓐ Ⓑ Ⓒ Ⓓ | Ⓐ Ⓑ Ⓒ Ⓓ | Ⓐ Ⓑ Ⓒ Ⓓ | Ⓐ Ⓑ Ⓒ Ⓓ | Ⓐ Ⓑ Ⓒ Ⓓ | Ⓐ Ⓑ Ⓒ Ⓓ | Ⓐ Ⓑ Ⓒ Ⓓ | Ⓐ Ⓑ Ⓒ Ⓓ | Ⓐ Ⓑ Ⓒ Ⓓ | Ⓐ Ⓑ Ⓒ Ⓓ | Ⓐ Ⓑ Ⓒ Ⓓ | Ⓐ Ⓑ Ⓒ Ⓓ | Ⓐ Ⓑ Ⓒ Ⓓ | Ⓐ Ⓑ Ⓒ Ⓓ | Ⓐ Ⓑ Ⓒ Ⓓ | Ⓐ Ⓑ Ⓒ Ⓓ | Ⓐ Ⓑ Ⓒ Ⓓ | Ⓐ Ⓑ Ⓒ Ⓓ | Ⓐ Ⓑ Ⓒ Ⓓ | Ⓐ Ⓑ Ⓒ Ⓓ | Ⓐ Ⓑ Ⓒ Ⓓ | Ⓐ Ⓑ Ⓒ Ⓓ | Ⓐ Ⓑ Ⓒ Ⓓ | Ⓐ Ⓑ Ⓒ Ⓓ | Ⓐ Ⓑ Ⓒ Ⓓ | Ⓐ Ⓑ Ⓒ Ⓓ | Ⓐ Ⓑ Ⓒ Ⓓ | Ⓐ Ⓑ Ⓒ Ⓓ | Ⓐ Ⓑ Ⓒ Ⓓ | Ⓐ Ⓑ Ⓒ Ⓓ | Ⓐ Ⓑ Ⓒ Ⓓ | Ⓐ Ⓑ Ⓒ Ⓓ | Ⓐ Ⓑ Ⓒ Ⓓ |

Date Taken _____

Number Correct

Section 1 _____

Section 2 _____

Section 3 _____

# 12

# Practice Test 3 (PBT Style)

## SECTION 1

### LISTENING COMPREHENSION

This test is written to represent the PBT in terms of numbers of questions, types of questions, and length of time for each section. You can simulate actual TOEFL testing conditions by using the recordings that accompany this book. If you do not have the recordings, ask a friend to read the transcript for the Listening Comprehension section of Practice Test 3 in Part 3 of this book, "Transcripts for Practice Tests."

The Listening Comprehension section includes three parts. In Part A, you hear conversations between two people. Each conversation is followed by one question. In Part B, you hear longer conversations followed by several questions. In Part C, you hear talks given by a single person followed by several questions.

**Now listen to the directions for each part.**

**If you have the CD version, this test can be found on disc 1.**

## Part A

In Part A, you will hear short conversations between two people. After each conversation, a third person will ask a question about what was said. You will hear the conversation only one time, so you must listen carefully. After you hear a question, read the four possible answers in your test book, and decide which one is the best answer. Then, on your answer sheet, fill in the oval of the answer you have chosen. Answer all questions based on what is stated or implied by the speakers.

**Now, listen to an example. You will hear:**

You will read the answer choices in your test book:

- (A)   He will call Pete before he goes home.
- (B)   He will call Pete after he gets home.
- (C)   He called Pete at home.
- (D)   He will call Pete tomorrow.

You learn from the conversation that the man will call Pete as soon as he gets home. The best answer to the question "What does the man mean?" is choice (B), "He will call Pete after he gets home."

**Now continue listening to the recording and begin the test.**

1.  (A)   Adam will repair the car.
    (B)   Adam helped pull the car to the repair shop.
    (C)   Fred already had the car repaired.
    (D)   The car cannot be fixed anymore.

2.  (A)   Jeff agreed to take the oral exam again.
    (B)   Jeff passed the oral exam and went on a vacation.
    (C)   It took Jeff a long time to pass his exam.
    (D)   Jeff didn't take the oral exam.

3.  (A)   He has been waiting for Ron for a long time.
    (B)   Ron is not a new librarian.
    (C)   Ron did a lot of work for the man.
    (D)   He needs to collect some information from Ron.

4.  (A)   He would like to help the woman with the article.
    (B)   He's sure that she'll have trouble with the article.
    (C)   He wants the woman to help him with the article.
    (D)   He's not sure that he wants any help with the article.

5.  (A)   Why the man needs to return to the classroom
    (B)   Why the man is going to the bookstore
    (C)   Which classroom the man is going to
    (D)   What book the man needs to get

6.  (A)    Mary is going to get her driver's license soon.

    (B)    Mary is not going to the party.

    (C)    Mary can't drive because she doesn't have a car.

    (D)    Mary should not be driving without a license.

7.  (A)    She doesn't mind showing the man where the Humanities building is.

    (B)    She wants the man to go away.

    (C)    She would like the man to show her where the Humanities building is.

    (D)    She's not sure she wants to go to the Humanities building.

8.  (A)    The fee for charging is more than $15.

    (B)    He cannot use a credit card if he spends less than $15.

    (C)    The bookstore does not accept credit cards.

    (D)    They cannot accept cash.

9.  (A)    The woman has to wait in line to register.

    (B)    It may be too late for the woman to get into the speech class.

    (C)    The woman needs to take another class before registering for this class.

    (D)    The woman shouldn't wait to give her speech.

10. (A)    Students can consult their books during the final exam.

    (B)    The department will not allow Dr. Jones to give a final exam.

    (C)    Dr. Jones will not give an open-book exam for the final.

    (D)    Dr. Jones is sorry that the exam will be on Tuesday.

11. (A)    He's glad that the woman will be away.

    (B)    He's not sure if he'll be able to help her.

    (C)    He will do what the woman requested of him.

    (D)    He would be glad to help the woman if he weren't going to be away.

12. (A)    She can't eat anymore pizza.

    (B)    She'll eat another piece, but no more after that.

    (C)    She doesn't care for this pizza very much.

    (D)    She'll give the man one more slice.

13. (A)    He's getting some new roommates.

    (B)    He lives alone without anybody to bother him.

    (C)    Things are all right at this point.

    (D)    Things are far from good.

14. (A)    He thinks the university policy hasn't changed a lot.

    (B)    He agrees with the woman's opinion.

    (C)    He doesn't know what the old policy was.

    (D)    He thinks the university has to change their policy.

15. (A)    She was very nervous.
    (B)    She had a heart problem.
    (C)    She failed to give her presentation.
    (D)    She wasn't scared at all.

16. (A)    He thinks it's not a good time or place to talk.
    (B)    He thinks he can make the place better.
    (C)    He thinks it's a good place for a conversation.
    (D)    He thinks they had better leave the place now.

17. (A)    It's expensive to get a 10-speed bicycle.
    (B)    He commutes to school by bike.
    (C)    He would really like a fast bicycle.
    (D)    He can borrow his friend's bicycle whenever he wants.

18. (A)    She doesn't like cheap things.
    (B)    It was two dollars cheaper than usual.
    (C)    It was too expensive.
    (D)    She bought something cheaper.

19. (A)    She was expecting the class to start earlier.
    (B)    She set her alarm for 8 a.m.
    (C)    She got up early and she ate.
    (D)    She had a date before the lab.

20. (A)    Jim graded his assistant's paper.
    (B)    The papers were not graded.
    (C)    Jim didn't grade the papers.
    (D)    Jim always needs assistance grading the papers.

## PART B

In this part of the test, you will hear longer conversations between two people and class discussions. After each conversation or discussion, you will be asked some questions. You will hear the conversations or discussions and the questions only once, so listen carefully. After you hear a question, read the four possible answers in your test book, and decide which one is the best answer. Then, on your answer sheet, find the number of the question and fill in the oval of the answer you have chosen. Answer all questions based on what is stated or implied by the speakers.

**Listen to the example. You will hear:**

**Questions 1 and 2 are based on the following conversation between two friends at school.**

**Now listen to sample question number 1.**

1. Where is the woman going?

   You will read the answer choices in your test book:

   (A)   To the cafeteria

   (B)   To the movie theater

   (C)   To her dorm room

   (D)   To the library

   The correct answer to the question "Where is the woman going?" is choice (D), "To the library."

**Now listen to sample question number 2.**

2. Which best describes the man's feelings about his classes?

   You will read the answer choices in your test book:

   (A)   Term papers are easy for him.

   (B)   He has a lot of essay exams.

   (C)   He finds lab experiments easier than writing term papers.

   (D)   He is busier this semester than last semester.

   The best answer to the question "Which best describes the man's feelings about his classes?" is choice (C), "He finds lab experiments easier than writing term papers."

**Now listen to the test. Remember, you are not allowed to take any notes or write in your test book.**

21. (A)   Why and how Levi Strauss developed his line of blue jeans

    (B)   How Levi's jeans have changed since 1930

    (C)   Successful and unsuccessful inventions

    (D)   Strauss's designer jeans

22. (A)   It's always necessary for mothers to be inventive.

    (B)   Inventiveness is inspired by the need for something.

    (C)   Necessity is born out of new inventions.

    (D)   Most inventions are inspired by mothers.

23. 1) Rivets scratched their saddles.

    2) They got soiled too quickly.

    3) The pockets often tore.

    4) The blue color faded.

       (A)   1 and 2

       (B)   1 and 4

       (C)   2 and 3

       (D)   2 and 4

24. (A)  His original fabric was too stiff.
    (B)  His original fabric got dirty too quickly.
    (C)  The French fabric was cheaper and more durable.
    (D)  The French fabric was 100 percent polyester.

25. (A)  He added front and back pockets.
    (B)  He dyed the fabric off-white.
    (C)  He added the name "denim."
    (D)  He added rivets on the pockets.

26. (A)  They were no longer necessary after the gold mines closed.
    (B)  They made noise on the classroom chairs.
    (C)  They scratched the surface of things when people sat down.
    (D)  They were uncomfortable for school children.

27. (A)  Strauss had successfully improved on a product.
    (B)  Strauss had captured the market like a mouse in a trap.
    (C)  Strauss also invented devices for catching rodents.
    (D)  Necessity is the mother of invention.

28. (A)  Because all jeans are the same
    (B)  Because "Levi's" is easier to pronounce than other brand names
    (C)  Because the name "Levi's" has become synonymous with "blue jeans"
    (D)  Because Levi's jeans are the only jeans available today

29. (A)  In a restaurant
    (B)  In a classroom
    (C)  In a library
    (D)  At a park

30. (A)  Study
    (B)  Eat dinner
    (C)  See a movie
    (D)  Work

31. (A)  Working
    (B)  Studying
    (C)  Dancing
    (D)  Eating

32. (A)  To set a time to meet again
    (B)  To complain about school
    (C)  To explain working hours
    (D)  To request help in finding books

33. (A) Canada

    (B) Alaska

    (C) Alabama

    (D) Washington

34. (A) That he was a president

    (B) That he was a scientist

    (C) That he liked peanuts

    (D) That he was Native American

35. (A) Dedicated

    (B) Angry

    (C) Excited

    (D) Uninformed

# PART C

In this part of the test, you will hear segments read by a single person. After each segment, you will be asked some questions. You will hear the segments and the questions only once, so listen carefully. After you hear a question, read the four possible answers in your test book, and decide which one is the best answer. Then find the number of the question on your answer sheet, and fill in the oval that corresponds to the letter of the answer you have chosen. Answer all questions based on what is stated or implied in the talk.

**Listen to this sample talk. You will hear:**

**Questions 1–2 are based on the following announcement.**

**Now listen to sample question number 1.**

1. [What is the main purpose of this announcement?]

   You will read the answer choices in your test book:

   (A) To demonstrate tutoring techniques

   (B) To explain school policies

   (C) To recruit childcare workers

   (D) To explain a service

   The best answer to the question "What is the purpose of this announcement?" is (D), "To explain a service."

**Now listen to sample question number 2.**

2. What does the speaker recommend?

   You will read the answer choices in your test book:

   (A) Give your child extra tutoring.

   (B) Take your child to the program today.

   (C) Apply as soon as you can.

   (D) Pay next month.

The best answer to the question "What does the speaker recommend?" is (C), "Apply as soon as you can."

**Now, listen to the talks. Remember, you are not allowed to write any notes in your test book.**

36. (A)  History of the Smithsonian
    (B)  Introduction to archaeology
    (C)  Native Americans in the Western States
    (D)  Hiking and backpacking techniques

37. (A)  To the university
    (B)  To a lecture
    (C)  To Wyoming
    (D)  To the Smithsonian Institute

38. (A)  Searching for plant and animal fossils
    (B)  Planting a field
    (C)  Climbing rocks
    (D)  Working at the Smithsonian Museum

39. (A)  $1,250
    (B)  $1,500
    (C)  $2,000
    (D)  $2,500

40. (A)  Her work was promoted by Alfred Stieglitz.
    (B)  She taught at the Art Institute of Chicago.
    (C)  She began spending time in Mexico after her husband's death.
    (D)  She refrained from using vivid colors in her flower paintings.

41. (A)  Her adobe house in New Mexico
    (B)  Her vivid flower paintings
    (C)  Her work in the art department at Texas State Normal College
    (D)  Her commemorative stamp

42. (A)  Southwestern architecture
    (B)  Wisconsin farmland
    (C)  Her studies under Alfred Stieglitz
    (D)  Mexico City skyscrapers

43. (A)  An art gallery
    (B)  The night sky
    (C)  An adobe house
    (D)  A commemorative stamp

44. (A) European expeditions in the 1700s
    (B) The growth of Los Angeles
    (C) Famous sites in Los Angeles
    (D) The entertainment industry

45. (A) The oceans and the gold rush
    (B) Tourism and the entertainment industry
    (C) The railroads and the discovery of oil
    (D) Sea trade and the airplane industry

46. (A) 50 years
    (B) 100 years
    (C) 200 years
    (D) 300 years

47. (A) In a tropical rain forest
    (B) In a Ugandan village
    (C) In a farm community
    (D) In the American Southwest

48. (A) All of the animals living there are endangered.
    (B) It is located southwest of Uganda.
    (C) Half of the remaining mountain gorilla population lives there.
    (D) It is known for its lack of biodiversity.

49. (A) They returned to their camp outside the forest at the end of each day.
    (B) They brought food to the gorillas to supplement their diet.
    (C) They often stayed in the forest at night because they were too far away from their camp.
    (D) They often had to hike all morning because they were unfamiliar with the forest.

50. (A) She thinks that each one is unique.
    (B) She thinks that they all look the same.
    (C) She thinks that their personalities are similar to ours.
    (D) She thinks that they are fascinated by the researchers.

# SECTION 2

# STRUCTURE AND WRITTEN EXPRESSION

## Time—25 minutes

## Part 1—Sentence Completion

**Directions:** Questions 1–15 are not complete sentences. One or more words are left out of each sentence. Under each sentence, you will see four words or phrases, marked (A), (B), (C), and (D). Choose the one word or phrase that completes the sentence correctly. Then, on your answer sheet, find the number of the question and fill in the oval that corresponds to the letter of your answer choice.

**Sentence Completion example questions:**

1. Birds make nests in trees _____ hide their young in the leaves and branches.

    (A)    can where they

    (B)    where they can

    (C)    where can they

    (D)    where can

    The sentence should read, "Birds make nests in trees where they can hide their young in the leaves and branches." Therefore, you should select choice (B).

2. Sleeping, resting, and _____ are the best ways to care for a cold.

    (A)    to drink fluids

    (B)    drank fluids

    (C)    one drink fluids

    (D)    drinking fluids

    The sentence should read, "Sleeping, resting, and drinking fluids are the best ways to care for a cold." Therefore, you should select choice (D).

**Now begin with the questions.**

1. A log grabber has a long arm _____, which stretches out to pick up logs.

    (A)    calls a jib

    (B)    calling a jib

    (C)    a jib called

    (D)    called a jib

2. A home computer _____ an opportunity for convenient and efficient work at home.

   (A)  provides
   (B)  to be providing
   (C)  which provides
   (D)  providing it

3. Eli Whitney's milling machine remained unchanged for a century and a half because _____ was so efficient.

   (A)  it
   (B)  he
   (C)  of
   (D)  its

4. Some of the rainwater from clouds evaporates before _____.

   (A)  reaching the ground
   (B)  to reach the ground
   (C)  reach the ground
   (D)  the ground reaches

5. Once an offending allergen has been identified _____ tests, it is possible for the doctor to give specific desensitizing injections.

   (A)  means of
   (B)  by means of
   (C)  of the means by
   (D)  by means

6. Sometimes _____ wears people out and is worse than the lack of sleep itself.

   (A)  to sleep the desire
   (B)  the desire to sleep
   (C)  to desire sleep is
   (D)  the desire to sleep who

7. Although dissimilar in almost every other respect, birds and insects have both evolved efficient _____ capabilities.

   (A)  fly
   (B)  flying
   (C)  to fly
   (D)  is flying

8. Baby carriers and digging sticks _____ in many cultures today are examples of the earliest tools used by humans.

   (A)  that are still using
   (B)  which still used
   (C)  still used
   (D)  still using

9. _____ children master the basics, advanced development becomes easier.

    (A) The

    (B) Once

    (C) That

    (D) Even

10. _____ there is a close correlation between stress and illness.

    (A) Some psychologists believe

    (B) Believed some psychologists

    (C) Some psychologists to believe

    (D) Some psychologists believing

11. _____ is often used in soups and sauces.

    (A) Parsley, an inexpensive herb,

    (B) Parsley is an inexpensive herb

    (C) Inexpensive parsley, herb

    (D) An herb is inexpensive parsley,

12. Perspiration increases _____ vigorous exercise or hot weather.

    (A) during

    (B) when

    (C) at the time

    (D) for

13. Goddard developed the first rocket to fly faster _____.

    (A) than sound is

    (B) does sound

    (C) sound

    (D) than sound

14. Even if the unemployment rate _____ sharply, the drop may still be temporary.

    (A) will drop

    (B) dropping

    (C) have dropped

    (D) drops

15. Studies indicate _____ collecting art today than ever before.

    (A) there are that more people

    (B) more people that are

    (C) that there are more people

    (D) people there are more

## Part 2—Error Identification

**Directions:** In questions 16 to 40, each sentence has four underlined words or phrases, marked (A), (B), (C), and (D). Choose the one word or phrase that must be changed in order for the sentence to be correct. Then, on your answer sheet, find the number of the question and fill in the oval that corresponds to the letter of your answer choice.

**Error Identification example questions.**

1.  Aspirin is <u>recommend</u> to <u>many</u> people for <u>its</u> ability <u>to thin</u> the blood.
       (A)        (B)           (C)          (D)

    The sentence should read, "Aspirin is recommended to many people for its ability to thin the blood." Therefore, you should select choice (A).

2.  Some people <u>believe that</u> human beings will never <u>use away</u> all <u>the</u> natural
                  (A)                                       (B)         (C)

    resources <u>on earth</u>.
              (D)

    The sentence should read, "Some people believe that human beings will never use up all the natural resources on earth." Therefore, you should select choice (B).

**Now begin work on the questions.**

16.  The surface of <u>the</u> tongue <u>covered</u> with <u>tiny</u> taste <u>buds</u>.
                     (A)          (B)          (C)        (D)

17.  <u>Cosmic</u> distance <u>is</u> measured <u>on</u> light-<u>years</u>.
      (A)              (B)            (C)       (D)

18.  <u>A</u> million <u>of</u> tourists from <u>all over</u> the world <u>visit</u> New York every year.
      (A)     (B)                  (C)                  (D)

19.  <u>Whereas</u> Earth <u>has</u> one moon, the planet <u>call</u> Mars has two small <u>ones</u>.
      (A)          (B)                          (C)                        (D)

20.  An ardent feminist, Margaret Fuller, <u>through</u> her literature, asked <u>that</u> women
                                          (A)                        (B)

     <u>be</u> given a <u>fairly</u> chance.
     (C)          (D)

21.  <u>No</u> longer <u>scientific discovery is</u> a <u>matter of</u> one person <u>working alone</u>.
      (A)           (B)                  (C)                  (D)

22.  The <u>scientific</u> method <u>consists of</u> forming hypotheses, <u>collect</u> data, and
           (A)                  (B)                                  (C)

     testing <u>results</u>.
             (D)

23. All data <u>in computer</u> are changed <u>into</u> electronic pulses <u>by</u> an input <u>unit</u>.
               (A)                (B)                 (C)        (D)

24. The basic <u>law</u> of addition, subtraction, multiplication, and <u>division</u> are <u>taught</u>
           (A)                                   (B)      (C)
to all elementary <u>school</u> students.
                 (D)

25. A <u>largely</u> percentage <u>of</u> Canadian export business <u>is</u> <u>with</u> the United States.
     (A)             (B)                       (C) (D)

26. <u>The famous</u> Jim Thorpe <u>won</u> both the pentathlon <u>or</u> decathlon <u>in</u> the 1912
    (A)              (B)                (C)       (D)
Olympic Games.

27. Acute pharyngitis pain <u>is</u> most often <u>caused</u> by a viral infection, for <u>who</u>
                     (A)         (B)                  (C)
antibiotics <u>are ineffective</u>.
        (D)

28. <u>Knowledges</u> about cultures provides <u>insight into</u> the <u>learned</u> <u>behavior</u> of
   (A)                        (B)      (C)   (D)
groups.

29. A fiber-optic cable <u>across</u> the Pacific <u>went into</u> service <u>in</u> April 1989, <u>link</u> the
               (A)           (B)      (C)      (D)
United States and Japan.

30. <u>Dislike</u> the gorilla, the <u>male</u> adult chimpanzee weighs <u>under</u> 200 <u>pounds</u>.
   (A)             (B)                     (C)      (D)

31. <u>Before</u> lumberjacks had mechanical <u>equipments</u>, they <u>used</u> horses and ropes
   (A)                      (B)        (C)
to <u>drag</u> logs.
  (D)

32. George Gershwin not only <u>composed</u> popular songs <u>for</u> musicals, <u>also</u> wrote
                      (A)         (B)     (C)
<u>more serious</u> concerts.
   (D)

33. <u>Born</u> sometime <u>between</u> the eleventh and the sixteenth centuries, Deganawidah
  (A)        (B)
came to <u>be known</u> as "The Peacemaker" among <u>tribal</u> of the American
       (C)                        (D)
Northeast.

34. Caricature, a <u>type of</u> comic <u>exaggeration</u>, is <u>common</u> used <u>in</u> political
                 (A)            (B)        (C)     (D)
    cartoons.

35. One <u>and</u> more sentences <u>related to</u> the <u>same</u> topic <u>form</u> a paragraph.
      (A)                 (B)      (C)     (D)

36. Mirrors <u>that made</u> of shiny metal <u>were used</u> by the Egyptians <u>in</u> ancient <u>times.</u>
            (A)                 (B)                (C)    (D)

37. Mark Twain's novel, "The Adventures of Huckleberry Finn," <u>are</u> one <u>of</u>
                                                  (A)   (B)
    America's <u>national</u> <u>treasures</u>.
           (C)    (D)

38. In <u>his</u> early days as a <u>direct</u>, Charlie Chaplin produced 62 <u>short, silent</u> comedy
    (A)              (B)                         (C)
    films <u>in four</u> years.
        (D)

39. Some studies show <u>that young babies</u> prefer the <u>smell</u> of milk to <u>those</u> of <u>other</u>
                       (A)               (B)        (C)
    <u>liquids</u>.
    (D)

40. Plants <u>absorb water</u> and nutrients and <u>anchoring themselves</u> in <u>the soil</u> with
            (A)                     (B)        (C)
    their roots.
       (D)

# SECTION 3

## READING COMPREHENSION

## Time—55 minutes

> **Directions:** In this section, you will read several passages. Each passage is followed by questions about it. Choose the one best answer, (A), (B), (C), or (D), for each question. Then, on your answer sheet, find the number of the question and fill in the space that corresponds to the letter of your answer choice. Answer all questions based on what is stated or implied in the passage.

**Reading Comprehension example passage and questions**

### Read the following passage:

A new hearing device is now available for some hearing-impaired people. This device uses a magnet to hold the detachable sound-processing portion in place. Like other aids, it converts sound into vibrations. But it is unique in that it can transmit the vibrations directly to the magnet and then to the
(5)  inner ear. This produces a clearer sound. The new device will not help all hearing-impaired people — only those with a hearing loss caused by infection or some other problem in the middle ear. It will probably help no more than 20 percent of all people with hearing problems. Those people who often have persistent ear infections, however, should find relief and restored
(10) hearing with the new device.

1.  What is the author's main purpose in this passage?

    (A)    To describe a new cure for ear infections

    (B)    To inform the reader of a new device

    (C)    To urge doctors to use a new device

    (D)    To explain the use of a magnet

The author's main purpose is to inform the reader of a new device for hearing-impaired people. Therefore, you should select choice (B).

2.  The word "relief" in the last sentence means

    (A)    Less distress

    (B)    Assistance

    (C)    Distraction

    (D)    Relaxation

The phrase "less distress" is similar in meaning to "relief" in this sentence. Therefore, you should select choice (A).

**Now begin with the questions.**

**Questions 1–12 are based on the following passage.**

Another common blues instrument that flourished in the rural South during the 1920s and 1930s was the blues harp, or harmonica. It was played mainly in bands called jug bands that commonly performed on street corners, in saloons, and in country stores. Jug bands used a variety of instruments,
(5) including the banjo, guitar, washboard, kazoo, fiddle, jugs, and blues harp. In these bands, the blues harp was used primarily for melodic and rhythmic support. The earliest evidence of the harp used as a solo or lead instrument in the jug bands was in the late 1920s, as heard in the recordings of George "Bullet" Williams. Other good harp men, such as Sonny Terry, Little
(10) Walter, and Sonny Boy Williamson, followed Williams, revolutionizing the harp's role as a lead instrument.

1.  What does the passage mainly discuss?

    (A)   Twentieth-century music of the South

    (B)   A change in the role of the blues harp

    (C)   Good harp men of the traditional blues harp

    (D)   The variety of instruments in jug bands

2.  The blues harp is another name for which of the following?

    (A)   Harpsichord

    (B)   Guitar

    (C)   Harmonica

    (D)   Banjo

3.  The word "flourished" as used in line 1 could best be replaced by which of the following?

    (A)   Became widely popular

    (B)   Was invented

    (C)   Appeared briefly

    (D)   Was prohibited

4.  The author uses the phrase "rural South" in line 1 to refer to the Southern

    (A)   landscape.

    (B)   metropolis.

    (C)   countryside.

    (D)   nation.

5.  What can be inferred about George "Bullet" Williams?

    (A)   He was the best blues harp player.

    (B)   He became friends with later harp men.

    (C)   He played lead guitar in his band.

    (D)   He influenced some of the later harp men.

6. As used in line 6, the word "primarily" could best be replaced by which of the following?

   (A)    Chiefly

   (B)    Peculiarly

   (C)    Favorably

   (D)    Advantageously

7. According to the author, when was the harp first used as a lead instrument?

   (A)    1920–1925

   (B)    1925–1930

   (C)    1930–1935

   (D)    1935–1940

8. The word "lead" as used in line 11 is closest in meaning to which of the following?

   (A)    Metallic

   (B)    Secondary

   (C)    Percussion

   (D)    Principal

9. Where in the passage is the best place to add the following sentence?

   "In time, however, musicians began to incorporate blues harp solos into their music."

   (A)    In line 4 after the word "stores"

   (B)    In line 5 after the word "harp"

   (C)    In line 7 after the word "support"

   (D)    In line 11 after the word "instrument"

10. The word "revolutionizing" in line 10 could best be replaced by which of the following?

   (A)    Reforming

   (B)    Fighting

   (C)    Resisting

   (D)    Turning

11. Which of the following would most likely be the topic of the previous paragraph?

   (A)    The use of instruments for rhythmic support in America

   (B)    Blues instruments in rural Southern music of the 1920s and 1930s

   (C)    American music before 1920

   (D)    Jug bands and their role in 1920s Southern music

12. According to the passage, jug bands were likely to perform in all of the following places EXCEPT

    (A)    on street corners.

    (B)    in country stores.

    (C)    in concert halls.

    (D)    in saloons.

**Questions 13–24 are based on the following passage.**

Over the past 600 years, English has grown from a language of few speakers to become the dominant language of international communication. English as we know it today emerged around 1350, after having incorporated many elements of French that were introduced following the Norman invasion of
(5) 1066. Until the 1600s, English was, for the most part, spoken only in England and had not extended even as far as Wales, Scotland, or Ireland. However, during the course of the next two centuries, English began to spread around the globe as a result of exploration, trade (including slave trade), colonization, and missionary work. Thus, small enclaves of English
(10) speakers became established and grew in various parts of the world. As these communities proliferated, English gradually became the primary language of international business, banking, and diplomacy.

Currently, more than 80 percent of the information stored on computer systems worldwide is in English. Two thirds of the world's science writing
(15) is in English, and English is the main language of technology, advertising, media, international airports, and air traffic controllers. Today there are more than 700 million English users in the world, and over half of these are nonnative speakers, constituting the largest number of nonnative users of any language in the world.

13. What is the main topic of this passage?

    (A)    The number of nonnative users of English

    (B)    The French influence on the English language

    (C)    The expansion of English as an international language

    (D)    The use of English for science and technology

14. The word "emerged" in line 3 could best be replaced by which of the following?

    (A)    Appeared

    (B)    Joined

    (C)    Frequented

    (D)    Engaged

15. As used in line 4, the word "elements" is most similar to which of the following?

    (A)    Declarations

    (B)    Features

    (C)    Curiosities

    (D)    Customs

16. Which lines in the passage best summarize how English was initially extended to many areas of the world?

    (A)  Lines 1–4

    (B)  Lines 5–9

    (C)  Lines 6–9

    (D)  Lines 22–26

17. Approximately when did English begin to be used beyond England?

    (A)  In 1066

    (B)  Around 1350

    (C)  Before 1600

    (D)  After 1600

18. According to the passage, all of the following contributed to the spread of English around the world EXCEPT

    (A)  the slave trade.

    (B)  the Norman invasion.

    (C)  missionaries.

    (D)  colonization.

19. As used in line 7, which of the following is closest in meaning to the phrase "the course of?"

    (A)  The subject of

    (B)  The policy of

    (C)  The time of

    (D)  The end of

20. The word "enclaves" in line 9 could best be replaced by which of the following?

    (A)  Communities

    (B)  Organizations

    (C)  Caves

    (D)  Countries

21. The word "proliferated" in line 11 is closest in meaning to which of the following?

    (A)  Contracted

    (B)  Organized

    (C)  Disbanded

    (D)  Expanded

22. Which of the following is closest in meaning to the word "stored" as used in line 13?

    (A)  Bought

    (B)  Saved

    (C)  Spent

    (D)  Valued

23. Which of the following is closest in meaning to the word "constituting" in line 18?

(A) Eliminating

(B) Segregating

(C) Surpassing

(D) Composing

24. According to the passage, approximately how many nonnative users of English are there in the world today?

(A) A quarter million

(B) Half a million

(C) 350 million

(D) 700 million

**Questions 25–36 are based on the following passage.**

As heart disease continues to be the number-one killer in the United States, researchers have become increasingly interested in identifying the potential risk factors that trigger heart attacks. High-fat diets and "life in the fast lane" have long been known to contribute to the high incidence of heart failure.
(5) But according to new studies, the list of risk factors may be significantly longer and quite surprising.

Heart failure, for example, appears to have seasonal and temporal patterns. A higher percentage of heart attacks occur in cold weather, and more people experience heart failure on Monday than on any other day of the
(10) week. In addition, people are more susceptible to heart attacks in the first few hours after waking. Cardiologists first observed this morning phenomenon in the mid-1980s and have since discovered a number of possible causes. An early morning rise in blood pressure, heart rate, and concentration of heart-stimulating hormones, plus a reduction of blood flow to the heart, may all
(15) contribute to the higher incidence of heart attacks between the hours of 8 a.m. and 10 a.m. In other studies, both birthdays and bachelorhood have been implicated as risk factors. Statistics reveal that heart attack rates increase significantly for both females and males in the few days immediately preceding and following their birthdays. And unmarried men are more
(20) at risk for heart attacks than their married counterparts. Though stress is thought to be linked in some way to all of the aforementioned risk factors, intense research continues in the hope of further comprehending why and how heart failure is triggered.

25. What does the passage mainly discuss?

(A) Risk factors in heart attacks

(B) Seasonal and temporal patterns of heart attacks

(C) Cardiology in the 1980s

(D) Diet and stress as factors in heart attacks

26. In line 2, the word "potential" could best be replaced by which of the following?

   (A)   Harmful

   (B)   Primary

   (C)   Unknown

   (D)   Possible

27. The word "trigger" as used in line 3 is closest in meaning to which of the following?

   (A)   Involve

   (B)   Affect

   (C)   Cause

   (D)   Encounter

28. What do the second and third paragraphs of the passage mainly discuss?

   (A)   The link between heart attacks and marriage

   (B)   Unusual risk factors in heart attacks

   (C)   Age and gender factors in heart attacks

   (D)   Myths about lifestyle and heart attacks

29. The author uses the word "temporal" in line 7 to mean which of the following?

   (A)   Time related

   (B)   Weather related

   (C)   Temporary

   (D)   Irregular

30. The phrase "susceptible to" in line 10 could best be replaced by which of the following?

   (A)   Aware of

   (B)   Suspected of

   (C)   Accustomed to

   (D)   Prone to

31. According to the passage, which of the following is NOT a possible cause of many heart attacks?

   (A)   Decreased blood flow to the heart

   (B)   Increased blood pressure

   (C)   Lower heart rate

   (D)   Increase in hormones

32. The word "phenomenon" in line 11 refers to which of the following?

   (A)   Habit

   (B)   Illness

   (C)   Occurrence

   (D)   Activity

33. The word "implicated" in line 17 could best be replaced by which of the following?

    (A)    Indicated

    (B)    Disregarded

    (C)    Investigated

    (D)    Discovered

34. Which of the following is NOT cited as a possible risk factor?

    (A)    Having a birthday

    (B)    Getting married

    (C)    Eating fatty foods

    (D)    Being under stress

35. Which of the following is inferred in the passage?

    (A)    We now fully understand how risk factors trigger heart attacks.

    (B)    We recently began to study how risk factors trigger heart attacks.

    (C)    We have not identified many risk factors associated with heart attacks.

    (D)    We do not fully understand how risk factors trigger heart attacks.

36. As used in line 17, which of the following could best replace the word "reveal"?

    (A)    Show

    (B)    Observe

    (C)    Cover

    (D)    Explain

**Questions 37–48 are based on the following passage.**

Baseball has been dubbed "America's favorite pastime," and many fans contend that there is no greater thrill than watching a good pitcher throw a skillfully delivered fastball or curveball. Two such pitches, the "rising fastball" and the "breaking curveball," are particularly difficult for batters
(5) to hit because these balls seem to veer in one direction or the other just as they reach home plate. The "rising fastball" zooms forward, then appears to jump up and over the bat as the batter swings. The "breaking curveball curves toward home plate, but seems to plunge downward unexpectedly at the last moment. Batters attempt to anticipate these pitches and respond accord-
(10) ingly.

However, according to studies conducted by a team of engineers and psychologists, the "rising fastball" and the "breaking curveball" do not actually exist; they are merely optical illusions. The studies revealed that batters think the ball is approaching more slowly or falling more quickly
(15) than it actually is, and this misperception creates the visual illusion. Also, batters tend to have difficulty tracking the ball continuously as it approaches

and so, they will briefly divert their eyes to the spot where they think the ball will cross the plate. When a batter misjudges the speed or angle of a pitch, and glances down for a second, the ball will appear to suddenly rise or dip—
(20) and the batter will often miss.

How will this finding affect "America's favorite pastime?" No doubt some fans will vehemently reject the notion that the "rising fastball" and the "breaking curveball" are mere illusions. But for others, the research findings may imbue the game with a new level of intrigue as batters attempt to
(25) respond to pitches that don't exist.

37. What does this passage mainly discuss?

(A) The difference between fastballs and curveballs

(B) America's favorite pastime

(C) Optical illusions and the movements of pitched balls

(D) Vision problems among baseball players

38. As used in line 2, the word "contend" could best be replaced by which of the following?

(A) Maintain

(B) Operate

(C) Disagree

(D) Suppose

39. Which of the following words could best replace the word "thrill" in line 2?

(A) Activity

(B) Excitement

(C) Remedy

(D) Issue

40. In line 5, the word "veer" could best be replaced by which of the following?

(A) Pause temporarily

(B) Stop suddenly

(C) Drop sharply

(D) Turn slightly

41. As used in line 6, the word "zooms" is closest in meaning to which of the following?

(A) Falls

(B) Rolls

(C) Speeds

(D) Bounces

42. Which of the following words could best replace the word "plunge" as used in line 8?

    (A) Drop

    (B) Withdraw

    (C) Emerge

    (D) Tip

43. According to the author, why is it difficult for the batter to hit the "rising fastball" and the "breaking curveball?"

    (A) Because the ball approaches too quickly

    (B) Because the ball slows down just before reaching home plate

    (C) Because the batter misjudges the pitcher's motives

    (D) Because the batter misjudges the speed and angle of the ball

44. In line 13, what does the word "they" refer to?

    (A) The "rising fastball" and the "breaking curveball"

    (B) The engineers and psychologists

    (C) The research studies

    (D) The optical illusions

45. Which of the following is closest in meaning to the word "glances" as used in line 19?

    (A) To gaze

    (B) To stare

    (C) To peek briefly

    (D) To look steadily

46. According to the passage, how is the illusion of the "rising fastball" and the "breaking curveball" produced?

    (A) By the pitcher throwing the ball erratically

    (B) By the batter failing to track the ball accurately

    (C) By the location and angle of home plate

    (D) By the studies of engineers and psychologists

47. Which paragraph or paragraphs best explain the actual reasons why batters often miss the "rising fastball" and the "breaking curveball?"

    (A) Paragraphs 1 and 2

    (B) Paragraphs 2 and 3

    (C) Paragraph 1

    (D) Paragraph 2

48. The word "imbue" in line 24 is closest in meaning to which of the following?

    (A) Enhance

    (B) Spoil

    (C) Alter

    (D) Change

**Questions 49–60 are based on the following passage.**

The Timber rattlesnake, once widespread throughout the Eastern United States, is now on the endangered species list and is already extinct in some of the Eastern states in which it once thrived. Compared to its Western cousins, the Timber rattlesnake may be especially vulnerable because of
*(5)* certain behaviors adapted for coping with the cold climate in which it lives.

Rattlesnakes are generally found in warm climates because, like all reptiles, they cannot generate or regulate their own body temperature internally and must rely on the sun's warmth for heat. But Timber rattlesnakes migrated into colder Northern areas about 8,000 years ago when
*(10)* glaciers retreated. In these Northern regions, the snakes developed a number of adaptive strategies to survive the cold, but ultimately these behaviors make them more vulnerable to human predation, their main threat.

One survival strategy the snakes have developed is hibernation. For approximately eight months of the year, the rattlers remain motionless in
*(15)* deep frost-free crevices, with their body temperature dropping as low as 40 degrees. In the spring, when they emerge, they must warm their chilled bodies by sunning for three or four days on rocks in the open. This behavior, coupled with the fact that Timber rattlesnakes tend to concentrate in large numbers at their wintering sites, makes them easy prey. Gestating females
*(20)* are particularly vulnerable because they spend much of their time basking in the sun in order to produce live young from eggs. In addition, females have very long interbirth intervals, producing live young only every three to five years. If a frost or cold spell comes late in the year, the entire litter of 6 to 12 young may die.

*(25)* Efforts are underway to protect the Timber rattlesnake and its habitat from further human depredation, but in many states it is already too late.

49. What is the main topic of the passage?

    (A)    Why Timber rattlesnakes hibernate

    (B)    How Timber rattlesnakes are surviving

    (C)    How Timber rattlesnakes adapted to northern climates

    (D)    Why Timber rattlesnakes are endangered

50. Which of the following is closest in meaning to the word "vulnerable" in line 4?

    (A)    Unprotected

    (B)    Impervious

    (C)    Insensitive

    (D)    Deprived

51. Which of the following is true about Timber rattlesnakes?

    (A)    They migrated to Eastern states.

    (B)    They migrated northward during a warming period.

    (C)    They migrated to escape a cold climate.

    (D)    They migrated to the South to seek a warmer climate.

52. Which part of the passage gives reasons why Timber rattlesnakes are more vulnerable to human predation than other rattlesnake species?

    (A) Lines 4–5

    (B) Lines 10–13

    (C) Lines 13–19

    (D) Lines 1–3

53. Which of the following could best replace the word "emerge" in line 16?

    (A) Come out

    (B) Set off

    (C) Get up

    (D) See through

54. In which of the following places might a person be most likely to find Timber rattlesnakes in the spring?

    (A) In forests

    (B) In open meadows

    (C) In deep crevices

    (D) In caves

55. Which of the following could best replace the phrase "coupled with" in line 18?

    (A) Compared with

    (B) Combined with

    (C) Controlled with

    (D) Supplied with

56. The phrase "easy prey" in line 19 could best be replaced by which of the following?

    (A) Relaxed

    (B) Protected

    (C) Vulnerable

    (D) Sociable

57. Which of the following words can best replace the word "basking" in line 20?

    (A) Washing

    (B) Eating

    (C) Crawling

    (D) Lying

58. According to the passage, which of the following does NOT contribute to the rattlesnake being an endangered animal?

    (A) Hibernating in crevices

    (B) Basking in the sun

    (C) Congregating together

    (D) Having long intervals between births

59. Which of the following could best replace the word "depredation" in line 26?

    (A) Fear

    (B) Habitation

    (C) Destruction

    (D) Depression

60. What is the author's tone?

    (A) Accusative

    (B) Nostalgic

    (C) Informational

    (D) Humorous

# ANSWER KEY

## SECTION 1—LISTENING COMPREHENSION

### Part A

| | | | |
|---|---|---|---|
| 1. A | 6. D | 11. C | 16. C |
| 2. C | 7. C | 12. B | 17. C |
| 3. B | 8. B | 13. C | 18. C |
| 4. C | 9. B | 14. B | 19. A |
| 5. A | 10. C | 15. A | 20. C |

### Part B

| | | |
|---|---|---|
| 21. A | 26. C | 31. A |
| 22. B | 27. A | 32. A |
| 23. C | 28. C | 33. C |
| 24. A | 29. C | 34. B |
| 25. D | 30. A | 35. D |

### Part C

| | | |
|---|---|---|
| 36. B | 41. B | 46. B |
| 37. C | 42. A | 47. A |
| 38. A | 43. C | 48. C |
| 39. B | 44. B | 49. A |
| 40. A | 45. C | 50. A |

## SECTION 2: STRUCTURE AND WRITTEN EXPRESSION

### PART 1—SENTENCE COMPLETION

| | | |
|---|---|---|
| 1. D | 6. B | 11. A |
| 2. A | 7. B | 12. A |
| 3. A | 8. C | 13. D |
| 4. A | 9. B | 14. D |
| 5. B | 10. A | 15. C |

## PART 2—ERROR IDENTIFICATION

| | | | | |
|---|---|---|---|---|
| 16. B | 21. B | 26. C | 31. B | 36. A |
| 17. C | 22. C | 27. C | 32. C | 37. A |
| 18. B | 23. A | 28. A | 33. D | 38. B |
| 19. C | 24. A | 29. D | 34. C | 39. C |
| 20. D | 25. A | 30. A | 35. A | 40. B |

# SECTION 3—READING COMPREHENSION

| | | | | | |
|---|---|---|---|---|---|
| 1. B | 11. B | 21. D | 31. C | 41. C | 51. B |
| 2. C | 12. C | 22. B | 32. C | 42. A | 52. C |
| 3. A | 13. C | 23. D | 33. A | 43. D | 53. A |
| 4. C | 14. A | 24. C | 34. B | 44. A | 54. B |
| 5. D | 15. B | 25. A | 35. D | 45. C | 55. B |
| 6. A | 16. C | 26. D | 36. A | 46. B | 56. C |
| 7. B | 17. D | 27. C | 37. C | 47. D | 57. D |
| 8. D | 18. B | 28. B | 38. A | 48. A | 58. A |
| 9. C | 19. C | 29. A | 39. B | 49. D | 59. C |
| 10. A | 20. A | 30. D | 40. D | 50. A | 60. C |

# EXPLANATORY ANSWERS

## SECTION 1—LISTENING COMPREHENSION

## Part A —Listening Comprehension

1. **The correct answer is (A).** The construction "to have someone do something" means to ask someone to do something.

2. **The correct answer is (C).** The meaning of this sentence is in the intonation of the man, and the word "finally," which indicate that it took Jeff a long time, but he finally passed the exam.

3. **The correct answer is (B).** The man's comment "he's been here as long as I have," and his tone of voice indicate that Ron is not a new employee.

4. **The correct answer is (C).** "The answer is shown both by the tone of voice of "Would I!" and the positive response of "Please do." The exclamation "Would I!" actually means "I really would." Also, he says, "Please do," meaning, "Please help me."

5. **The correct answer is (A)**. The question "What's up?" means, "What is going on?" or "What is the matter?" or "Why?" The woman means, "Why do you need to go back to the classroom?"

6. **The correct answer is (D)**. Because the man says that Mary does not have a driving license, we can assume that Mary should not be driving. The man doesn't mention when Mary will get her driver's license, or whether or not she has a car.

7. **The correct answer is (C)**. When the woman says "if you don't mind," she means, "Yes, I would like you to show me where the building is if it is no trouble for you."

8. **The correct answer is (B)**. The woman says that they will accept a credit card only if the man spends more than $15. If he spends less than $15, he cannot use credit.

9. **The correct answer is (B)**. When the man says there is a waiting list, he means that there are no more spaces left for students in the speech class, but a list has been made of students who would like to take the class. If she's on the waiting list, the woman may still be able to join the class if one of the registered students decides not to take it.

10. **The correct answer is (C)**. Because Dr. Jones says, "department regulations don't allow that…," we can assume that Dr. Jones will follow department policy and not allow books to be opened during the exam. An open-book exam is an exam in which the students can look for information in their books (or consult their books) during the test.

11. **The correct answer is (C)**. The man answers, "Sure," so he is agreeing to help the woman. He says that he'll be glad to do what she has requested.

12. **The correct answer is (B)**. When the woman says, "I just can't stop eating. …," we can assume that she has already eaten a lot of pizza and wants to continue to eat it. She says that she'll eat one more slice (or piece), and that will be her last one ("then that's it"). The phrase "that's it" means "that's all" or "that's the end."

13. **The correct answer is (C).** The expression "so far, so good" means, "At this point in time, things are fine."

14. **The correct answer is (B)**. This is a question for which the speaker's tone of voice is important He is repeating the verb of the woman's comment that the policy "has changed." His statement "Hasn't it!" is an expression of strong agreement, not a question.

15. **The correct answer is (A)**. This is a question for which the speaker's tone of voice is important. In fact, the speaker says the opposite of what she means. Her exclamation "Not much, I wasn't!" actually means "Yes, I was very scared!"

16. **The correct answer is (C).** If there is "no better place then here," then the place is the best place in this area to sit and talk.

17. **The correct answer is (C).** A racing bike is a bike that can go very fast. The man says that he has always wanted a racing bike. He does not say that it is expensive (although it probably is) or that he commutes to school by bike (although he might).

18. **The correct answer is (C).** The woman says that she would have bought the item if it had been ten dollars less. We can infer that it is too expensive for her to buy.

19. **The correct answer is (A).** To say "I thought the lab started at 8 a.m." implies that, in fact, it didn't start at the time she expected. The man's questions "Why did you get up so early?" suggests that Marie thought the class started early in the morning.

20. **The correct answer is (C).** The word "but" is an indication that the sentence expresses an opposite idea. Usually Jim grades the papers, but this time he didn't; he had his assistant grade them.

## Part B

21. **The correct answer is (A).** This is a main idea question. The discussion centers on the invention of Levi's jeans: why he made them, what they were like, and how they've changed since the 1850s. Choices (B) and (D) contain an error, and choice (C) is too general.

22. **The correct answer is (B).** This is a restatement question. The student states that people are inspired to create new things when there is a need. Choice (C) means the opposite. The idiom to be "born out of" means to "came from" or "be the result of."

23. **The correct answer is (C).** This is a restatement question. The word "soiled" means "became dirty." Choices (A), (B), and (D) are incorrect because the first Levi's didn't have rivets, and a color fading problem wasn't mentioned in the discussion.

24. **The correct answer is (A).** This is an inference question. The professor confirms that the original canvas fabric was too stiff and said that Strauss found another softer fabric from France. The sentence implies that Strauss began using it for his jeans All of the other answers contain errors. The original color (off white) got dirty too quickly. The price of the fabric wasn't mentioned, and the professor said that the fabric from France was equally durable, not more durable. The French fabric was 100 percent cotton, not polyester.

25. **The correct answer is (D).** This is a restatement question. Strauss added rivets to the original design because miners complained that the pants pockets tore. Choices (A), (B), and (C) are false.

26. **The correct answer is (C)**. This is a restatement question. The professor states that the rivets scratched saddles and classroom chairs. Choice (A) is not a true statement, and choices (B) and (D) are not mentioned in the discussion.

27. **The correct answer is (A)**. This is a restatement question. The professor says that "to build a better mousetrap" means to make a better product or have an idea that better meets people's needs. Choices (B) and (C) are not mentioned in the discussion; choice (D) is an expression that has a different meaning.

28. **The correct answer is (C)**. This is an inference question. The professor implies that Strauss's Levi's have been so popular and widely used for so long that the name "Levi's" has come to mean "blue jeans," just as many nouns have come from the names of products. Some examples are: "Kleenex," "Xerox," and "Frigidaire." Choices (A), (B) and (D) are false.

29. **The correct answer is (C)**. This is a restatement question. The woman says that she has to stay late at the library.

30. **The correct answer is (A)**. This is a restatement question. The woman says that she is going to study until eleven o'clock.

31. **The correct answer is (A)**. This is a restatement question. The man states that he has to work at the library until eleven o'clock.

32. **The correct answer is (A)**. This is an inference question. Although the woman may be interpreted as making a complaint about school, and although the man does talk about the hours he is working, the best answer is that the two people are making a date and time to meet again. The man first asks her if she wants to meet at eleven o'clock, and then the woman asks the man if he wants to get together on another day.

33. **The correct answer is (C)**. This is a restatement question. The woman states that Tuskegee is in the state of Alabama.

34. **The correct answer is (B)**. This is a restatement question. The woman says that George Washington Carver was a great scientist.

35. **The correct answer is (D)**. This is an inference question. The man indicates that he does not know where Tuskegee is, why it is famous, or who Carver is. He is uninformed about all of these facts.

## Part C

36. **The correct answer is (B)**. This is an inference question. The announcer talks about archaeological digs and paleontology. She also says that this trip would be a good way to learn about archaeology and that students will get class credit from their department.

37. **The correct answer is (C)**. This is a restatement question. The announcer says that the volunteers will explore some current archaeological digs in Wyoming.

38. **The correct answer is (A).** This is a restatement question. The announcer says that the volunteer field workers will search for fossil remains of plants and animals.

39. **The correct answer is (B).** This is a restatement question. The woman says the trip will cost $1,500.

40. **The correct answer is (A).** This is a restatement question. To "promote" can mean to actively help and encouraging the success of a business or venture. Stieglitz exhibited O'Keeffe's art, thereby actively helping her to become better known. Choices (B), (C), and (D) are false.

41. **The correct answer is (B).** This is a restatement question. The speaker states that O'Keeffe's flower paintings are her most well known, meaning that many people are familiar with these paintings.

42. **The correct answer is (A).** This is a restatement question. The speaker states that Southwest architecture was depicted often in her paintings. There is no mention of Wisconsin farmland influencing her work, though she was born in that state. Choices (C), and (D) each contain an error.

43. **The correct answer is (C).** This is a restatement question. The speaker refers to "Black Patio Door" as one of the paintings that featured O'Keeffe's own adobe house.

44. **The correct answer is (B).** This is a main idea question. The lecture begins and ends with information about the size of Los Angeles and discusses how the town developed.

45. **The correct answer is (C).** This is a restatement question. The tour guide describes these two factors as the cause of the beginning of the city's growth in the late 1800s. Later, the entertainment industry caused further growth.

46. **The correct answer is (B).** This is a restatement question. The speaker ends by saying that Los Angeles has grown into a sprawling metropolis in the past 100 years. The word "sprawling" means "spreading out in an irregular pattern." A metropolis is a large city.

47. **The correct answer is (A).** This is a restatement question. The woman says that she did field research in Bwindi National Park, which is a tropical rain forest. The park is in Uganda, but she was not doing research in a village or a farm community.

48. **The correct answer is (C).** This is a restatement question. The woman says that of the approximately 600 remaining mountain gorillas in the world, half of them live in Bwindi National Park.

49. **The correct answer is (A).** This is an inference question. Because the woman says that she woke up every morning and left the camp with the others, we can assume that they all returned to the camp at the end of each day. She makes no mention of taking food to the gorillas or staying in the forest at night.

Regarding choice (D), we can assume that the trackers are familiar with the forest, and that the team sometimes hiked all morning because, as the woman says, the gorilla group lived deep within the forest.

50. **The correct answer is (A).** This is an inference question. The woman states that the gorillas have very distinctive faces and personalities, which means that each gorilla is different from the others, with unique features and personality. So, we can assume that she finds each one unique. Choice (B) contains an error. She doesn't think that they look the same. Though she says that the gorillas have diverse personalities, she does not mention any similarity to human personalities. Choice (D) is not stated in the talk.

# SECTION 2—STRUCTURE AND WRITTEN EXPRESSION

## Part 1—Sentence Completion

1. **The correct answer is (D).** Adjective phrase. The phrase "called a jib" could also be "which is called a jib." It describes the arm of the log grabber.

2. **The correct answer is (A).** Verb. The subject of the sentence is "computer," and the verb "provides" is present tense.

3. **The correct answer is (A).** Pronoun. The word "it" refers to the main noun, "machine."

4. **The correct answer is (A).** Gerund. After the preposition "before," the gerund (-ing) form of the verb is used.

5. **The correct answer is (B).** The phrase "by means of" refers to how something is done.

6. **The correct answer is (B).** Noun phrase. The complete phrase "the desire to sleep" is the subject of this sentence. The main verb is a two-word verb "to wear out,' which means "to become very tired or exhausted."

7. **The correct answer is (B).** Adjective. Although usually the word "flying" is a verb, in this sentence it is an adjective that describes the type of capabilities

8. **The correct answer is (C).** Reduced adjective clause. In this sentence, the full clause would read "which are still used," but here the clause is reduced. In the clause, the passive form of the verb "to use" is required because the tools are used (by someone).

9. **The correct answer is (B).** Adverb. The word "once" means "as soon as" or "whenever."

10. **The correct answer is (A).** Subject and verb. This is the main subject and verb of the sentence.

11. **The correct answer is (A).** Noun phrase The main noun of the sentence is "parsley," and the noun phrase after "parsley" describes what it is.

12. **The correct answer is (A).** Preposition. The word "during" is correct because it precedes two nouns (exercise and weather). Choice (C) would be correct if it said "at the time of." Choice (B) is incorrect because in this sentence it must be followed by a verb. Choice (D) does not make sense because perspiration doesn't increase for exercise.

13. **The correct answer is (D).** Comparison. After the -er form, the word "than" must be used. Choice (A) is incorrect; "is" could be replaced by "does," although this would create an awkward sentence.

14. **The correct answer is (D).** Verb. The verb "drops" is the regular present-tense verb used in the "if" clause of a conditional sentence that expresses a true situation or fact.

15. **The correct answer is (C).** Word order. The verb "indicate" must be followed by the word "that" in this sentence. Another possible answer could be "…there are more people..." (omitting the word "that").

# Part 2—Error Identification

16. **The correct answer is (B).** Verb. The correct answer is "is covered," a passive voice verb. To use the active voice, the sentence must read, "Taste buds cover the surface of the tongue."

17. **The correct answer is (C).** Preposition. The correct answer is "is measured in light-years." The preposition "in" follows the verb "measured" to indicate the form of measurement.

18. **The correct answer is (B).** Preposition/unnecessary word. The correct answer is "a million tourists." There should be no preposition following the noun "million."

19. **The correct answer is (C).** Verb. The correct answer is "planet called Mars." This is a passive verb used in a reduced adjective clause. The complete clause would be " . . .that is called Mars has two small ones."

20. **The correct answer is (D).** Word form. The correct answer is "given a fair chance." The adjective "fair" modifies the noun "chance."

21. **The correct answer is (B).** Word order. The correct answer is "scientific discovery is". In this sentence the subject "scientific discovery" and the verb "is" are reversed after the negative expression "No longer."

22. **The correct answer is (C).** Parallel construction. The correct answer is "collecting data." The series of verbs is "forming… collecting…, and testing…"

23. **The correct answer is (A)**. Singular/plural noun. The correct answer is "all data in computers are…." The verb "are" is plural, so the noun must also be plural. It is also possible in this sentence to say "All data in the computer…" In this case, "computer" is used as a non-count noun.

24. **The correct answer is (A)**. Singular/plural noun. Because the verb is "are," the subject must be plural: "laws."

25. **The correct answer is (A)**. Word form. The correct phrase is "a large percentage." The word "large" is an adjective that means "big" or "great" and describes the noun "percentage." The word "largely" is an adverb that means "much" or "mainly."

26. **The correct answer is (C)**. Conjunction. The correct word is "and." Because the sentence says that Jim Thorpe won both events, the word "and" is necessary.

27. **The correct answer is (C)**. Adjective clause. The correct word is "which," and it is part of the adjective clause describing infection. In casual speaking, it is possible to say "…which antibiotics are ineffective for." The word "who" refers to people, not things.

28. **The correct answer is (A)**. Singular/plural noun. The correct word is "knowledge," a non-count noun that does not have a plural -s form.

29. **The correct answer is (D)**. Word form. The correct answer is "linking," a participle that begins an adjective phrase that describes the cable.

30. **The correct answer is (A)**. Verb/adjective. The correct answer is "Unlike the gorilla." The word "dislike" is a verb that means "do not like." The word "unlike" is an adjective that means "different from," "having little resemblance to" or "not alike."

31. **The correct answer is (B)**. Singular/plural noun. The correct answer is "equipment," a non-count noun that does not have a plural -s form.

32. **The correct answer is (C)**. Omitted word. The correct answer is either "he also wrote" or "but also wrote" or "but he also wrote." The phrase "not only" in the beginning of the sentence is a clue. After "not only," you will usually find "but also."

33. **The correct answer is (D)**. Noun. The correct answer is "among tribes of the..." A noun is needed after the word "among" in this sentence. The word "tribal" is an adjective.

34. **The correct answer is (C)**. Word form. The correct answer is "commonly," an adverb that describes how often caricature is used.

35. **The correct answer is (A)**. Conjunction. The correct word is "or." The phrase "one or more" is used with the plural noun in this sentence to mean one sentence or more sentences.

36. **The correct answer is (A).** Adjective clause. The correct answer is "that were made of…" or the reduced form "made of…" The verb in the adjective clause is in the passive form.

37. **The correct answer is (A).** Verb. The correct answer is "is." The subject of this sentence is the name of one book, so the verb must be singular.

38. **The correct answer is (B).** Word form. The correct answer is "director," a noun that describes a person.

39. **The correct answer is (C).** Pronoun. The correct phrase is "to that of other liquids." Because "that" refers to "the smell", a singular noun, the pronoun must also be singular.

40. **The correct answer is (B).** Verb/parallel construction. The correct phrase is "anchor themselves." This sentence is describing two things that plants do: (1) absorb water and (2) anchor themselves in the soil. The verbs must both be simple present tense.

## Section 3—Reading Comprehension

1. **The correct answer is (B).** This is a main idea question. The main topic is the evolution of the blues harp into a lead instrument. The final sentences of the passage emphasize the change from a support to a lead instrument.

2. **The correct answer is (C).** In the first sentence, the word "or" indicates that the blues harp is another name for the harmonica.

3. **The correct answer is (A).** This is a vocabulary question. The verb "to flourish" means to thrive, to be successful or to grow well. In this sentence, it specifically means "to grow in popularity."

4. **The correct answer is (C).** This is a vocabulary question. The word "rural" means "country" or "countryside." It is the opposite of "urban" or "city."

5. **The correct answer is (D).** This is an inference question. The best clue to the answer is the word "followed" in the final sentence. Because they came after Williams, these other men either had heard his music or had heard of it, and they were probably influenced by their knowledge of what Williams did. While it is possible that Williams may have become friends with some of these men, this is not mentioned in the passage. Although the passage infers that Williams was a good player, it does not say that he was the best player (choice (A)). Choice (C) is incorrect because it refers to Williams as playing a guitar, not a harp.

6. **The correct answer is (A).** This is a vocabulary question. The word "primarily" means "mainly" or "chiefly."

7. **The correct answer is (B).** In lines 9–10, the author states that "Bullet" Williams made recordings in the late 1920s, which is closest to the years 1925–1930.

8. **The correct answer is (D).** The word "lead" in this sentence refers to the use of the blues harp as the main instrument for melody. The word "principal" also refers to being the main or most important thing. Choice (A) refers to something that is made of or looks like metal. Choice (B) means "not primary" or "not most important." Choice (C) refers to instruments such as drums.

9. **The correct answer is (C).** This is a sentence insertion question. The sentence best fits into the passage in line 7. The words "In time, however," mark this sentence as a transition between the earlier role of the blues harp as melodic and rhythmic support, and the later role as a lead instrument.

10. **The correct answer is (A).** This is a vocabulary question. The words "revolutionizing" and "reforming" both refer to making a change in something.

11. **The correct answer is (B).** This is a question about the previous possible topic. The first sentence implies that the previous topic was also about rural Southern music in the 1920s and 1930s. And the last two sentences focus on the role of the blues harp in its change to becoming a lead instrument. From this, we can infer that the previous topic was also about other rural instruments that were blues instruments.

12. **The correct answer is (C).** According to the third sentence, jug bands commonly played "on street corners, in saloons, and in country stores." There is no mention of performing in a concert hall.

13. **The correct answer is (C).** This is a main idea question. Choices (A), (B), and (D) are all mentioned in the passage but are too narrow to be the general idea.

14. **The correct answer is (A).** This is a vocabulary question. The words "emerged" and "appeared" both refer to something gradually coming into view. In this sentence, the meaning is that the English we use today began to be used around the year 1350.

15. **The correct answer is (B).** This is a vocabulary question. The words "elements" and "features" both mean "parts of" something. In this sentence, the "parts of" may be any part of a language: words, structures, pronunciation, spelling, and so forth.

16. **The correct answer is (C).** This is a summary question. The description of how English initially spread around the globe can be found in lines 6–9.

17. **The correct answer is (D).** This is a restatement question. The passage states that English began to spread beyond England during the two centuries after 1600.

18. **The correct answer is (B).** The Norman invasion brought French influence to the English language, but it did not contribute to the spread of English worldwide, as did choices (A), (C), and (D).

19. **The correct answer is (C).** This is a vocabulary question. In this sentence, the phrase "the course of" is similar in meaning to the "time period of." It is used to imply that something changed or developed during the "next two centuries."

20. **The correct answer is (A).** This is a vocabulary question. The word "enclaves" refers to small groups or communities that share some commonality.

21. **The correct answer is (D).** This is a vocabulary question. The verb proliferated means grew, expanded, or increased in number.

22. **The correct answer is (B).** This is a vocabulary question. The verb "to store" means "to save" or "to keep for later use."

23. **The correct answer is (D).** This is a vocabulary question. The verbs "constituting" and "composing" both mean consisting of, comprising, or forming the basis of something.

24. **The correct answer is (C).** This is a restatement/computation question. The passage states that about half of the 700 million speakers of English are nonnative speakers, which is approximately 350 million.

25. **The correct answer is (A).** This is a main idea question. Choices (B) and (D) refer only to portions of the passage but not the main idea. Choice (C) is too general.

26. **The correct answer is (D).** This is a vocabulary question. The word "potential" in this context refers to possible, but not yet confirmed, factors.

27. **The correct answer is (C).** This is a vocabulary question. The word "trigger" when used as a verb means "to set off" or "to cause something to begin."

28. **The correct answer is (B).** This is a paragraph focus sentence. Paragraphs 2 and 3 talk about some surprising and unexpected risk factors linked to heart attacks.

29. **The correct answer is (A).** This is a vocabulary question. In this sentence, the word "temporal" refers to time. Choice (B) refers to climate. Choice (C) means not permanent, and choice (D) means not regular or consistent.

30. **The correct answer is (D).** This is a vocabulary question. The phrases "susceptible to" and "prone to" both mean that one is "vulnerable to" something.

31. **The correct answer is (C).** Choices (A), (B), and (D) are all mentioned as possible causes of heart attacks in the early morning.

32. **The correct answer is (C).** This is a vocabulary question. The word "phenomenon" means an event or happening; that is, something that occurs.

33. **The correct answer is (A).** This is a vocabulary question. The words "implicate" and "indicate" can both mean "suggest" or "infer."

34. **The correct answer is (B).** Choices (A), (C), and (D) are all mentioned as possible factors in the increase of heart attacks. Choice (B) is the opposite of what is stated.

35. **The correct answer is (D).** This is an inference question. The final sentence of the passage indicates that many risk factors have been identified over the years, but how these factors actually trigger heart attacks is not clearly understood and is still being studied.

36. **The correct answer is (A).** This is a vocabulary question. The words "reveal" and "show" both mean "to disclose" or "to give information about" something. Choice (B) means "to see." Choice (C) means "to conceal" or "to hide." Choice (D) means "to give more information." However, the statistics do not "explain" the heart attacks—instead, they make certain facts known to all.

37. **The correct answer is (C).** This is a main idea question. The main idea of this passage is that the pitched balls, called "fastballs" and "curveballs," are not really thrown faster or more curved by the pitcher; rather, it is the batter who sees them as faster or curved because of the visual illusion, not vision problems.

38. **The correct answer is (A).** This is a vocabulary question. The verbs "contend" and "maintain" in this context both mean "to declare" or "to insist."

39. **The correct answer is (B).** This is a vocabulary question. The word "thrill" refers to a feeling of sudden intense excitement, joy, or sometimes fear.

40. **The correct answer is (D).** This is a vocabulary question. The word "veer" means to turn slightly to the right or left away from a straight trajectory.

41. **The correct answer is (C).** This is a vocabulary question. The word "zoom" means "to go fast," or "speed."

42. **The correct answer is (A).** This is a vocabulary question. In this context, the words "to plunge" and "to drop" both refer to something falling suddenly or rushing downward.

43. **The correct answer is (D).** This is a restatement question. In the second paragraph of the passage, the author states that the batter's misperception makes the balls hard to hit. In the first paragraph, the author describes what the batter thinks and what many people think they see, but the second paragraph of this passage states that this is only an optical illusion.

44. **The correct answer is (A).** The word "they" refers to the closest, previous main noun phrase, which, in this sentence, is the phrases "the 'rising fastball' and the 'breaking curveball.'"

45. **The correct answer is (C).** This is a vocabulary question. The word "glance" refers to a look that is brief. Each of the others refers to a steady look.

46. **The correct answer is (B).** This is a restatement question. In the second paragraph, the author states that the batter's inability to follow the ball accurately is what causes the illusion. The batter briefly looks away from the ball and as a result, misjudges the angle and speed of the ball. The way the pitcher throws the ball and the location and angle of home plate do not create the illusion. Nor do the studies of engineers and psychologists produce the illusion.

47. **The correct answer is (D).** This is a summary question. Although paragraph 1 describes why batters think they can't hit the "fast" and "curve" balls, paragraph 2 gives the scientific explanation for this phenomenon and explains that what the batters think they see is actually an illusion.

48. **The correct answer is (A).** This is a vocabulary question. The verb "imbue" means "to penetrate, add to, or fill with ideas or feelings." "Spoil" means ruin or rot; "alter" and "change" both mean transform.

49. **The correct answer is (D).** This is a main idea question. The first paragraph introduces the topic of the Timber rattlesnake as an endangered species. The following paragraphs explain why they are endangered, what they have done to adapt to cold weather, and how their behavior contributes to their being endangered. Choices (A), (B), and (C) are too narrow; they are specific issues discussed in the passage but they are not the main topic.

50. **The correct answer is (A).** The word "vulnerable" refers to "subject to danger, injury, or attack." The word "unprotected" is the closest synonym. Choice (B) means "incapable of being penetrated or affected." Choice (C) means "incapable of intense feelings." Choice (D) means "not having" or "not able to have."

51. **The correct answer is (B).** This is an inference question. The passage states that Timber rattlesnakes migrated northward as glaciers retreated or melted, which can happen only during a warming period.

52. **The correct answer is (C).** This is a summary question. Although choices (A) and (B) mention that, in general, adaptive behaviors make the Timber rattlesnake more vulnerable, lines 13–19 give some reasons why this occurs. The term "make them easy prey" in line 19 means "make them easy to catch or kill."

53. **The correct answer is (A).** The words "emerge" and "come out" both mean "to rise into view" or "to appear." Choice (B) means "to start" or "to begin" something. Choice (C) means "to stand up." Choice (D) has many meanings, including "to perceive."

54. **The correct answer is (B).** This is an inference question. The passage states that the rattlesnakes warm themselves by lying on rocks in open areas, which means areas that get direct sun. Of these answers, the most open area would be a meadow. In forests, crevices, and caves there is little or no direct sunlight.

55. **The correct answer is (B)**. This is a vocabulary question. The phrase "coupled with" means "joined" or "combined," or "the bringing together of two or more factors" (ideas, people, etc.).

56. **The correct answer is (C)**. In this sentence, the word "prey" refers to an animal that is killed by another animal. The phrase "easy prey" refers to the fact that it is easy for an animal to find and kill the snakes while they are lying in the sun in large numbers. The best synonym is "vulnerable."

57. **The correct answer is (D)**. The word "to bask" means "to relax in the warmth of the sun." The best choice is "lying" because the snakes lie still while basking.

58. **The correct answer is (A)**. Of all the options, choices (B), (C), and (D) are reasons that make the snake vulnerable, and therefore, endangered. The only protective measure is choice (A), because the snakes are hidden in the rocks when they hibernate.

59. **The correct answer is (C)**. This is a vocabulary question. The word "depredation" refers to complete destruction.

60. **The correct answer is (C)**. The author may express some feeling of regret in the last line by stating that it's already too late to save some rattlesnakes. However, the overall tone is simply informative, offering information and explanation about the status of Timber rattlesnakes. The author does not seem to accuse people of killing rattlesnakes (choice (A)), to yearn for the past

# ANSWER SHEET FOR PRACTICE TEST 4

## Section 1: Listening Comprehension

1 2 3 4 5 6 7 8 9 10 11 12 13 14 15 16 17 18 19 20 21 22 23 24 25 26 27 28 29 30 31 32 33 34 35 36 37 38 39 40 41 42 43 44 45 46 47 48 49 50

Ⓐ Ⓑ Ⓒ Ⓓ (for each item)

## Section 2: Structure and Written Expression

1 2 3 4 5 6 7 8 9 10 11 12 13 14 15 16 17 18 19 20 21 22 23 24 25 26 27 28 29 30 31 32 33 34 35 36 37 38 39 40

Ⓐ Ⓑ Ⓒ Ⓓ (for each item)

## Section 3: Reading Comprehension

1 2 3 4 5 6 7 8 9 10 11 12 13 14 15 16 17 18 19 20 21 22 23 24 25 26 27 28 29 30 31 32 33 34 35 36 37 38 39 40 41 42 43 44 45 46 47 48 49 50 51 52 53 54 55 56 57 58 59 60

Ⓐ Ⓑ Ⓒ Ⓓ (for each item)

Date Taken _____

Number Correct

Section 1 _____

Section 2 _____

Section 3 _____

# Practice Test 4 (PBT Style)

## SECTION 1

### LISTENING COMPREHENSION

### Time—approximately 30 minutes

This test is written to represent the PBT in terms of numbers of questions, types of questions, and length of time for each section. You can simulate actual TOEFL testing conditions by using the recordings that accompany this book. If you do not have the recordings, ask a friend to read the transcript for the Listening Comprehension section of Practice Test 3 in Part 3 of this book, "Transcripts for Practice Tests."

The Listening Comprehension section includes three parts. In Part A, you hear conversations between two people. Each conversation is followed by one question. In Part B, you hear longer conversations followed by several questions. In Part C, you hear talks given by a single person followed by several questions.

**Now listen to the directions for each part.**

**If you have the CD version, this test can be found on Disc 1.**

## Part A

In Part A, you will hear short conversations between two people. After each conversation, a third person will ask a question about what was said. You will hear the conversation only one time, so you must listen carefully. After you hear a question, read the four possible answers in your test book, and decide which one is the best answer. Then, on your answer sheet, fill in the oval of the answer you have chosen. Answer all questions based on what is stated or implied by the speakers.

**Now, listen to an example. You will hear:**

**You will read the answer choices in your test book:**

    (A) He will call Pete before he goes home.

    (B) He will call Pete after he gets home.

    (C) He called Pete at home.

    (D) He will call Pete tomorrow.

You learn from the conversation that the man will call Pete as soon as he gets home. The best answer to the question "What does the man mean?" is choice (B), "He will call Pete after he gets home."

**Now continue listening to the recording and begin the test.**

1.  (A)    Lisa is having a hard time in school.

    (B)    Lisa is expecting a baby.

    (C)    Lisa is very busy this term.

    (D)    Lisa is often very tired.

2.  (A)    Her major was not chemistry.

    (B)    She is an excellent student in chemistry.

    (C)    She wanted to change her major.

    (D)    She likes chemistry classes more than computer science classes.

3.  (A)    Mark has quit smoking.

    (B)    Mark doesn't like to share a room with someone smoking.

    (C)    Mark shouldn't smoke in the classroom.

    (D)    Mark helped his roommate quit smoking.

4.  (A)    Not many people attended the workshop.

    (B)    There were not many workshops available last night.

    (C)    The workshop is more interesting than the show.

    (D)    Last night's show was one of the few good ones.

5.  (A)    He didn't do well in school.

    (B)    He won't graduate this summer.

    (C)    Steve needs some hands-on classes.

    (D)    Steve is able to apply his knowledge.

6. (A)    Rent a videotape

   (B)    Fix the brakes on the car

   (C)    Begin packing for their move

   (D)    See a film

7. (A)    She will return the man's favor.

   (B)    She will return the book on her way to work.

   (C)    She can't return the book for the man.

   (D)    She works at the school library.

8. (A)    He's going to leave the room.

   (B)    He's going to sit down.

   (C)    He's going to buy a new chair.

   (D)    He's going to bring the chair back.

9. (A)    The man was excited by the lecture.

   (B)    The man was very interested in the speech.

   (C)    The man gave a long speech.

   (D)    The man is tired.

10. (A)    She wants to continue her studies right away.

    (B)    She wants a break from studying.

    (C)    She hasn't decided yet.

    (D)    She'll find a job right after graduation.

11. (A)    Choose one class or the other.

    (B)    Ask his adviser.

    (C)    Let the professors make the decision.

    (D)    Take both classes.

12. (A)    He doesn't have the book.

    (B)    He had the book, but lost it.

    (C)    He wants to read it again.

    (D)    He has not read the book.

13. (A)    He'll take his car and give the woman a ride.

    (B)    He'll take his bicycle to school, too.

    (C)    He'll join her at her exercise class.

    (D)    He'll teach the woman how to ride a bicycle.

14. (A)    She didn't think the books would have to be returned so soon.

    (B)    She doesn't want to keep these books.

    (C)    She doesn't think her library card is valid.

    (D)    She has finished reading these books already.

15. (A) It will probably take 5 minutes to fix it.

    (B) She fixed it a few minutes ago.

    (C) Her machine is connected to the man's.

    (D) The electrical connection might be the problem.

16. (A) Thank you for dropping by.

    (B) Thank you for picking it up.

    (C) No thanks, I don't want any.

    (D) No thanks, I'm not going.

17. (A) Show her how to make it work right

    (B) Invite her as a guest

    (C) Tell the woman the directions

    (D) Take her there, if necessary

18. (A) He already has a job.

    (B) He will probably work at the library.

    (C) He needs to study full time.

    (D) He plans to work at the library in the summer.

19. (A) He enjoys working on weekends.

    (B) He is different from the other workers.

    (C) He works at a different time on Saturdays and Sundays.

    (D) He's going out of town this weekend.

20. (A) Whether she'll have enough time to do it

    (B) Whether the professor will approve it

    (C) Whether she'll change her mind

    (D) Whether she has enough knowledge to do it

# PART B

In this part of the test, you will hear longer conversations between two people and class discussions. After each conversation or discussion, you will be asked some questions. You will hear the conversations or discussions and the questions only once, so listen carefully. After you hear a question, read the four possible answers in your test book, and decide which one is the best answer. Then, on your answer sheet, find the number of the question and fill in the oval of the answer you have chosen. Answer all questions based on what is stated or implied by the speakers.

**Listen to the example. You will hear:**

**Questions 1 and 2 are based on the following conversation between two friends at school.**

**Now listen to sample question number 1.**

1. Where is the woman going?

    You will read the answer choices in your test book:

    (A)    To the cafeteria

    (B)    To the movie theater

    (C)    To her dorm room

    (D)    To the library

    The correct answer to the question "Where is the woman going?" is choice (D), "To the library."

**Now listen to sample question number 2.**

2. Which best describes the man's feelings about his classes?

    You will read the answer choices in your test book:

    (A)    Term papers are easy for him.

    (B)    He has a lot of essay exams.

    (C)    He finds lab experiments easier than writing term papers.

    (D)    He is busier this semester than last semester.

    The best answer to the question "Which best describes the man's feelings about his classes?" is choice (C), "He finds lab experiments easier than writing term papers."

**Now listen to the test. Remember, you are not allowed to take any notes or write in your test book.**

21. (A)    Playing the guitar

    (B)    Working at a restaurant

    (C)    Singing in a rock concert

    (D)    Dancing in a ballet recital

22. (A)    San Francisco

    (B)    Washington

    (C)    Chicago

    (D)    New York

23. (A)    In a restaurant

    (B)    In a book shop

    (C)    In a record store

    (D)    In a theater

24. (A)    New York

    (B)    Chicago

    (C)    Washington

    (D)    San Francisco

25. (A)    Nantucket

    (B)    Woods Hole

    (C)    Her father's restaurant

    (D)    On the coast

26. (A)   Woods Hole
    (B)   New York
    (C)   His uncle's restaurant
    (D)   His father's restaurant

27. (A)   Sea birds
    (B)   Sharks
    (C)   Whales
    (D)   Crabs

28. (A)   Because he will be visiting his grandparents
    (B)   Because he will be working for his uncle
    (C)   Because she will be working on a boat
    (D)   Because she will be working in a laboratory

29. (A)   American history
    (B)   American literature
    (C)   English literature
    (D)   Chemistry

30. (A)   To visit relatives
    (B)   To give a lecture
    (C)   To meet her publisher
    (D)   To see museum exhibits

31. (A)   To speak to his class
    (B)   To deliver a message for him
    (C)   To review an article for him
    (D)   To lend him 5 dollars

32. (A)   The shape and makeup of the DNA molecule
    (B)   The difference between a chromosome and a protein
    (C)   The study of genetic engineering
    (D)   The parts of a ladder

33. (A)   One "rung" on the DNA "ladder"
    (B)   A segment of the DNA molecule
    (C)   The "packaging" for the DNA molecule
    (D)   The "double helix"

34. (A)   To help students visualize the shape of the DNA molecule
    (B)   To help students understand the step-by-step process in genetics
    (C)   To explain the tools used by genetic engineers
    (D)   To demonstrate how a protein is made

35. (A)     It is located within the gene.

    (B)     It is inside the chromosome.

    (C)     It can be represented as a twisted rope.

    (D)     It is made up of several genes.

# PART C

In this part of the test, you will hear segments read by a single person. After each segment, you will be asked some questions. You will hear the segments and the questions only once, so listen carefully. After you hear a question, read the four possible answers in your test book, and decide which one is the best answer. Then find the number of the question on your answer sheet, and fill in the oval that corresponds to the letter of the answer you have chosen. Answer all questions based on what is stated or implied in the talk.

**Listen to this sample talk. You will hear:**

**Questions 1–2 are based on the following announcement.**

**Now listen to sample question number 1.**

1.  What is the main purpose of this announcement?

    You will read the answer choices in your test book:

    (A)     To demonstrate tutoring techniques

    (B)     To explain school policies

    (C)     To recruit childcare workers

    (D)     To explain a service

    The best answer to the question "What is the purpose of this announcement?" is choice (D), "To explain a service."

**Now listen to sample question number 2.**

2.  What does the speaker recommend?

    You will read the answer choices in your test book:

    (A)      Give your child extra tutoring.

    (B)     Take your child to the program today.

    (C)     Apply as soon as you can.

    (D)     Pay next month.

    The best answer to the question "What does the speaker recommend?" is (C), "Apply as soon as you can."

**Now, listen to the talks. Remember, you are not allowed to write any notes in your test book.**

36. (A)     To give background of the life of James Joyce

    (B)     To introduce the book Dubliners

    (C)     To give an overview of James Joyce's novels

    (D)     To explain why Joyce left Ireland

37. (A)    It focuses on Catholic schools in Dublin.

    (B)    It was written while Joyce was tending to his mother.

    (C)    It was published in London.

    (D)    It concerns language and philosophy in Ireland.

38. (A)    He did not like his family.

    (B)    He did not manage his money well.

    (C)    He and Nora were not happy together.

    (D)    He did not enjoy school.

39. (A)    Dublin

    (B)    Paris

    (C)    London

    (D)    Zurich

40. (A)    To give a background of Dr. Sawyer

    (B)    To discuss the field of paleontology

    (C)    To give some background about the Institute

    (D)    To introduce students to fossil research

41. (A)    They wrote and published some articles together.

    (B)    They grew up as childhood friends.

    (C)    They did research together in Kazahkstan.

    (D)    They both went to the University of Cambridge.

42. (A)    Documenting ancient cultures

    (B)    Studying the prehistory of Africa

    (C)    Authoring books on paleontology

    (D)    Conducting research on fossils

43. (A)    Fossils from the late Cambrian era

    (B)    Prehistoric sites in Egypt

    (C)    Fossil remains from Antarctica

    (D)    Dr. Sawyer's world travels

44. (A)    It is the oldest public university.

    (B)    It is the largest public university.

    (C)    It is the least expensive public university.

    (D)    It is the most beautiful university.

45. (A)    The university's forty-one campuses

    (B)    The university's numerous monuments

    (C)    The university's community programs

    (D)    The university's heritage

46. (A)    It has two stories and is made of brick.

    (B)    It was where the first students graduated.

    (C)    It was built in 1800.

    (D)    It is situated on the main corner of the campus.

47. (A)  Music

    (B)  Science

    (C)  Baseball

    (D)  Arts

48. (A)  In a cafeteria

    (B)  In an auditorium

    (C)  In a classroom

    (D)  In a gymnasium

49. (A)  To be camp counselors

    (B)  To maintain the equipment

    (C)  To drive the campers

    (D)  To work as teachers

50. (A)  To California

    (B)  To high school

    (C)  To Washington

    (D)  To college

# SECTION 2

## STRUCTURE AND WRITTEN EXPRESSION

## Time—25 minutes

## Part 1—Sentence Completion

**Directions:** Questions 1–15 are not complete sentences. One or more words are left out of each sentence. Under each sentence, you will see four words or phrases, marked (A), (B), (C), and (D). Choose the one word or phrase that completes the sentence correctly. Then, on your answer sheet, find the number of the question and fill in the oval that corresponds to the letter of your answer choice.

**Sentence Completion example questions:**

1.  Birds make nests in trees _____ hide their young in the leaves and branches.

    (A)  can where they

    (B)  where they can

    (C)  where can they

    (D)  where can

    The sentence should read, "Birds make nests in trees where they can hide their young in the leaves and branches." Therefore, you should select choice (B).

2. Sleeping, resting, and _____ are the best ways to care for a cold.

   (A) to drink fluids

   (B) drank fluids

   (C) one drink fluids

   (D) drinking fluids

   The sentence should read, "Sleeping, resting, and drinking fluids are the best ways to care for a cold." Therefore, you should select choice (D).

## Now begin with the questions.

1. Because aluminum is lighter and cheaper _____, it is frequently used for high-tension power transmission.

   (A) as copper

   (B) than copper

   (C) for copper

   (D) more copper

2. It is only recently that ballets have been based on themes _____ American life.

   (A) that reflect

   (B) reflects

   (C) is reflecting

   (D) reflected

3. Poison oak generates irritating poisons _____ even if people merely brush against the plants.

   (A) they can affect people

   (B) that can affect people

   (C) what can effect people

   (D) which do they affect

4. _____ ants live in colonies, keep farms, go to war, carry off slaves, and have a society somewhat like human beings.

   (A) Studies of ant life show that

   (B) Studies of ant life that

   (C) That is studied

   (D) That the studies of ant life

5. Generic medications are just as _____, and much less expensive.

   (A) effectively brand-name products

   (B) brand-name products effective

   (C) brand-name products as effective

   (D) effective as brand-name products

6. _____ is no way to tell the exact number of heroin addicts in the United States.

    (A)    It

    (B)    There

    (C)    What

    (D)    Each

7. Ernest Hemingway is _____ of modern fiction.

    (A)    one of the molders

    (B)    the molders one

    (C)    who is one of the molders

    (D)    the molders who is the one

8. _____ occasions for congratulations.

    (A)    Birthdays that usually considered

    (B)    Usually considering birthdays

    (C)    Birthdays are usually considered

    (D)    That considered birthdays usually

9. "Forty-niners" _____ to California for gold in 1848.

    (A)    rushed

    (B)    are rushed

    (C)    have rushed

    (D)    rushing

10. In order for people to work together effectively, they need _____ each other's needs.

    (A)    to be sensitive to

    (B)    is sensitive for

    (C)    sensitivity

    (D)    sensitive

11. It is good form to use the name of the person _____.

    (A)    who are greeting

    (B)    you are greeting

    (C)    which you are greeting

    (D)    greeting for you

12. _____ the promotion of health and to helping people avoid injury and disease.

    (A)    To commit the Red Cross

    (B)    The Red Cross to commit

    (C)    Committed to the Red Cross is

    (D)    The Red Cross is committed to

13. People usually can get a sufficient amount of the calcium their bodies _____ from the food they consume.

   (A)   need

   (B)   needs

   (C)   needing

   (D)   to need

14. It is possible _____ may assist some trees in saving water in the winter.

   (A)   the leaves are lost

   (B)   when leaves have lost

   (C)   that the loss of leaves

   (D)   to lose leaves

15. Hollywood, the heart of America's motion picture industry, _____ of Los Angeles a century ago.

   (A)   was only a quiet suburb

   (B)   only quiet suburb was

   (C)   quiet suburb only was

   (D)   suburb was quiet only

## Part 2—Error Identification

**Directions:** In questions 16 to 40, each sentence has four underlined words or phrases, marked (A), (B), (C), and (D). Choose the one word or phrase that must be changed in order for the sentence to be correct. Then, on your answer sheet, find the number of the question and fill in the oval that corresponds to the letter of your answer choice.

**Error Identification example questions.**

1. Aspirin is <u>recommend</u> to <u>many</u> people for <u>its</u> ability <u>to thin</u> the blood.
               (A)        (B)         (C)       (D)

The sentence should read, "Aspirin is recommended to many people for its ability to thin the blood." Therefore, you should select choice (A).

2. Some people <u>believe that</u> human beings will never <u>use away</u> all <u>the</u> natural
            (A)                         (B)     (C)
resources <u>on earth</u>.
        (D)

The sentence should read, "Some people believe that human beings will never use up all the natural resources on earth." Therefore, you should select choice (B).

**Now begin work on the questions.**

## Part 2—Error Identification

**Directions:** In questions 16 to 40, each sentence has four underlined words or phrases, marked (A), (B), (C), and (D). Choose the one word or phrase that must be changed in order for the sentence to be correct. Then, on your answer sheet, find the number of the question and fill in the oval that corresponds to the letter of your answer choice.

**Error Identification example questions.**

1. Aspirin is <u>recommend</u> to <u>many</u> people for <u>its</u> ability <u>to thin</u> the blood.
       (A)   (B)   (C)  (D)

   The sentence should read, "Aspirin is recommended to many people for its ability to thin the blood." Therefore, you should select choice (A).

2. Some people <u>believe that</u> human beings will never <u>use away</u> all <u>the</u> natural
        (A)         (B)  (C)

   resources <u>on earth</u>.
      (D)

   The sentence should read, "Some people believe that human beings will never use up all the natural resources on earth." Therefore, you should select choice (B).

**Now begin work on the questions.**

16. <u>How</u> the Earth is <u>in the shadow</u> of <u>the</u> moon, we see <u>an</u> eclipse of the sun.
     (A)     (B)  (C)    (D)

17. <u>The children's</u> television program <u>called</u> Sesame Street <u>has broadcast</u> through
      (A)       (B)      (C)

    out <u>the</u> world.
      (D)

18. Some <u>research</u> suggests <u>what</u> there is a <u>link between</u> the body's calcium
       (A)    (B)    (C)

    balance <u>and</u> tooth decay.
       (D)

19. Luther Burbank earned <u>the funds</u> to <u>go west</u> by <u>sale</u> his new ideas <u>about</u>
            (A)   (B)  (C)     (D)

    growing potatoes.

20. Louisa May Alcott infused <u>her</u> own life <u>into</u> the character <u>of</u> Jo <u>in book</u> *Little*
            (A)   (B)    (C)  (D)

    *Women.*

21. <u>Rock music</u> was <u>original</u> a mixture of <u>country music</u> and rhythm <u>and</u> blues.
    (A)        (B)             (C)           (D)

22. An <u>increasing</u> number <u>of</u> office <u>works</u> in developing countries use computer
    (A)        (B)    (C)
programs as <u>daily</u> routine.
        (D)

23. <u>Traveling</u> ballet companies <u>were</u> uncommon before <u>her</u> Augusta Maywood
    (A)            (B)           (C)
formed the first <u>traveling</u> troupe.
        (D)

24. <u>The</u> virtues of <u>ordinary</u> life <u>is</u> the focus of <u>many</u> poems.
    (A)        (B)   (C)     (D)

25. Economic <u>goods</u> often consist <u>to</u> material items, <u>but</u> they can also <u>be</u> services
       (A)       (B)      (C)     (D)
to people.

26. Moby Dick is a <u>novel</u> that <u>telling</u> the story of a ship captain's <u>single-minded</u>
          (A)    (B)              (C)
hatred <u>of</u> a huge white whale.
    (D)

27. <u>Earwax lubricates</u> and protects the ear from <u>foreign</u> matter <u>such</u> water and
     (A)                      (B)    (C)
<u>insects</u>.
 (D)

28. Before <u>creating</u> the telegraph, Samuel Morse <u>made</u> <u>their</u> living <u>as</u> a painter.
      (A)                     (B) (C)   (D)

29. Some jellyfish <u>make</u> daily journeys <u>from deep</u> water to the surface and back,
         (A)          (B)
<u>while</u> others migrate <u>horizontal</u>.
 (C)         (D)

30. <u>To putting</u> a large amount of information <u>on</u> a map, a <u>variety</u> of symbols must
    (A)                  (B)    (C)
<u>be used</u>.
  (D)

31. <u>Before</u> the nineteenth century, <u>it</u> was <u>rarely</u> to find organized <u>systems</u> of adult
    (A)            (B)   (C)         (D)
education.

32. <u>Smoking</u> is <u>the</u> number one <u>prevent</u> cause <u>of death</u> in the United States.
      (A)     (B)         (C)         (D)

33. <u>Not</u> single alphabet has ever <u>perfectly</u> represented the <u>sounds</u> of <u>any of</u> Earth's
      (A)                (B)         (C)   (D)
    natural languages.

34. <u>When</u> the Second World War, <u>almost</u> a third <u>of</u> a million people <u>were killed</u>.
      (A)            (B)    (C)         (D)

35. The ozone layer <u>must be protected</u> because <u>it</u> shields the Earth <u>from</u> excessive
                   (A)         (B)      (C)
    ultraviolet <u>radiate</u>.
          (D)

36. Carbohydrates <u>and fats</u> are two essential <u>sources</u> of energy <u>for</u> animal <u>grow</u>.
             (A)           (B)     (C)   (D)

37. <u>By passing</u> sunlight <u>through</u> a prism, the light <u>is separate</u> into a <u>spectrum of</u>
      (A)        (B)            (C)     (D)
    colors.

38. <u>In spite</u> modern medical technology, <u>many</u> diseases caused <u>by viruses</u> are still
      (A)               (B)         (C)
    <u>not</u> curable.
    (D)

39. <u>Though</u> Pablo Picasso was <u>primarily</u> a <u>painting</u>, he also became a <u>fine</u>
      (A)        (B)   (C)         (D)
    sculptor, engraver, and ceramist.

40. People who live in <u>small towns</u> often <u>seem</u> more warm and friendly than
             (A)     (B)
    people <u>who</u> live in <u>populated densely</u> areas.
      (C)      (D)

# SECTION 3

# READING COMPREHENSION

## Time—55 minutes

**Directions:** In this section, you will read several passages. Each passage is followed by questions about it. Choose the one best answer, (A), (B), (C), or (D), for each question. Then, on your answer sheet, find the number of the question and fill in the space that corresponds to the letter of your answer choice. Answer all questions based on what is stated or implied in the passage.

**Reading Comprehension example passage and questions**

**Read the following passage:**

A new hearing device is now available for some hearing-impaired people. This device uses a magnet to hold the detachable sound-processing portion in place. Like other aids, it converts sound into vibrations. But it is unique in that it can transmit the vibrations directly to the magnet and then to the
(5) inner ear. This produces a clearer sound. The new device will not help all hearing-impaired people — only those with a hearing loss caused by infection or some other problem in the middle ear. It will probably help no more than 20 percent of all people with hearing problems. Those people who often have persistent ear infections, however, should find relief and restored
(10) hearing with the new device.

1. What is the author's main purpose in this passage?
   (A)   To describe a new cure for ear infections
   (B)   To inform the reader of a new device
   (C)   To urge doctors to use a new device
   (D)   To explain the use of a magnet

   The author's main purpose is to inform the reader of a new device for hearing-impaired people. Therefore, you should select choice (B).

2. The word "relief" in the last sentence means:
   (A)   Less distress
   (B)   Assistance
   (C)   Distraction
   (D)    Relaxation

   The phrase "less distress" is similar in meaning to "relief" in this sentence. Therefore, you should select choice (A).

**Now begin with the questions.**

**Questions 1–12 are based on the following passage.**

What happened to Amelia Earhart? One of the mysteries of history is that no conclusive answer has been found to this question. In 1928, Amelia Earhart was the first woman to fly across the Atlantic, and in 1932, she was the first to fly alone across the Atlantic. Earhart continued to break records.
(5) In 1935, she was the first person to fly alone from Hawaii to California. Later, in 1937, she and her navigator, Frederick Noonan, set off in hopes of being the first to fly around the world. They never made it. Somewhere in the Pacific between New Guinea and Howland Island, Earhart's plane disappeared.

(10)  Conventional wisdom has it that Earhart's plane ran out of fuel and crashed into the ocean, but some refuse to believe this. People still continue to look for clues about the disappearance of the plane. In 1992, one search party reported finding remnants of what could be Earhart's plane on the island of Nikumaroro, but people who originally worked on Earhart's plane
(15) disputed that evidence. There have been other search expeditions to Nikumaroro, some funded by an organization formed specifically to search for historic plane wrecks. Two people of this group, Ric Gillespie and Pat Thrasher, have spent years looking for evidence, and their theory is that Earhart ran out of fuel and landed on Nikumaroro, only to die later of disease
(20) or starvation. They don't have much to go on. There are a few bones that were found on the island in 1940 that could possibly have come from either Earhart or Noonan. They have found some crumbling fragments of a woman's shoe that could possibly have belonged to Earhart. And there is a sheet of aluminum that might possibly have come from her plane if only the
(25) rivet pattern was different. The evidence is minimal. But Gillespie and Thrasher keep looking. Maybe the conclusive piece of evidence is just around the corner. Until then, the mystery continues.

1. What is the mystery that the author refers to?

   (A)   Why are people still looking for Earhart?

   (B)   What happened to Amelia Earhart?

   (C)   Whose shoe was found on the island?

   (D)   Why was Earhart flying in the Pacific?

2. What phrase could best be substituted for the phrase in line 4 "break records?"

   (A)   Surpass the standard

   (B)   Destroy old evidence

   (C)   Hide previous information

   (D)   Establish new rules

3. What does the sentence "They never made it" refer to in line 7?

   (A)   They couldn't find a place to land.

   (B)   They ran out of fuel.

   (C)   They could not fix the plane.

   (D)   They did not achieve their goal.

4. Why does the author mention "conventional wisdom" in line 10?

   (A) To indicate what many people believe

   (B) To point to something that is wise

   (C) To show that not everyone knows

   (D) To demonstrate seriousness

5. What is the purpose of paragraph 2?

   (A) To give details about the mystery

   (B) To indicate conventional wisdom

   (C) To dispute current theories

   (D) To add to historical evidence

6. Which of the following is closest in meaning to the word "disputed" in line 15?

   (A) Dispersed

   (B) Disrupted

   (C) Disagreed with

   (D) Disposed of

7. What does the author say about Ric Gillespie and Pat Thrasher?

   (A) They found clear evidence of Earhart's disappearance.

   (B) An organization supported their search efforts.

   (C) They think she crashed into the Pacific Ocean.

   (D) A group of people on the island assisted them.

8. The word "crumbling" in line 22 is closest in meaning to which of the following?

   (A) Tearing apart at the seams

   (B) Looking like dry sand

   (C) Smelling like rotten fruit

   (D) Breaking into small pieces

9. Which of the following is NOT true according to the passage?

   (A) Earhart and Noonan wanted to fly around the world.

   (B) Earhart's plane was shot down over the Pacific.

   (C) Earhart was the first woman to fly alone from Hawaii to California.

   (D) Earhart was an accomplished pilot.

10. According to the passage, what would most likely make Gillespie and Thrasher very happy?

    (A) To find a small piece of Earhart's plane

    (B) To find people to talk to on Nikumaroro

    (C) To get the funding to continue their search

    (D) To get more free time to be able to search

11. Which of the following is NOT mentioned as a possible piece of evidence?

   (A)   A part of a woman's shoe

   (B)   A piece of a bone

   (C)   A piece of metal

   (D)   A part of an engine

12. The author uses the phrase "just around the corner" in line 27 to mean

   (A)   they cannot go straight.

   (B)   there is an intersection.

   (C)   something is close.

   (D)   it is dependent on others.

**Questions 13–24 are based on the following passage.**

About 200 million years ago, as the Triassic Period came to a close, many species of animals disappeared from the face of the Earth. Scientists previously believed that the series of extinctions happened over a period of 15 to 20 million years. Recent discoveries in Nova Scotia suggest, however,
(5) that the extinctions may have happened over a much shorter period of time, perhaps less than 850,000 years.

   Evidence for a rapid extinction of species at the end of the Triassic Period is found in the McCoy Brook Formation along the Bay of Fundy in Nova Scotia. Fossils found in this formation indicate a rapid disappearance of
(10) species rather than a slow and gradual change over time. One explanation for a relatively sudden extinction at the end of the Triassic may be that a large meteorite struck the earth at the time and is responsible for a 70-kilometer hole nearby. If geologists and other researchers can find evidence, such as shocked quartz in the rock formations, that a meteorite did strike the earth,
(15) it would give more credence to the theory of rapid Triassic extinctions. It is possible, however, that even if a rapid extinction happened in and around Nova Scotia, it did not necessarily occur in the rest of the world.

13. What is the main topic of this passage?

   (A)   The disappearance of animal species at the end of the Triassic Period

   (B)   Evidence of a relatively sudden extinction of species

   (C)   The possibility of an extinction happening simultaneously throughout the world

   (D)   A meteorite hole in the Bay of Fundy in Nova Scotia

14. Which of the following could best replace the word "close" as used in line 1?

   (A)   Connection

   (B)   Dispersion

   (C)   Separation

   (D)   End

15. The author uses the phrase "the face of the Earth" in line 2 in order to

    (A)    emphasize the disappearance.

    (B)    focus on one part of the Earth.

    (C)    focus on one period of time.

    (D)    point out the reference to land, not water.

16. All of the following are mentioned in the passage EXCEPT

    (A)    the extinction of late Triassic animals.

    (B)    the duration of time for the extinction.

    (C)    a large meteorite hitting the Earth 10 million years ago.

    (D)    the use of types of rock in scientific research.

17. Which of the following is closest in meaning to the word "relatively" in line 11?

    (A)    Comparatively

    (B)    Independently

    (C)    Phenomenally

    (D)    Visibly

18. Where in the passage does the author give evidence for the argument?

    (A)    Lines 1–6

    (B)    Lines 10–15

    (C)    Lines 7–9

    (D)    Lines 16–17

19. According to the passage, what would give evidence that a meteorite struck the earth?

    (A)    A gradual change in species over time

    (B)    A change in the quartz

    (C)    Gold deposits in the veins of rocks

    (D)    A change in the waters of the Bay of Fundy

20. Which of the following could best replace the word "struck" as used in line 12?

    (A)    Affected

    (B)    Discovered

    (C)    Devastated

    (D)    Hit

21. Where is the best place in the passage to add the following sentence?

"A comparison of fossils from sites around the world could provide new answers to this question of extinction."

    (A)    In line 4 after the words "20 million years"

    (B)    In line 6 after the words "850,000 years"

    (C)    In line 9 after the words "Nova Scotia"

    (D)    In line 17 after the word "world"

22. In line 15, the first "it" refers to:

    (A)    Evidence

    (B)    An extinction

    (C)    The Earth

    (D)    A meteorite

23. Which of the following could best replace the word "credence" in line 15?

    (A)    Demonstration

    (B)    Elevation

    (C)    Suitability

    (D)    Credibility

24. Which of the following best describes the author's tone?

    (A)    Aggressive

    (B)    Explanatory

    (C)    Apologetic

    (D)    Cynical

**Questions 25–36 are based on the following passage.**

Alzheimer's disease impairs a person's ability to recall memories, both distant memories and memories as recent as a few hours before. Although there is not yet a cure for the illness, there may be hope for a cure with a protein called nerve growth factor. The protein is produced by nerve cells in
(5)  the same region of the brain where Alzheimer's occurs. Based on this relationship, scientists from the University of Lund in Sweden and the University of California at San Diego designed an experiment to test whether doses of nerve growth factor could reverse the effects of memory loss caused by Alzheimer's. Using a group of rats with impaired memory,
(10) the scientists gave half of the rats doses of nerve growth factor while giving the other half a blood protein as a placebo, thus creating a control group. At the end of the four-week test, the rats given the nerve growth factor performed equally to rats with normal memory abilities. While the experiments do not show that nerve growth factor can stop the general process of
(15) deterioration caused by Alzheimer's, they do show potential as a means to slow the process significantly.

25. With what topic is this passage mainly concerned?

    (A)    Impaired memory of patients

    (B)    Cures for Alzheimer's disease

    (C)    The use of rats as experimental subjects

    (D)    Nerve growth factor as a cure for Alzheimer's

26. The word "impairs" in line 1 is most similar to which of the following?

    (A) Affects

    (B) Destroys

    (C) Enhances

    (D) Diminishes

27. According to the passage, where is nerve growth factor produced in the body?

    (A) In nerve cells in the spinal column

    (B) In red blood cells in the circulatory system

    (C) In nerve cells in the brain

    (D) In the pituitary gland

28. Which of the following is closest in meaning to the word "region" as used in line 5?

    (A) Vicinity

    (B) Plain

    (C) Expanse

    (D) Orbit

29. Which of the following is closest in meaning to the word "doses" in line 8?

    (A) Measures

    (B) Pieces

    (C) Injections

    (D) Stipends

30. Which lines in the passage best describe the effect of nerve growth factor on the test rats?

    (A) Lines 1–3

    (B) Lines 4–6

    (C) Lines 11–13

    (D) Lines 13– 16

31. Which of the following can be inferred from the passage?

    (A) Alzheimer's disease is deadly.

    (B) Though unsuccessful, the experiments did show some benefits derived from nerve growth factor.

    (C) The experiments did not show any significant benefits from nerve growth factor.

    (D) More work needs to be done to understand the effects of nerve growth factor.

32. The passage most closely resembles which of the following patterns of organization?

  (A)  Chronological order

  (B)  Statement and illustration

  (C)  Cause/effect

  (D)  Alphabetical order

33. Which of the following is closest in meaning to the word "deterioration" in line 15?

  (A)  Depression

  (B)  Deduction

  (C)  Decline

  (D)  Disconnection

34. Which of the following could best replace the word "potential" in line 15?

  (A)  Possibility

  (B)  Capability

  (C)  Dependability

  (D)  Creativity

35. Which of the following could best replace the word "significantly" in line 16?

  (A)  Considerably

  (B)  Knowingly

  (C)  Suggestively

  (D)  Tirelessly

36. The relationship between nerve growth factor and a protein is similar to the relationship between Alzheimer's and

  (A)  forgetfulness.

  (B)  a disease.

  (C)  a cure.

  (D)  a cancer.

**Questions 37–48 are based on the following passage.**

Until recently, hunting for treasure from shipwrecks was mostly fantasy; with recent technological advances, however, the search for sunken treasure has become more popular as a legitimate endeavor. This has caused a debate between those wanting to salvage the wrecks and those wanting to preserve
(5) them.

Treasure hunters are spurred on by the thought of finding caches of gold coins or other valuable objects on a sunken ship. One team of salvagers, for instance, searched the wreck of the RMS *Republic*, which sank outside the Boston harbor in 1909. The search party, using side-scan sonar, a device that
(10) projects sound waves across the ocean bottom and produces a profile of the

sea floor, located the wreck in just two and a half days. Before the use of this new technology, such searches could take months or years. The team of 45 divers searched the wreck for two months, finding silver tea services, crystal dinnerware, and thousands of bottles of wine, but they did not find the five *(15)* and a half tons of American Gold Eagle coins they were searching for.

Preservationists focus on the historic value of a ship. They say that, even if a shipwreck's treasure does not have a high monetary value, it can be an invaluable source of historic artifacts that are preserved in nearly mint condition. But once a salvage team has scoured a site, much of the *(20)* archaeological value is lost. Maritime archaeologists who are preservationists worry that the success of salvagers will attract more treasure-hunting expeditions and thus threaten remaining undiscovered wrecks. Preservationists are lobbying their state lawmakers to legally restrict underwater searches and unregulated salvages. To counter their efforts, treasure hunters *(25)* argue that without the lure of gold and million-dollar treasures, the wrecks and their historical artifacts would never be recovered at all.

37. What is the main idea of this passage?

    (A)    Searching for wrecks is much easier with new technologies like side-scan sonar.

    (B)    Maritime archaeologists are concerned about the unregulated searching of wrecks.

    (C)    The search of the RMS *Republic* failed to produce the hoped-for coins.

    (D)    The popularity of treasure seeking has spurred a debate between preservationists and salvagers.

38. The word "sunken" in line 2 is closest in meaning to which of the following words?

    (A)    Broken

    (B)    Underwater

    (C)    Ancient

    (D)    Hollow

39. Which of the following is closest in meaning to the word "legitimate" in line 3?

    (A)    Justified

    (B)    Innocent

    (C)    Prudent

    (D)    Fundamental

40. What does the second paragraph mainly discuss?

    (A)    How side-scan sonar works to find a shipwreck

    (B)    How the Boston salvage team located the ship's gold

    (C)    A specific salvage operation that took place in 1909

    (D)    A specific salvage operation that used new technology to locate a shipwreck

41. Which of the following statements is best supported by the author?

    (A)   The value of a shipwreck depends on the quantity of its artifacts.

    (B)   Preservationists are fighting the use of technological advances such as side-scan sonar.

    (C)   Side-scan sonar has helped to legitimize salvaging.

    (D)   The use of sound waves is crucial to locating shipwrecks.

42. The author uses the word "services" in line 13 to refer to which of the following?

    (A)   Cups

    (B)   Sets

    (C)   Containers

    (D)   Decorations

43. The author uses the phrase "mint condition" in lines 18-19 to describe

    (A)   something perfect.

    (B)   something significant.

    (C)   something tolerant.

    (D)   something magical.

44. All of the following were found on the RMS *Republic* EXCEPT

    (A)   wine bottles.

    (B)   silver tea services.

    (C)   American Gold Eagle coins.

    (D)   crystal dinnerware.

45. From the passage, you can infer that a preservationist would be most likely to

    (A)   shun treasure-seeking salvagers.

    (B)   be a diver.

    (C)   put treasures in a museum.

    (D)   do archaeological research.

46. The word "scoured" in line 19 is most similar to which of the following?

    (A)   Scraped away

    (B)   Scratched over

    (C)   Scrambled around

    (D)   Searched through

47. In line 25, what is the closest meaning to the word "lure"?

    (A)   Knowledge

    (B)   Attraction

    (C)   Luxury

    (D)   Glare

48. The second and third paragraphs are an example of

    (A)    chronological order.

    (B)    explanation.

    (C)    specific to general.

    (D)    definition.

**Questions 49–60 are based on the following passage.**

Are you interested in seeing the beautiful fall foliage of New England but tired of traffic jams and overbooked hotels? Then this year, forget the crowds in New England and see the beautiful colors of autumn in the Catskills.

(5)     These rugged mountains in New York State, just 90 miles northwest of New York City, are famous for the legendary tales of Rip Van Winkle and more recently for the summer hotels that sprang up in the region during the 1940s, 1950s, and 1960s. Families trying to escape the heat of New York City found the Catskills to be the perfect place to stay for a month or so each (10) summer. By the late 1950s, there were over 500 resorts and hotels offering nighttime entertainment as well as all kinds of outdoor activities. Famous comedians like Jackie Gleason, Joan Rivers, and Sid Caesar all got their start touring the hotel clubs here. Since the introduction of air-conditioning and cheaper air travel, however, families have stopped coming to the Catskills (15) in such large numbers, choosing instead more distant locations at different times of the year. Many of the Catskill hotels closed in the 1970s, but some remain and have expanded and changed their facilities to meet the needs of today's visitors.

        Currently, there are many activities available to the traveler besides (20) witnessing the changing colors of the leaves. There is an all-organic sheep farm where visitors can see how a traditional sheep farm operates. There are also hundreds of miles of scenic drives in the area. Route 42, for instance, is an excellent site for spotting bald eagles. For more information on vacations in the Catskills, call the Office of Public Information.

49. What is the author's main purpose in this passage?

    (A)    To promote the Catskills as a vacation destination

    (B)    To introduce visitors to famous Catskills entertainers

    (C)    To describe the history of the Catskills region

    (D)    To compare the Catskills to New England

50. The word "rugged" in line 5 could be best replaced by which of the following?

    (A)    Barren

    (B)    Rough

    (C)    Tall

    (D)    Lush

51. According to the passage, which of the following caused the decline in the number of resorts in the 1970s?

    (A) Television

    (B) Shorter vacations

    (C) Affordable air travel

    (D) More traffic

52. Which of the following is closest in meaning to the word "legendary" in line 6?

    (A) Foolish

    (B) Perplexing

    (C) Mythical

    (D) Humorous

53. The phrase "sprang up" in line 7 most probably refers to something that has done which of the following?

    (A) Burst forth

    (B) Spread out

    (C) Operated vigorously

    (D) Joined together

54. In what season would a tourist most likely have visited the Catskills in the 1950s?

    (A) Fall

    (B) Winter

    (C) Spring

    (D) Summer

55. Which of the following most reflects the author's tone in this passage?

    (A) Light and encouraging

    (B) Informative and scientific

    (C) Humorous and skeptical

    (D) Regretful and reminiscent

56. What does the passage imply that a visitor might be lucky enough to do?

    (A) See fall leaves in color

    (B) See a kind of bird

    (C) Work on a sheep farm

    (D) Drive on scenic roads

57. Where is the best place in the passage to add the following sentence?

    "For the bird-watcher, the Catskills offer a habitat rich in both common and rare bird species."

    (A)   In line 4 after the word "Catskills"

    (B)   In line 8 after the words "and 1960s"

    (C)   In line 22 after the word "area"

    (D)   In line 24 after the words "public information"

58. As used in line 23, which of the following could best replace the word "drives"?

    (A)   excursions.

    (B)   tracks.

    (C)   paths.

    (D)   canyons.

59. As used in line 23, which of the following could best replace the word "spotting"?

    (A)   Photographing

    (B)   Seeing

    (C)   Painting

    (D)   Shooting

60. The author implies that in the Catskills there are few

    (A)   leaves.

    (B)   eagles.

    (C)   people.

    (D)   sheep.

# ANSWER KEY

## SECTION 1—LISTENING COMPREHENSION

### Part A

| | | | |
|---|---|---|---|
| 1. C | 6. D | 11. A | 16. B |
| 2. A | 7. C | 12. D | 17. C |
| 3. A | 8. B | 13. B | 18. A |
| 4. A | 9. D | 14. A | 19. C |
| 5. D | 10. A | 15. D | 20. A |

### Part B

| | | |
|---|---|---|
| 21. C | 26. C | 31. A |
| 22. B | 27. C | 32. A |
| 23. C | 28. C | 33. B |
| 24. D | 29. B | 34. A |
| 25. B | 30. C | 35. B |

### Part C

| | | |
|---|---|---|
| 36. A | 41. A | 46. A |
| 37. C | 42. D | 47. B |
| 38. B | 43. A | 48. C |
| 39. B | 44. A | 49. A |
| 40. A | 45. D | 50. C |

## SECTION 2—STRUCTURE AND WRITTEN EXPRESSION

### Part 1—Sentence Completion

| | | |
|---|---|---|
| 1. B | 6. B | 11. B |
| 2. A | 7. A | 12. D |
| 3. B | 8. C | 13. A |
| 4. A | 9. A | 14. C |
| 5. D | 10. A | 15. A |

## Part 2—Error Identification

| | | | | |
|---|---|---|---|---|
| 16. A | 21. B | 26. B | 31. C | 36. D |
| 17. C | 22. C | 27. C | 32. C | 37. C |
| 18. B | 23. C | 28. C | 33. A | 38. A |
| 19. C | 24. C | 29. D | 34. A | 39. C |
| 20. D | 25. B | 30. A | 35. D | 40. D |

## Section 3—Reading Comprehension

| | | | | | |
|---|---|---|---|---|---|
| 1. B | 11. D | 21. D | 31. D | 41. C | 51. C |
| 2. A | 12. C | 22. A | 32. B | 42. B | 52. C |
| 3. D | 13. B | 23. D | 33. C | 43. A | 53. A |
| 4. A | 14. D | 24. B | 34. A | 44. C | 54. D |
| 5. A | 15. A | 25. D | 35. A | 45. A | 55. A |
| 6. C | 16. C | 26. D | 36. B | 46. D | 56. B |
| 7. B | 17. A | 27. C | 37. D | 47. B | 57. C |
| 8. D | 18. B | 28. A | 38. B | 48. B | 58. A |
| 9. B | 19. B | 29. A | 39. A | 49. A | 59. B |
| 10. A | 20. D | 30. C | 40. D | 50. B | 60.C |

# EXPLANATORY ANSWERS

## SECTION 1—LISTENING COMPREHENSION

## Part A

1. **The correct answer is (C).** A "tight schedule" refers to a very busy schedule. The two speakers agree that Lisa is busy.

2. **The correct answer is (A).** The man says he thinks her major is computer science, so he must think that it is not chemistry.

3. **The correct answer is (A).** When the man says "not anymore," he means, "Mark doesn't smoke a lot anymore." The man's comment could mean that Mark has quit smoking. It could also mean that now Mark smokes less than he did before, but this is not an answer choice. So, choice (A) is the best answer.

4. **The correct answer is (A).** "Only a few showed up" means that not many people were there.

5. **The correct answer is (D).** The phrase "using what he's learned" means the same thing as "applying his knowledge."

6. **The correct answer is (D).** The words "movies" and "film" are often used interchangeably in the United States. If the speakers were going to rent a videotape, they would say, "Let's go *get* a movie" rather than "Let's go *to* a movie."

7. **The correct answer is (C).** The woman is using the conditional tense. She means, "I would (return your book) if I were going to the library, but I am not going to the library."

8. **The correct answer is (B).** When a person asks, "Is this seat taken?" it usually means that the person wants to sit there. This is a polite question to ask before sitting down next to someone in a public place.

9. **The correct answer is (D).** When the man says, "so am I," he means that he is feeling the same thing. The word "exhausted" means "very tired."

10. **The correct answer is (A).** The woman's response, "actually I do," means that she feels the opposite of what the man says. The man asked a negative question, "you don't want to . . .?" and the woman's response is positive.

11. **The correct answer is (A).** The woman means that the man needs to make a decision about which class to take, because two of them are at the same time.

12. **The correct answer is (D).** The man's statement is a conditional. If he wishes he had done something, it means that he has not done it.

13. **The correct answer is (B).** The man's response is positive, as shown by his use of the word "sure."

14. **The correct answer is (A).** The woman's tone of voice is important in this conversation. Her word "Already?" could be expanded to "Are these books already due at the library?"

15. **The correct answer is (D).** The words "a bad connection" refer to a connection between electric wires.

16. **The correct answer is (B).** We can assume that the man has just picked up something the woman dropped, and she is thanking him for picking it up.

17. **The correct answer is (C).** The woman is asking for directions, so we can assume that the man will give her the directions.

18. **The correct answer is (A).** When the word "thank you" is said as "but thank you anyway," it means that the speaker is being polite in saying no.

19. **The correct answer is (C).** The weekend is Saturday and Sunday. The man says that his working hours are different on these days. He works either more or fewer hours.

20. **The correct answer is (A).** The word "feasible" means "possible." The man is questioning whether or not one year will be enough time to finish the project.

# Part B

21. **The correct answer is (C).** This is a restatement question. The woman says, "Your singing was great."

22. **The correct answer is (B).** This is a restatement question. The man says, "maybe you can see us next week when we play in Washington."

23. **The correct answer is (C).** This is an inference question. The woman tries to help the man find a record in the store and then directs him to try another record store to find the album. It is implied from this conversation that she works in a store selling records.

24. **The correct answer is (D).** This is a restatement question. The woman says that she will be going to San Francisco for vacation.

25. **The correct answer is (B).** This is a restatement question. The woman says she is going to Woods Hole, Massachusetts, to study whales.

26. **The correct answer is (C).** This is a restatement question. Tom states he will be working in his uncle's restaurant.

27. **The correct answer is (C).** This is a restatement question. The woman states that she will be studying whales.

28. **The correct answer is (C).** This is a restatement question. The woman says she will be away on a boat for the month of July.

29. **The correct answer is (B).** This is an inference question. The woman is writing a book about an American poet, and the man is teaching a class in American literature. Based on this information, it can be inferred that the teachers are most likely teaching American literature.

30. **The correct answer is (C).** This is a restatement question. The woman is traveling to meet a publisher and discuss the last chapter of the book she is writing.

31. **The correct answer is (A).** This is a restatement question. The man asks the woman to speak to his American literature class.

32. **The correct answer is (A).** This is a main idea question. The discussion focuses on the "twisted ladder" shape and the components of the DNA molecule.

33. **The correct answer is (B).** This is a restatement question. The professor states that a gene is a segment, or section, of the DNA molecule. Choice (A) refers to "bases," choice (C) refers to the chromosome, and choice (D) describes the shape of DNA.

34. **The correct answer is (A).** This is a restatement question. The professor reminds students that he is using the analogy of the "ladder" to help them picture the shape of DNA.

35. **The correct answer is (B).** This is a restatement question. DNA is found within the chromosome, not the gene. It is represented by a ladder not a rope. It has thousands of genes, not several.

# Part C

36. **The correct answer is (A).** This is a main purpose question. The professor begins by saying that he will give "a bit of background about James Joyce." He goes on to talk about Joyce's family, education, and marriage and about some of Joyce's books.

37. **The correct answer is (C).** This is a restatement question. The professor says that he could not find any publisher in Ireland, and that it was published in London.

38. **The correct answer is (B).** This is an inference question. The professor says that Joyce squandered his money, which means to waste it or use it wastefully. He also says that Joyce was often poor.

39. **The correct answer is (B).** This is a restatement question. The professor says that Joyce spent later years living in Paris. The term "later years" refers to the years when one is elderly.

40. **The correct answer is (A).** This is a main topic question. The main topic of the discussion is to introduce Dr. Sawyer. Choice (B) is too broad, and choice (C) is not discussed. Choice (D) is possible, but is not the best answer since the talk may be open to more than just students, and also the talk seems to be more advanced than a general introduction to fossil research.

41. **The correct answer is (A).** This is a restatement question. The speaker says that he and Dr. Sawyer co-authored some articles.

42. **The correct answer is (D).** This is a restatement question. The speaker says that Dr. Sawyer is well known for his work on documenting prehistory through fossil research.

43. **The correct answer is (A).** This is a question about a following topic. The speaker ends by introducing Dr. Sawyer, and states that Dr. Sawyer will now explain his findings from southern Kazahkstan where he has found some late Cambrian assemblages. The word "assemblage" refers to a collection of items. The word "Cambrian" refers to the geologic era of 3,800 – 700 million years ago.

44. **The correct answer is (A).** This is a restatement question. The speaker says that the school is the oldest public university in the United States.

45. **The correct answer is (D).** This is an inference question. The speaker says that the university has "quite a heritage" and the he gives some of the history of the university. Choice (A) is wrong because the speakers said 41 students, not 41 campuses. Choice (B) is wrong since the speaker did not mention monuments, though he did mention one building that is a historic building. And the speaker did not mention community programs.

46. **The correct answer is (A).** This is a restatement question. The speaker says that university began with this two-story brick building. Choice (B) may be correct, but the passage does not state this. Choice (C) is wrong since the speaker says the building was begun in 1793. Choice (D) is wrong because the passage does not state where the building is located, though it does refer to "a cornerstone." A cornerstone is one of the first stones that is laid in the foundation of a building, often in a corner of the building, which often has writing on it that gives the date of the construction of the building.

47. **The correct answer is (B).** This is a main idea question. The teacher is announcing that a summer science camp is looking for students to serve as camp counselors.

48. **The correct answer is (C).** This is a location question. The most likely location would be a classroom because the teacher says he is about to begin today's lecture.

49. **The correct answer is (A).** This is a restatement question. The announcement is calling for students to apply for jobs as counselors.

50. **The correct answer is (C).** This is a restatement question. The speaker says that the campers are scheduled to travel to Washington.

# SECTION 2: STRUCTURE AND WRITTEN EXPRESSION

## Part 1—Sentence Completion

1. **The correct answer is (B).** Comparison. After the comparative ending -er, the word "than" is necessary.

2. **The correct answer is (A).** Adjective phrase. The phrase "that reflect American life" describes the noun "themes."

3. **The correct answer is (B).** Connecting word/adjective clause. The clause "that can affect people" describes the noun "poisons."

4. **The correct answer is (A).** Subject + verb. The main subject and verb of the sentence are "Studies . . . show." The rest of the sentence is a clause that begins with the word "that" and describes what the studies show.

5. **The correct answer is (D).** Comparison. This is an "as . . . as" comparison. Two things are compared: generic medications and brand-name medications. A "generic" medication is one that is not produced and sold by a specific company but is the general medicine that is used by all the companies.

6. **The correct answer is (B).** Subject. The expletive "there" is the subject of this sentence. The main verb is "is." Choice (C) is incorrect because the word "what" before "is" would begin a question, and this is not a question. Choice (D) is incorrect because it does not make sense to say, "each is no way."

7. **The correct answer is (A).** The word "one" refers to Ernest Hemingway. The sentence means that Hemingway is one of the many writers who shaped modern writing.

8. **The correct answer is (C).** Subject + verb. The main verb of the sentence is "considered." Choices (A) and (D) incorrectly add the word "that," which is a connecting word for a clause. They are incorrect because there is no other verb for a clause. Choice (B) is incorrect because it does not bring a main verb to the sentence.

9. **The correct answer is (A).** Verb. This is a past-tense sentence that can have only a past-tense verb.

10. **The correct answer is (A).** The verb "need" in this sentence must be followed by the preposition "to."

11. **The correct answer is (B).** The word "you" in choice (B) is a general word that refers to all people. The sentence could also be "the person that you are greeting." Choice (C) is incorrect because "which" does not refer to people.

12. **The correct answer is (D).** Subject + verb. This sentence is a parallel construction: "committed to the promotion of health and [committed] to helping people."

13. **The correct answer is (A).** The verb "need" is a present-tense verb that goes with "bodies."

14. **The correct answer is (C).** The clause "that the loss of leaves may assist" follows "possible that." The other answers add another verb.

15. **The correct answer is (A).** Verb. The main noun of this sentence is "Hollywood," and the main verb is "was." The other answers have an incorrect order of adjectives.

## Part 2—Error Identification

16. **The correct answer is (A).** Adverb. The wrong word has been put in this sentence. The correct word is "when," which tells the time at which we can see an eclipse of the sun.

17. **The correct answer is (C).** Verb. The correct verb tense is either "is broadcasted" or "has been broadcasted." Both of these answers are in the passive voice.

18. **The correct answer is (B).** Connecting word/noun clause. The correct word is "that," which answers the question "what," as in, "What does some research suggest? Some research suggests that . . .?"

19. **The correct answer is (C).** Word form. After the word "by" must be the -ing form: "selling." This is an adverb phrase that answers the question "how?" as in, "How did Luther Burbank earn the funds to go west? By selling his new ideas . . .."

20. **The correct answer is (D).** Omitted word/article. The correct phrase is "in the book." There must be an article before the singular noun "book."

21. **The correct answer is (B).** Word form. An adverb is needed to refer to the time that rock music was a combination of country music and blues. The correct answer is "originally."

22. **The correct answer is (C).** Word form. The sentence is referring to people, so the correct word is "workers."

23. **The correct answer is (C).** Unnecessary word. The word "her" is not needed in this sentence because both the pronoun "her" and the name refer to the same person. The correct phrase is "before Augusta Maywood formed . . .."

24. **The correct answer is (C).** Verb. Because the subject is "virtues," a plural noun, the verb must be "are."

25. **The correct answer is (B).** Preposition. After the verb "consist" comes the preposition "of."

26. **The correct answer is (B).** Word form. The correct phrase is "that tells the story." This begins an adjective clause that answers the question "what kind of," as in, "What kind of novel is Moby Dick? It is a novel that tells the story of a ship captain . . . " The verb "tells" is the simple present tense.

27. **The correct answer is (C).** Omitted word. The correct answer is "such as," as a connecting phrase that introduces an example.

28. **The correct answer is (C).** Pronoun. Because Samuel Morse is one person, the pronoun must be singular. The correct answer is "made his living."

29. **The correct answer is (D).** Word form. The correct word is "horizontally," an adverb that describes how the jellyfish migrate.

30. **The correct answer is (A).** Infinitive/gerunds. The correct answer is "To put." This sentence could also be written, "In order to put a large amount of information on a map…" It answers the question "why," as in, "Why must a variety of symbols be used" to put a large amount of information on a map?

31. **The correct answer is (C).** Word form. This sentence needs the adjective "rare," not the adverb. The phrase "it was rare" is grammatically similar to a sentence such as "it was beautiful" or "it was funny."

32. **The correct answer is (C).** Word form. The correct word is "preventable," an adjective that describes the noun "cause."

33. **The correct answer is (A).** Negative adverb. The correct answer is "no single alphabet." It would also be correct to say, "not a single alphabet." The word "not" cannot come directly before a noun.

34. **The correct answer is (A).** Adverb. The correct word to make sense in the sentence is "during," which begins an adverb phrase that answers the question "when," as in, "When were . . . people killed? During the Second World War." It would also be correct to begin this sentence with a clause, such as, "When the Second World War ended, almost a third of a million people had been killed."

35. **The correct answer is (D).** Word form. The word "radiate" is a verb, but the sentence requires the noun form, "radiation."

36. **The correct answer is (D).** Word form. This sentence should end in a noun, "growth." The phrase "for animal growth" describes the reason that energy is essential. The word "animal" in this sentence is used as an adjective that describes the type of growth.

37. **The correct answer is (C).** Verb. The correct answer is "is separated," a passive form of the verb. The active voice could be, "something separates the light into . . . colors."

38. **The correct answer is (A).** Connecting phrase/omitted word. The correct phrase is "in spite of." It would also be correct to say, "Despite modern medical technology . . . "

39. **The correct answer is (C).** Word form. Because Picasso is a person, the word to describe him must be "painter."

40. **The correct answer is (D).** Reversed words. The correct phrase is "densely populated areas." The adverb "densely" describes the word "populated."

## SECTION 3—READING COMPREHENSION

1. **The correct answer is (B).** This is an inference question. The author states that no conclusive answer has been found to the question of what happened to Amelia Earhart.

2. **The correct answer is (A).** When someone "breaks a record," they do something better or different than anyone has ever done before. Earhart was the first woman to fly across the Atlantic, and she was the first to fly several long distances alone. The verb "to surpass" means "to do or be better than."

3. **The correct answer is (D).** The idiom "to make it" means to complete something or to do something that is difficult, so "never make it" is the opposite. Whereas choices (A), (B), and (C) might be true, they do not refer specifically to the sentence in this part of the passage. The sentence "They never made it" comes right after the statement of their goal: to be the first to fly around the world."

4. **The correct answer is (A).** This is a vocabulary question. The term "conventional wisdom" refers to knowledge that many people have that may or may not be supported by facts.

5. **The correct answer is (A).** This is an inference question. In paragraph 2, the author discusses several aspects of the mystery, including two theories: (1) that the airplane crashed into the ocean and (2) that they landed on an island when they ran out of fuel. The paragraph goes on to give details, especially about the second theory.

6. **The correct answer is (C).** This is a vocabulary question. When someone *disputes* another person, it means that she does not agree with that person or that idea.

7. **The correct answer is (B).** This is a restatement question. The passage states that they belong to a group that is funded by an organization that was formed specifically to search for historic plane wrecks.

8. **The correct answer is (D).** The verb "to crumble" means to fall apart into little pieces, as a cookie might if it is held for a while.

9. **The correct answer is (B).** This is an inference question. The author says that not all people believe that Earhart's plane crashed into the ocean, and that some people are looking for other evidence, especially on the island of Nikumaroro.

10. **The correct answer is (A).** This is an inference question. What Gillespie and Thrasher want is to find evidence to support their theory that Earhart and Noonan landed on the island. The other answer choices are not mentioned.

11. **The correct answer is (D).** This is a negative question. All of the other choices are mentioned in the passage except choice (D). Choice (C) refers to a piece of aluminum and a rivet; these would probably come for the exterior of the plane, not the engine. A rivet is a metal pin used to fasten two things together.

12. **The correct answer is (C).** The idiom "It's just around the corner" means that you hope that whatever you are looking for is very near, but you cannot see it yet.

13. **The correct answer is (B).** The author begins the passage by explaining that recent discoveries suggest that extinctions may have happened over a much shorter period of time than had previously been thought.

14. **The correct answer is (D).** The word "close" can be a noun, an adjective, or a verb. In this sentence, it is a noun and it means the same as "the end."

15. **The correct answer is (A).** The phrase "the face of the Earth" does not mean anything different from the phrase "the Earth." It is used only to emphasize that many species of animals completely disappeared from the Earth.

16. **The correct answer is (C).** The passage states that a large meteorite may have struck the Earth at the end of the Triassic Period. The beginning of the passage states that the Triassic Period was 200 million years ago, not 10 million years ago.

17. **The correct answer is (A).** This is a vocabulary question. The words "relatively" and "comparatively" both mean "considering something in comparison with another thing."

18. **The correct answer is (B).** The author states in lines 10–15 that the evidence is in the McCoy Brook Formation along the Bay of Fundy in Nova Scotia.

19. **The correct answer is (B).** The final paragraph mentions shocked quartz as an example of evidence that a meteorite struck the earth.

20. **The correct answer is (D).** The word "struck" is to the past tense of "strike," which means "to hit." Both words in this sentence mean "to collide with."

21. **The correct answer is (D).** This is a sentence insertion question. The sentence best fits at the end of the passage because the final sentence in the passage introduces the idea that extinction may have occurred at a different rate elsewhere in the world.

22. **The correct answer is (A).** The head noun before the word "it" is "evidence." The word "meteorite" explains the "evidence," and the word "Earth" is connected in meaning to "meteorite." The word "extinction" follows the word "it" and does not explain it.

23. **The correct answer is (D).** This is a vocabulary question. The words "credence" and "credibility" are similar in meaning to "belief," "confidence," and "trust."

24. **The correct answer is (B).** This question asks for the author's tone. The author is primarily concerned with a description of the evidence for a new theory. There are no words to suggest any of the other answers.

25. **The correct answer is (D).** This is a main idea question. Both choices (A) and (B) are more general than the scope of the passage. Choice (C) is not relative to the main idea.

26. **The correct answer is (D).** In the context of this passage, the word "impair" means "to cause a deterioration in memory." Choice (A) is not specific enough, and choice (B) is too extreme. Choice (C) is the opposite of deterioration.

27. **The correct answer is (C).** This is a restatement question. Lines 2–5 of the passage state that the nerve growth factor is produced in the same part of the brain in which Alzheimer's occurs.

28. **The correct answer is (A).** This is a vocabulary question. The words "region" and "vicinity" both refer to a locality around something. Choice (B) refers to a flat level area, choice (C) refers to a large area, and choice (D) refers to the revolving or circular path of an object.

29. **The correct answer is (A).** This is a vocabulary question. The words "measures" and "doses" both refer to "quantities" or "amounts" of something, often medicines. Choice (B) refers to bits of solid material. Choice (C) refers to a syringe or needle that forces a drug into the body. Choice (D) generally refers to a regular or fixed payment such as a salary.

30. **The correct answer is (C).** This question is a summary question. The results of the test showing the effects of nerve growth factor on rats are summarized in lines 11–13. Other sentences do not discuss the effects of nerve growth on rats; lines 13–16 present the overall implications of the test for humans.

31. **The correct answer is (D).** This is an inference question. Choice (A) is not true; the passage describes the disease only in terms of a gradual deterioration of memory. Choices (B) and (C) each contain some information that is false according to the passage. Choice (D) can be inferred because the final sentence of the passage states that there is potential in this experiment. This implies that we do not yet know enough about it.

32. **The correct answer is (B).** This is an organization question. Neither choice (A) nor choice (D) is correct because the passage is not ordering things chronologically or alphabetically. Choice (C) is not correct because the passage does not focus on the experiments and the results. Instead, there is a statement of the main idea, which is that there is a potential cure for Alzheimer's disease, followed by a discussion of nerve growth factor, which illustrates this potential cure.

33. **The correct answer is (C).** This is a vocabulary question. The words "deterioration" and "decline" both mean that something is "getting worse."

34. **The correct answer is (A).** This is a vocabulary question. The word "potential" refers to the possibility of something developing in the future.

35. **The correct answer is (A).** This is a vocabulary question. The word "significantly" indicates that there is enough of something to make it important. The word "considerably" means "enough" or "importantly."

36. **The correct answer is (B).** This is an analogy question. For this type of question, the answer must form a parallel sentence with the question. A nerve growth factor is an example of a protein, just as Alzheimer's is an example of a disease.

37. **The correct answer is (D).** This is a main idea question. The other choices are ideas presented in the passage, but they are only part of the main idea.

38. **The correct answer is (B).** This is a vocabulary question. The word "sunken" comes from the verb "to sink," which implies that an object has gone underwater.

39. **The correct answer is (A).** The words "legitimate" and "justified" both refer to something that has been shown to have value or has been approved. In this case, the use of new technological devices has given credence and respectability to the act of searching for sunken treasure because it now can be done scientifically.

40. **The correct answer is (D).** This is a paragraph focus question. Choice (D) best summarizes the central idea of the paragraph. Although choice (A) is mentioned within the paragraph, it is not the focus.

41. **The correct answer is (C).** This is an author's support question. The first sentence states that treasure seeking is now seen as legitimate because of new technology. The fifth sentence states that one of the new technological advances is side-scan sonar. Choice (A) is not correct because the passage infers that a sunken ship may have value as an historic object, even if it has no monetary value from treasures. Choice (B) is not correct; it may be inferred, but it is not "best supported" by the author. Choice (D) is not correct because the use of sound waves is not stated as being crucial, only as being a new advance that has improved and sped up the process of discovery.

42. **The correct answer is (B).** A "tea service" refers to a group of items, such as a tray containing a teapot, a small bowl for sugar, a small jug for cream, and maybe a spoon.

43. **The correct answer is (A).** The phrase "mint condition" refers to something that is "like new" or "in perfect condition." It comes from the noun and verb "mint," which refers to the place and process of producing coins. At a mint, all coins are brand new and in perfect condition.

44. **The correct answer is (C).** This is a negative question. The answer lies in lines 12–15, where the author lists the items found and states that the crew did not find any American Gold Eagle coins.

45. **The correct answer is (A).** This is an inference question. Because preservationists are critical of the activities of treasure hunters and because the passage says that they are fighting each other in the courts, it would be most likely that preservationists would shun salvagers. The verb "to shun" means "to avoid deliberately."

46. **The correct answer is (D).** In this sentence, the verbs "to scour" and "to search through" mean "to comb through" or "to rummage through." "Scour" infers that the search involves turning things over to look under them. In other instances, the verb "to scour" means "to wash vigorously."

47. **The correct answer is (B).** The nouns "lure" and "attraction" both refer to something that is appealing, such as a reward or pleasure.

48. **The correct answer is (B).** This is an organization question. The second and third paragraphs explain two opposing groups of people: preservationists and treasure seekers (also called "treasure hunters" and "salvagers"). Choice (D), "definition," is too narrow because the paragraphs supply more information than just a definition of the types of people.

49. **The correct answer is (A).** This is a question of the author's purpose. Choice (B) is incorrect because the entertainers are mentioned only as one reason to visit the Catskills. Choice (C) is also mentioned only as a way to promote the region. Choice (D) is incorrect because there is no similar discussion of New England's features as a vacation destination.

50. **The correct answer is (B).** This is a vocabulary question. The words "rugged" and "rough" both refer to something that is uneven or jagged, such as the mountains. Choice (A) refers to a place that has little vegetation growing. Choice (D) is just the opposite of choice (A) in that it refers to a place that is very green and filled with growing plants.

51. **The correct answer is (C).** This is a restatement question. Lines 13–16 give cheaper air travel and air-conditioning as reasons why families stopped coming to the hotels and why the hotels later closed.

52. **The correct answer is (C).** This is a vocabulary question. A "legendary" story is one that is probably not true but is well known in a particular culture. "Mythical" also refers to a story that is not true but is well known.

53. **The correct answer is (A).** The phrases "to spring up" and "to burst forth" both refer to something that appears suddenly.

54. **The correct answer is (D).** This is an inference question. Lines 8–11 describe the Catskills in the 1950s as a summer-vacation spot.

55. **The correct answer is (A).** This is an author's tone question. Throughout the passage, the author is speaking directly to the reader in a lighthearted way to encourage the reader to visit the Catskills. Whereas much of the passage is "informative," it is not written in a scientific way. There are no words to suggest humor, skepticism, regret, or reminiscence.

56. **The correct answer is (B).** This is an inference question. The final paragraph mentions several things that a visitor might be able to do. The only answer that implies being "lucky" is choice (B), "spotting bald eagles." An eagle is a bird. The word "spot" implies a quick look at something, which could also be "discern," "detect," or "pick out." All these verbs imply that it is not always easy to see the object, and one may get only a glance at it. Seeing the fall colors, as mentioned in choice (A), is written of as an expected activity, not a "lucky" one. Choices (C) and (D) are both mentioned as things visitors can do; there is no implication that the visitor must be "lucky" to do them.

57. **The correct answer is (C).** This is a sentence insertion question. The sentence best fits near the end of the passage after the word "area" and before the sentence beginning with "Route 42," which gives an example of a good birding site.

58. **The correct answer is (A).** This is a vocabulary question. In this sentence, the word "drives" refers to places that people can drive to in their cars for pleasure. The word "excursion" refers to the same activity. Choices (B) and (C) do not imply automobile tourism, as does "drives." One might walk on a track or path. On a scenic drive, a tourist might view a canyon, but the word "drive" refers to the road, not the canyon itself.

59. **The correct answer is (B).** This is a line focus question. The verb "to spot" refers to seeing or viewing something briefly or with difficulty.

60. **The correct answer is (C).** This is an inference question. The passage begins with the implication that few people go to the Catskills because there are no traffic jams or overbooked hotels.

# Transcripts for Practice Tests

## PART 4

**PREVIEW**

# Test 1 (CBT Style) Listening Script

## SECTION 1

### LISTENING

This test is written to represent the CBT in terms of the numbers of questions, types of questions, and length of time for each section. As on the CBT, the directions for both Parts A and B are given at the beginning of the test.

The Listening section includes two parts. In Part A, you hear conversations between two people. Sometimes the people speak only once, and at other times, they speak more than once. Each conversation is followed by one question. In Part B, you hear longer conversations and talks. Sometimes the talks are by professors in a classroom; for these, you might hear students in the classroom asking questions, answering questions, or giving comments. Each of the longer conversations and talks is followed by several questions.

**Now, listen to the directions for each part.**

## Part A

(*Narrator*):    In the first part of the Listening section, Part A, you will hear conversations between two people. You will hear the conversation only one time, so you must listen carefully to what is said. After each conversation, a third person will ask a question. On the computer test, you will see pictures of the speakers and see the questions on your screen. Next, you will see the answer choices. Decide which is the correct choice, and select your answer. Answer all questions based on what is stated or implied by the speakers. On the computer test, you will not be able to return to a question once you have confirmed your answer.

\* *Note to test taker:* *On the CBT, at this point you would see a picture of a man and woman talking outside on a university campus.*

(*Narrator*):    Now listen to an example.

(*Woman*):    Have you called Pete?

(*Man*):    I'll call him as soon as I get home.

(*Narrator*):    What does the man mean?

(*Narrator*):    Choose an answer in your book.

[**To the reader:** Pause for 12 seconds after each question is asked to allow time for the test taker to answer.]

(*Narrator*):    You learn from the conversation that the man will call Pete as soon as he gets home. The best answer to the question "What does the man mean?" is choice (B), "He will call Pete after he gets home."

(*Narrator*):    Now listen to the directions for Part B.

## Part B

(*Narrator*): In the second part of the Listening section, Part B, you will hear longer conversations and talks. You will hear the conversation or talk only once, so listen carefully to what is said. After each conversation or talk, you will be asked several questions. Answer all questions based on what is stated or implied by the speakers. On the computer test, you will see pictures of the speakers and see the questions on your screen. Next, you will see the answer choices. Decide which is the correct choice, and select your answer. On the computer test, you will not be able to return to a question once you have confirmed your answer.

| *(Narrator):* | Listen to the first example talk. There are two questions for this example. |
|---|---|
| **Example talk 1.** | Listen to a conversation between two friends at school. |
| *(Man):* | Hi, Joanie. Where are you going? |
| *(Woman):* | Oh, hi, Paul. I'm on my way to the library. |
| *(Man):* | Oh yeah? I just wondered if you wanted to go to a movie with me. |
| *(Woman):* | I'd love to, but I can't. I can't believe all the work I have this semester. I only have three classes, but in all of them I have lots of reading, term papers, reports, and essay exams. It's incredible! I feel like I'll never get through everything. |
| *(Man):* | That's terrible. I felt like that last year when I had term papers to write, but this semester seems easy now. I spend a lot of time in class, but most of it is in labs doing experiments. I hated writing all those term papers. But can't I talk you into going to the show anyway? I've heard that the movie over at the East Auditorium is really good. It's a murder mystery. |
| *(Woman):* | Oh, now I'm sure I won't go. I might go to a comedy, but I hate murder mysteries. |

**Now listen to example question number one.**

1. Where is the woman going?

   Choose an answer.

[**To the reader:** Pause for 12 seconds after each question is asked to allow time for the test taker to answer.]

> The correct answer to the question "Where is the woman going?" is choice (D), "To the library."

**Now listen to example question number two.**

2. Which best describes the man's feelings about his classes?

   Choose an answer.

[**To the reader:** Pause for 12 seconds after each question is asked to allow time for the test taker to answer.]

> The best answer to the question "Which best describes the man's feelings about his classes?" is choice (C), "He finds lab experiments easier than writing term papers."

**Now listen to the second example talk. There are two questions for this talk.**

**Example talk 2.** Listen to an announcement at a university.

*(Woman):* At this university, we offer three different programs for students who have children. For those of you with very young children, we have a day-care program for infants from 3 months to 24 months. We have another program for children between 2 and 5 years of age. And we also have an after-school program for school-aged children. This program offers sports, crafts, outings, and tutoring during after-school hours. Enrollment in these child-care programs is limited, so early application is essential, since our programs often have waiting lists. The fees are on an hourly basis. If any of you new students need these services, please let me know right away so I can get you an application form.

**Now listen to example question number one.**

1. What is the main purpose of this announcement?

Choose an answer.

[**To the reader:** Pause for 12 seconds after each question is asked to allow time for the test taker to answer.]

The best answer to the question "What is the main purpose of this announcement?" is choice (D), "To explain a service."

**Now listen to example question number two.**

2. What does the speaker recommend?

Choose an answer.

[**To the reader:** Pause for 12 seconds after each question is asked to allow time for the test taker to answer.]

The correct answer to the question "What does the speaker recommend?" is choice (C), "Apply as soon as you can."

**This is the end of the example questions for Listening Comprehension. Now begin the test 1 with Part A. Get ready to listen.**

# LISTENING

## Part A

[**To the reader:** Pause for 12 seconds after each question is asked to allow time for the test taker to answer.]

1. *(Woman):*     I'd like to go jogging, but I have to study for an exam.

   *(Man):*     Working out always helps me to relax when I'm stressed.

   *(Woman):*     That's a good point. Maybe I will go jogging, after all.

   *(Narrator):*     What does the man imply to the woman?

2. *(Man):*     These biology books are really expensive!

   *(Woman):*     I know. I barely had enough money to buy them.

   *(Narrator):*     What does the woman mean?

3. *(Man):*     I don't think I'll be able to go to that concert with you on Tuesday. I'm getting really busy with my school-work.

   *(Woman):*     Didn't you hear? It's been rescheduled for Wednesday.

   *(Man):*     Really? That's great! I'll be able to go then.

   *(Narrator):*     What does the woman mean?

4. *(Man):*     Do you want to get some lunch? I'm hungry!

   *(Woman):*     Me, too! I didn't have time for breakfast.

   *(Narrator):*     What does the woman imply?

5. *(Woman):*     Can you attend the conference next week?

   *(Man):*     Let me check my calendar. I'd really like to go. It sounds interesting.

   *(Narrator):*     What does the man imply?

6. *(Woman):*     Did you hear what happened to Steve?

   *(Man):*     No. What?

   *(Woman):*     He lost his whole term paper because he hadn't saved it on the computer.

   *(Narrator):*     What does the woman say about Steve?

7.  **(Man):**        Did you and Katy finish the article for today's class?

    **(Woman):**    Katy said that she couldn't complete it and neither could I.

    **(Man):**        It was difficult, wasn't it?

    **(Woman):**    It sure was!

    **(Narrator):**  What does the woman imply?

8.  **(Man):**        Professor, could I arrange to take a make-up exam? I won't be able to come to class on the day of the test.

    **(Woman):**    And why is that, Jason?

    **(Man):**        Well…my dad's having surgery that day, and I want to be there at the hospital.

    **(Woman):**    Oh, I'm sorry to hear that. I hope it all goes well. Certainly, we can work something out about the exam.

    **(Narrator):**  What does the woman mean?

9.  **(Woman):**    Have you seen the new science library yet?

    **(Man):**        No, is it nice?

    **(Woman):**    Nice! Wow, wait until you see it!

    **(Narrator):**  What does the woman mean?

10. **(Man):**        Aren't you almost ready to graduate, Robin?

    **(Woman):**    I thought I was, but I just found out that they've added an extra course requirement to my major.

    **(Narrator):**  What does the woman mean?

11. **(Woman):**    How's it going with your new roommate?

    **(Man):**        It's hard to say. He's seems okay, but he's a lot messier than I am. So, I don't know if we're really going to be compatible.

    **(Woman):**    Well, time will tell.

    **(Narrator):**  What does the woman mean?

12. **(Man):**        That study group last night was a real waste of time.

    **(Woman):**    Why? What do you mean?

    **(Man):**        Well, no one else had even read the material. So I was the only one prepared to talk about it, much less analyze it. I might as well have stayed home and studied by myself.

| (Narrator): | What does the man imply? |
|---|---|

13. **(Man):** Dr. Coltrain, is the new lab manual all ready for tomorrow?

**(Woman):** Yes it is, and I'd like you and the other teaching assistants to take a look at it this afternoon, so you'll be ready to help your students with it tomorrow.

**(Man):** I'm afraid I have an appointment off campus this afternoon. Could I come in early tomorrow morning?

**(Woman):** Sure. I'll be here by 8:30 tomorrow. You can come then.

**(Man):** Thanks. I'll be here bright and early.

**(Narrator):** What does the man mean?

14. **(Woman):** Hey Josh! When did you start working here?

**(Man):** Just a few days ago.

**(Woman):** Why did you want to work in the dining hall? This is the last place I'd want to work.

**(Man):** I didn't really have a choice. I was assigned to work here as part of my work-study program. But it's not so bad; it has its advantages.

**(Woman):** Advantages?

**(Man):** Yeah, free meals, if you work here.

**(Narrator):** What does the man mean?

15. **(Man):** I'll never get these formulas memorized by Friday.

**(Woman):** Well, why did you put off studying for the exam until now?

**(Narrator):** What does the woman imply?

## Part B

**Questions 16–18. Listen to two students talking about their involvement with music.**

| | |
|---|---|
| *(Woman):* | What are you doing after class? Do you want to go for a cup of coffee? |
| *(Man):* | Coffee sounds great, but I have to go to orchestra practice from 5 to 7 p.m. |
| *(Woman):* | Really? I didn't know you were a musician. |
| *(Man):* | Well, I'm not a professional musician. I'm just an amateur. I play the violin in the university orchestra. |
| *(Woman):* | When did you start playing? |
| *(Man):* | When I was seven. My elementary school had an orchestra program, and I always enjoyed playing the violin. |
| *(Woman):* | That's great! I wish I hadn't given up on the piano when I was young. |
| *(Man):* | It takes dedication, but it's never too late to learn. |

[**To the reader:** Pause for 12 seconds after each question is asked to allow time for the test taker to answer.]

16. What does the woman want to do after class?

17. How long has the man been playing the violin?

18. According to the discussion, what does the woman wish she had done?

**Questions 19–22. Listen to part of a class discussion in an environmental studies class. The professor is focusing on a controversy between economics and ecology.**

*(Male Professor):* Up to now in this class we've had a basic introduction to some of the issues in environmental studies, but we haven't yet examined the controversies that abound in this field. So today, we'll look at one of those. It centers on issues in economics as well as in ecology. Both of these words, in fact, stem from the same root word. Does anyone know what the Greek root word *eco-* means?

*(Female Student):*   I think it means house.

*(Male Professor):*   That's correct. So one might think that the two words, economy and ecology, wouldn't be in conflict. Yet, in many people's minds they represent conflicting views on how to approach our environment, both in terms of current needs and in terms of planning for the future. People coming from an ecological perspective have been widely labeled as the enemy of economic progress. And people who are concerned with progress are often seen as anti-environmental. Actually, this is not a new conflict. The first clash between economic advancement and preservation of the natural environment probably occurred thousands of years ago. Since humans first began to develop land for agriculture and permanent settlements, plants and animals and their natural ecological cycles have been affected. Of course, development at that time was on a small enough scale that its overall effect on the environment was minimal. But over time, with a massive increase in human population, and the widespread use of advanced technology, we have seen a startling rise in the number of plant and animal species that have become extinct or are seriously endangered. Scientists say that, in one day alone, about forty-five plant and animal species die out. And it is this issue—development versus environmental protection—that is the basis of the clash.

*(Male Student):*   Well, I don't know how this can be solved, but is there a way to stop the mass extinction of plants and animals?

*(Male Professor):*   Well, yes, at least to some extent. Conservation measures are being taken by some governments around the world. Years ago the U.S. government established the Endangered Species Act to protect plant and animal species that are in danger of extinction. This act has already helped save a number of species, for example, the blue whale, the bald eagle, and the peregrine falcon. It has also stopped or altered some land development that might endanger the environment.

*(Female Student):*   If we stop land development in order to protect plants and animals, how will we take care of the needs of a growing population?

*(Male Professor):* You've put your finger right on the issue here. As we examine economic and ecological issues, we must consider who will benefit and who will suffer from our actions. This is a difficult social and political issue as well, one that often divides factions both within a country and internationally. For instance, there is international concern about the destruction of the rain forest, but economic issues in rain forest areas must be considered. One example is the issue of how to allocate funds. Even though a government may want to spend money on protecting the environment, they may have more pressing needs, such as providing for people in dire need of food and clothing. So, the issue is complex. It's not a simple debate, and there are no easy solutions.

[**To the reader:** Pause for 12 seconds after each question is asked to allow time for the test taker to answer.]

19. What is the major issue that the professor is discussing?
20. What does the Greek root word eco- mean?
21. According to the professor, what has been the result of an increasing human population?
22. What is the main objective of the U.S. government's Endangered Species Act?

**Questions 23–26. Listen to two students talking about registering for classes.**

*(Man):* What a nightmare! I've been trying to register for classes all day, but a number of the classes I want are already full.

*(Woman):* I bet that plenty of other students are in the same boat.

*(Man):* Possibly. But I need to take these classes now if I'm going to graduate in June.

*(Woman):* I had the same dilemma when I was an undergraduate. But I had a fairly effective way of getting around the problem.

*(Man):* Really? What did you do? I'm open to ideas.

*(Woman):* Well, if a class was full, but I really needed it, I'd go to the first class meeting and sit in. Then, I'd explain the situation to the professor and ask if I could audit the class if no space opened up for me to join officially.

*(Man):* But you don't get credit or a grade when you audit a class.

*(Woman):*      That's true, but 95 percent of the time I ended up getting into the class.

*(Man):*      You did?

*(Woman):*      Yes. Sometimes the professor would just let me in, seeing how serious I was to take the class. But usually one or two of the students would drop the class in the first week, and there I'd be to take their place.

*(Man):*      Well, it sounds like a pretty good strategy.

*(Woman):*      It was for me. I found that just being there and speaking to the professor directly and showing an interest often got me into the class.

*(Man):*      Okay, I guess it's worth a try.

[**To the reader:** Pause for 12 seconds after each question is asked to allow time for the test taker to answer.]

23. What is the man's problem?

24. How did the woman handle this problem in the past?

25. What can we infer about the woman?

26. What will the man probably do?

**Questions 27–29. Listen to a discussion in a sociology class. The professor is reviewing basic concepts in the field of sociology.**

*(Male Professor):*      This morning let's begin by reviewing what we discussed on Friday. Does anyone remember how we defined sociology?

*(Female Student):*      It's the study of human society and social behavior, isn't it?

*(Male Professor):*      That's right. The way people behave is largely shaped by the groups they belong to and by the social interaction that takes place within these groups.

*(Male Student):*      So, you mean that I would behave differently if I were born in a different time and place, right?

*(Male Professor):*      Yes, according to sociologists, if you had been born in another country or another time in history, your personality, your opinions on life, and your social experiences would be quite different. This fact seems obvious enough, but it is easily overlooked. The way we were raised greatly affects the person we will become. Sociologists are mainly interested in social interaction, the ways in which people act toward, respond to, and influence one another. All types of social behavior, from greetings to religious practices to family roles, are ultimately the products of social groups.

[**To the reader:** Pause for 12 seconds after each question is asked to allow time for the test taker to answer.]

27. According to the first student's comment, what is the definition of sociology?

28. According to the discussion, what is the main focus of sociology?

29. Which of the following would be of most interest to sociologists?

**Questions 30–32. Listen to a conversation between two people about registering for courses.**

*(Man):* Excuse me.

*(Woman):* Yes, can I help you?

*(Man):* Yes, I would like to take an accounting course in September, and I need some information.

*(Woman):* Sure. Courses start on September 20 and finish right after Thanksgiving on November 30. The Introduction to Accounting class meets every Monday from 6 to 10 p.m. The Intermediate Accounting class meets every Wednesday from 6 to 10 p.m., and the Advanced Accounting class meets every Thursday from 6 to 10 p.m. Registration is one week before classes begin. So, that's September 13.

*(Man):* So, the classes only meet one night a week, and registration is on September 13?

*(Woman):* Yes, that's correct.

*(Man):* And how much is the tuition for one course?

*(Woman):* It's $550 per course. Are you interested in our Certificate Program in Accounting?

*(Man):* Maybe. Can you tell me something about it?

*(Woman):* Well, the coursework consists of the three classes I mentioned before. When you complete the program, you will be awarded a certificate. This program introduces the important theories and practices of accounting and is especially good for business owners, bookkeepers, or others who want to increase their basic knowledge of accounting. Would you like a brochure and an application explaining the program in more detail?

*(Man):* Yes, that would be great. Thank you so much. You've been very helpful.

*(Woman):* You're welcome.

[**To the reader:** Pause for 12 seconds after each question is asked to allow time for the test taker to answer.]

    30. What does the man want to do?

    31. How many days a week does each class meet?

    32. What will the man probably do next?

**Questions 33–36. Listen to a lecture on the history and development of written communication. The professor is giving an overview of the types of writing systems that have been used over time.**

*(Woman Speaker):* Good morning everyone. As you will notice I've written this week's topic on the blackboard. It says "The History and Development of Written Communication." But I didn't need to read it to you in order to communicate what our topic would be. Why not? Because the letters—or we could call them symbols—that I've used are also a form of communication. They convey information and meaning to you nonverbally.

When we think of written communication, we naturally envision complex systems, such as our alphabet in which individual letters represent sounds. Or you might think of a character system like Chinese in which characters represent syllables, words, or ideas. But long before the development of these complex systems, people were communicating via written forms. From prehistoric times people began using pictures, symbols, and signs to record events, keep accounts, and convey information. Ancient rock drawings, paintings, and carvings found all over the world are an example of very early forms of written communication. The general term for rock drawings and paintings is "pictograph," while the term "petroglyphs" refers specifically to rock carvings. The use of pictures to convey ideas was, and still is a very effective form of communication, which we continue to use liberally in our modern societies. For example, if you see a red circle with a red diagonal line across it you will recognize this to mean that something is prohibited or forbidden. If there is a picture of a burning cigarette inside the circle, you understand the meaning immediately: Smoking is prohibited here. Pictures are a very effective—and universal—form of communication. However, they are limited in their ability to express complex ideas. Even thousands of years ago, people realized this.

The Sumarians devised a fairly refined picture writing system about 5000 years ago that we call "logographs." In this system, pictures represented individual words in the language. Thus each picture, or logograph, corresponded to a key word in a sentence. But this system proved limited because it didn't allow for the expression of abstract ideas or the use of words that could not be represented by a picture, such as proper names. To overcome this limitation, a more complex, phonetic-based system eventually developed.

In phonetic-based writing systems, pictures could still be used to represent objects, but they could also be used to represent similar sounding words that could not be easily drawn. For example, if we used this type of phonetic-based system in English we would represent the word "belief" with a picture of a bee followed by a picture of a leaf. This form of writing is often called a "word-syllabic" system because objects, words, and syllables could be represented by pictures or symbols. Cuneiform, with its wedge-like symbols, and hieroglyphics, with its pictures, are both examples of early word-syllabic writing systems. Even more complex writing forms combine both the syllabic and pictographic systems. Chinese, developed over 4000 years ago, with as many as 50,000 characters is an example of this blended system.

Ultimately, alphabets like the one we use today, came into use. Our modern alphabet is a descendent of the Roman alphabet, which was developed about 2000 years ago. Today most languages of the world use an alphabetic form of writing in which one symbol or letter represents one or more sounds.

Now let me stop for a minute so I can answer any questions you have. And then we're going to watch a video, which is entitled "From Pictograph to Paragraph, the History of Writing".

[**To the reader:** Pause for 12 seconds after each question is asked to allow time for the test taker to answer.]

33. What is the main purpose of the Professor's lecture?

34. What does the professor say about the use of pictures and symbols to convey information?

35. According to the professor, what was one limitation of the "logograph" system of writing developed by the Sumarians?

36. According to the professor, how are cuneiform and hieroglyphics similar?

**Questions 37–41. Listen to part of a discussion in an archaeology class. The professor has invited a guest speaker to come in.**

[**To the reader:** Pause for 12 seconds after each question is asked to allow time for the test taker to answer.]

*(Male Professor):*  Okay everyone, if you'll have a seat now, we'll get started. I'd like to begin by introducing Dr. Marilyn Clearwater, head archaeologist for the Native Lands Recovery Project. She'll be telling you about one of the archaeological projects that you can get involved in to meet your field-study requirements for our class. Tomorrow we'll have Ben Allen, President of the State Historical Society, here to tell you about another project. Then you'll need to decide which one you want to volunteer for. But now, Dr. Clearwater, thank you for coming today.

*(Female Guest Speaker):*

It's my pleasure. Well, good afternoon everyone. As your professor may have told you, we've just begun the very time-consuming job of surveying and mapping the entire Yolo River archaeological site. This is the first stage of the project. The work requires a number of detail-oriented individuals and it involves walking very slowly over the entire site and recording on a grid any surface features or evidence you see that might indicate early human activity. For this phase, we need 20 volunteers for approximately three weeks.

*(Female Student):*  Dr. Clearwater, how will we know what to look for?

*(Female Guest Speaker):*

We'll train you. We'll show you what to look for, how to look, how to record your observations on a grid, and even how to walk when you're doing the survey.

*(Male Student):*  What if we find something like an arrowhead or piece of pottery? Should we just leave it there?

*(Female Guest Speaker):*

Well, first of all, I don't expect that you'll find anything of that sort lying on the surface at this particular site. But if you should see any possible evidence of early human habitation, such as fire-charred seeds or pieces of shellfish, you must not remove them or disturb them in any way. Just leave them as they are. During the survey and mapping phase of the project, you'll only note their location on the grid.

*(Male Student):* It sounds interesting but kind of tedious.

*(Female Guest Speaker):*

No question about it, it's tedious work and requires your undivided concentration. Remember, much of archaeological work is not the high-adventure "Indiana Jones" experience that you've seen in Hollywood films. It's often slow and exacting and involves a great deal of record keeping. But it's fascinating work and gives you a unique opportunity to peer into the past.

*(Female Student):* Where can we learn more about the Yolo river area and the people who used to live there?

*(Female Guest Speaker):*

I've brought with me a fact sheet about the history of the area and information about the Recovery Project. Help yourself to these, and if you're interested in volunteering for this project, sign up with your professor by the end of the week. Then I'll contact you to set up your work schedule. Any further questions?

[**To the reader:** Pause for 12 seconds after each question is asked to allow time for the test taker to answer.]

37. What is the main purpose of this talk?

38. What will the students do if they join the Yolo River Project?

39. Why are the students planning to do fieldwork?

40. Based on information from the talk, what can be implied about the early inhabitants of the Yolo River area?

41. How might students learn more about the Yolo River archaeological site?

**Questions 42–46. Listen to a presentation given to students in a Teacher Education Program.**

*(Female Speaker)* Good afternoon, and congratulations to all of you for successful completion of the first phase of the Teacher Education Program. I'm Deana Cantor, the director of Student Teaching, and I'm here to discuss the second phase of the program, and explain the academic requirements that you must fulfill before applying for your student teaching position. Overall, you'll need to complete 40 units, 10 of which can be elective courses. The required courses are as follows: Teaching Methodology 1 and 2, Classroom Management, Research Methods for Educators, Computers in the Classroom, and Materials Development. The two Methodology courses include instruction on teaching reading, writing, and mathematics, as well as general pedagogy.

Regarding your elective courses, you may choose them from any discipline that interests you, but you must have your elective choices approved by your adviser. In addition to the course requirements, you'll need to continue with your current observations in the public schools. But you should reduce your observation hours from 6 hours per week to 4 hours per week, because your course-load will now be heavier.

As you approach completion of this second phase of the program, your adviser and I will work with you to set up a student teaching assignment with a mentor teacher in a public school classroom. In some cases, it will be possible to do your student teaching in the same classroom where you are now observing. That's always nice, because you already know the teacher and the children. So, it's a little easier to adjust to the stress and responsibility of actually teaching for the first time. But that will come later when you've finished the coursework in phase 2. Now, let me stop here for a minute to answer any questions you might have.

[**To the reader:** Pause for 12 seconds after each question is asked to allow time for the test taker to answer.]

42. What is the purpose of the speaker's talk?

43. What courses can they choose for their two elective courses?

44. Based on the talk, what can we infer about the required courses for phase 2 of the Teacher Education Program?

45. Based on the talk, what can we assume about the students?

46. Why are students advised to reduce their observation hours in the public schools?

**Questions 47–50. Listen to a discussion in an American history course. The professor has been talking about indigenous people of North America.**

*(Male Professor):*  We've been talking about how environment shaped and dictated the lifestyles of indigenous peoples of North America. Now, with this in mind, we're going to look at a specific example, the California Indians, and discuss how environment and lifestyle led to the development of a rich tradition of basket making. And we should note that, although there were as many as 80 distinctly different language groups and thousands of separate tribal units in what is now California, all of these groups used baskets and other plant products extensively. In fact, some of the finest baskets ever produced were made by California Indians.

*(Female Student):* Professor, I've heard that California Indians never developed pottery. Is that true?

*(Male Professor):* No, not entirely. Some tribes did use pottery along with baskets. But others, such as the Central California Indians, developed no pottery at all. They used only baskets for both functional and ceremonial purposes. They had baskets of every size and shape for carrying, storing, and winnowing seeds. They had cone-shaped woven fish traps. They had funnel-shaped baskets with no bottoms for holding acorns or seeds as they pounded them on rocks. They had tightly woven baskets for carrying water and even baskets for cooking.

*(Male Student):* How could they cook in a basket? Wouldn't the basket burn?

*(Male Professor):* You would think so, but they had an ingenious technique. To cook, they would drop hot rocks into a basket filled with soup or porridge. The rocks heated the food, but to prevent burning the basket, they had to stir the rocks constantly. It was a very effective method. Now, in addition to baskets for food gathering and preparation, they made basket hats, baby carriers, mats, and housing materials. They even had canoes made entirely of reeds that were virtually unsinkable. Baskets for ceremonial use were often beautifully decorated with soft feathers and shell beads. Although men occasionally made baskets and nets for fishing, women did most of the basket making, and many women knew 15 to 20 different styles. [SPEAKER PAUSES] Okay, so why would such an elaborate basketry culture develop among the California Indians? What features of their environment and lifestyle contributed to this?

*(Female Student):* Well, I would guess that in California, they had a lot of plant materials handy all year round for making baskets. Is that right?

*(Male Professor):* Yes, absolutely, that's one factor. We're talking about a region with abundant natural resources. Basket making materials such as reeds, tules, and willow were plentiful and easily harvested. In addition, there were many rivers and streams, and a long coastline rich in sea life, birds, and coastal vegetation. So, procuring food did not require elaborate methods or technology. Baskets and woven items served the purpose well. The ease with which food could be procured plus a temperate climate in much of the region meant that people could spend more time on a skill such as basket making. So, we can see how environmental conditions and the necessities of their daily lives played a major role in the development of their sophisticated basketry tradition. Now, let's look at another example.

[**To the reader:** Pause for 12 seconds after each question is asked to allow time for the test taker to answer.]

47. What is the main focus of this lecture?

48. Why does the professor use the example of the California Indians?

49. What is true about the California Indians?

50. According to the talk, why did California Indians make boats out of reeds?

**This is the end of Section 1, Listening. Turn off the tape and continue with Section 2, Structure.**

# Test 2 (CBT Style) Listening Script

## SECTION 1

### LISTENING

This test is written to represent the CBT in terms of the numbers of questions, types of questions, and length of time for each section. As on the CBT, the directions for both Parts A and B are given at the beginning of the test.

The Listening section includes two parts. In Part A, you hear conversations between two people. Sometimes the people speak only once, and at other times, they speak more than once. Each conversation is followed by one question. In Part B, you hear longer conversations and talks. Sometimes the talks are by professors in a classroom; for these, you might hear students in the classroom asking questions, answering questions, or giving comments. Each of the longer conversations and talks is followed by several questions.

**Now, listen to the directions for each part.**

## Part A

*(Narrator):*    In the first part of the Listening section, Part A, you will hear conversations between two people. You will hear the conversation only one time, so you must listen carefully to what is said. After each conversation, a third person will ask a question. On the computer test, you will see pictures of the speakers and see the questions on your screen. Next, you will see the answer choices. Decide which is the correct choice, and select your answer. Answer all questions based on what is stated or implied by the speakers. On the computer test, you will not be able to return to a question once you have confirmed your answer.

*(Narrator):*        Now listen to an example.

*\* Note to test taker: On the CBT, at this point you would see a picture of a man and woman talking outside on a university campus.*

| | |
|---|---|
| *(Woman):* | Have you called Pete? |
| *(Man):* | I'll call him as soon as I get home. |
| *(Narrator):* | What does the man mean? |
| *(Narrator):* | Choose an answer in your book. |

**[To the reader:** Pause for 12 seconds after each question is asked to allow time for the test taker to answer.]

*(Narrator):*        You learn from the conversation that the man will call Pete as soon as he gets home. The best answer to the question "What does the man mean?" is choice (B), "He will call Pete after he gets home."

*(Narrator):*        Now listen to the directions for Part B.

## Part B

*(Narrator):* In the second part of the Listening section, Part B, you will hear longer conversations and talks. You will hear the conversation or talk only once, so listen carefully to what is said. After each conversation or talk, you will be asked several questions. Answer all questions based on what is stated or implied by the speakers. On the computer test, you will see pictures of the speakers and see the questions on your screen. Next, you will see the answer choices. Decide which is the correct choice, and select your answer. On the computer test, you will not be able to return to a question once you have confirmed your answer.

*(Narrator):*        Listen to the first example talk. There are two questions for this example.

**Example talk 1.** Listen to a conversation between two friends at school.

*\* Note to test taker: On the CBT, at this point you would see a picture of a man and woman talking outside on a university campus. Now, cover the answer choices below.*

*(Man):*      Hi, Joanie. Where are you going?

*(Woman):*    Oh, hi, Paul. I'm on my way to the library.

*(Man):*      Oh yeah? I just wondered if you wanted to go to a movie with me.

*(Woman):*    I'd love to, but I can't. I can't believe all the work I have this semester. I only have three classes, but in all of them I have lots of reading, term papers, reports, and essay exams. It's incredible! I feel like I'll never get through everything.

*(Man):*      That's terrible. I felt like that last year when I had term papers to write, but this semester seems easy now. I spend a lot of time in class, but most of it is in labs doing experiments. I hated writing all those term papers. But can't I talk you into going to the show anyway? I've heard that the movie over at the East Auditorium is really good. It's a murder mystery.

*(Woman):*    Oh, now I'm sure I won't go. I might go to a comedy, but I hate murder mysteries.

### Now listen to example question number one.

1. Where is the woman going?

   Choose an answer.

[**To the reader:** Pause for 12 seconds after each question is asked to allow time for the test taker to answer.]

The correct answer to the question "Where is the woman going?" is choice (D), "To the library."

### Now listen to example question number two.

2. Which best describes the man's feelings about his classes?

   Choose an answer.

[**To the reader:** Pause for 12 seconds after each question is asked to allow time for the test taker to answer.]

The best answer to the question "Which best describes the man's feelings about his classes?" is choice (C), "He finds lab experiments easier than writing term papers."

**Now listen to the second example talk. There are two questions for this talk.**

**Example talk 2.** Listen to an announcement at a university.

*\* Note to test taker: At this point on the CBT, you will see a picture of a woman speaking to a group of people. To simulate the computer-based test now, cover the questions and answer choices as you listen to the recording.*

*(Woman):*      At this university, we offer three different programs for students who have children. For those of you with very young children, we have a day-care program for infants from 3 months to 24 months. We have another program for children between 2 and 5 years of age. And we also have an after-school program for school-aged children. This program offers sports, crafts, outings, and tutoring during after-school hours. Enrollment in these child-care programs is limited, so early application is essential, since our programs often have waiting lists. The fees are on an hourly basis. If any of you new students need these services, please let me know right away so I can get you an application form.

**Now listen to example question number one.**

1. What is the main purpose of this announcement?

    Choose an answer.

[**To the reader:** Pause for 12 seconds after each question is asked to allow time for the test taker to answer.]

The best answer to the question "What is the main purpose of this announcement?" is choice (D), "To explain a service."

**Now listen to example question number two.**

2. What does the speaker recommend?

    Choose an answer.

[**To the reader:** Pause for 12 seconds after each question is asked to allow time for the test taker to answer.]

The correct answer to the question "What does the speaker recommend?" is choice (C), "Apply as soon as you can."

**This is the end of the example questions for Listening Comprehension. Now begin the test 1 with Part A. Get ready to listen.**

*Note to test taker: In order to practice your listening skills for the TOEFL, do not stop the recording or replay it while you are taking this practice test. To simulate the CBT, cover the questions and answer choices below as you listen to the recording. And do not look ahead at the next questions.*

## LISTENING

## Part A

[**To the reader:** Pause for 12 seconds after each question is asked to allow time for the test taker to answer.]

1. *(Man):*      Did you hear about Sylvia?

   *(Woman):*      No, what happened?

   *(Man):*      Jim says she got fired.

   *(Woman):*      Really?

   *(Narrator):*      What do the speakers mean?


2. *(Woman):*      How's the term going?

   *(Man):*      (groaning) Oh, I've got a midterm and two papers due this week.

   *(Woman):*      Well, perk up. The term will be over soon.

   *(Man):*      It doesn't seem like it!

   *(Narrator):*      What is the man's situation?


3. *(Man):*      Were you at Professor Jones' lecture yesterday?

   *(Woman):*      Yes, why?

   *(Man):*      Well, I was sitting up at the top in the last row, and I couldn't catch everything he said.

   *(Woman):*      Well, if you want, you can borrow my notes.

   *(Man):*      Thanks.

   *(Narrator):*      What will the man probably do?


4. *(Woman):*      I have to take my car in to get it fixed tomorrow morning, so I'll probably be a bit late to the study group. I'll get the bus as soon as I drop off the car.

   *(Man):*      OK. I'll tell the others.

   *(Narrator):*      What will the man do?


5. *(Man):*      I know you're looking for an exercise class. Did you hear about the new noontime stretch and fitness class at the gym?

   *(Woman):*      No, sounds interesting. Is it offered every day?

| | | |
|---|---|---|
| *(Man):* | I don't think so. I think it's two days a week. | |
| *(Woman):* | I'll look into it. | |
| *(Narrator):* | What does the woman mean? | |

6. *(Woman):* Hi Joe. How are things around your house?

   *(Man):* They have really changed. If only Laura would come back!

   *(Woman):* Yeah, I know. I feel the same.

   *(Narrator):* What does the woman mean?

7. *(Woman):* Barbara called to say that she sent the rent payment off today.

   *(Man):* She should have mailed the check a week ago.

   *(Woman):* I wonder what happened?

   *(Narrator):* What does the woman mean?

8. *(Man):* You know Jane, I've been looking for a new job, and I just found out that there might be a position for me in that new company, if all goes well.

   *(Woman):* Sounds fine, but you'd better hang on to your present job.

   *(Man):* Well, at least for a while.

   *(Narrator):* What does the man mean?

9. *(Woman):* Peter would be better now if he hadn't gone back to classes so soon.

   *(Man):* Yes, but we couldn't force him to stay home.

   *(Narrator):* What do the man and woman think?

10. *(Woman):* The recreation room is open four nights a week, isn't it?

    *(Man):* Let's find out.

    *(Narrator):* What does the man mean?

11. *(Man):* Hi, Linda. Good to see you again. How long are you staying this time?

    *(Woman):* Oh, I'm here for good now.

| *(Narrator):* | What does the woman mean? |
|---|---|

12. | *(Man):* | Sue, are you sure this is the right way to get to the library? |
|---|---|---|
| *(Woman):* | Sure. This is a shortcut; we'll be there in no time. |
| *(Narrator):* | What does the woman mean? |

13. | *(Woman):* | Did you finish the test? |
|---|---|---|
| *(Man):* | Finally! |
| *(Woman):* | What took you so long? |
| *(Man):* | I didn't think it would be so complicated. |
| *(Narrator):* | What does the man mean? |

14. | *(Man):* | Did you hear what happened in Roger's apartment? |
|---|---|---|
| *(Woman):* | Yeah. Wow! It was really a close call. |
| *(Man):* | I know. I'll bet they were all scared. |
| *(Narrator):* | What do the man and woman imply? |

15. | *(Man):* | Have you bought all your books for chemistry yet? |
|---|---|---|
| *(Woman):* | I'm waiting to buy back the ones from last year's students. |
| *(Narrator):* | What does the woman mean? |

# Part B

Now go on to Part B. Remember, you are not allowed to take any notes or write in your test book. To simulate the CBT, do not read the answer choices while you listen to the recording. Do not read ahead, and do not return to a question once you have answered it.

| *(Narrator):* | Questions 16–19. Listen to a class discussion about Jimmy Carter. |
|---|---|
| *(Female Professor):* | Let's continue with our discussion of American presidents by looking at Jimmy Carter. As you remember, he was president from 1977 to 1981, our thirty-ninth president. He was a modest man with a childhood that was quite unusual, especially for this day and age. He grew up on a peanut farm, where he did various jobs around the farm, such as picking cotton, milking cows, |

fertilizing crops, and harvesting fruit. For fun, he and his father used to go fishing and hunting. During his youth, his family followed the ideals of simplicity, frugality, and hard work. His family didn't even have electricity in their farmhouse when Carter was a young boy; so, they used kerosene lamps. And they got their water from a well. They also didn't have indoor plumbing, but used a privy. Yes, Ellen?

*(Female Student):* I know that it was a long time ago when Carter was a child, but it still sounds pretty strange that the Carters didn't have electricity or running water. Was this common then?

*(Female Professor):* Well, you're right to wonder about that. It was not common for most people in the U.S. then. But in farming areas, this was not unusual. Many families, both white and black, lived in such a way. At any rate, Jimmy never forgot this aspect of his upbringing, and his future work as president reflects it.

*(Male Student):* I've always thought it was strange that we call him "Jimmy." I think of that as a little boy's name, or a name that only close friends or family members use.

*(Female Professor):* This again reflects his attitude. When he became president, he said that he didn't want to be called "Jim" or "James," but he wanted everyone to call him the name he was most comfortable with. (pause) To move on, after high school, Carter attended the U.S. Naval Academy in Annapolis, Maryland. He graduated in 1946 and then went into the Navy. After that, in 1953 he went back to his family's peanut farm, and built it into a large, prosperous business. It was only later that he got into politics. He was the governor of Georgia from 1970 to 75, and he ran for president in 1976. It was a close campaign, but Carter beat the Republican candidate, then-president Gerald Ford. Carter only had one term as president. After that, he spent much of his time on human rights issues and projects such as building homes for working class people through the organization Habitat for Humanity.

[**To the reader:** Pause for 12 seconds after each question is asked to allow time for the test taker to answer.]

16. Which of the following most clearly reflects Jimmy Carter's childhood?

17. According to the speaker, which two of the following did Carter do with his father for recreation?

1.    Go fishing

2.    Go sailing

3.    Go hunting

4.    Go hiking

18. After his term of presidency ended, what activity did he get involved in?

19. When did Carter begin his term as president?

**Questions 20–22.  Listen to two students talk as they meet on campus.**

*(Woman):*    Hi George. What's going on? You look upset.

*(Man):*    Oh, hi, Jane. Well, I just got my history paper back, and Professor Adams wrote comments all over it. And they aren't very positive.  I feel pretty bad. I worked like crazy on that paper. I really don't understand why she didn't like it.

*(Woman):*    Maybe you should go see the TA and get some advice. At least that might help you write the next paper.

*(Man):*    I guess that's a good idea. It's just that I feel like I should be able to do this on my own. I don't usually need to go get extra help in doing assignments.

*(Woman):*    But I know that Professor Adams has specific things she's looking for. Maybe just a few suggestions would help you.

*(Man):*    OK. I'll give it a try anyway.

[**To the reader:** Pause for 12 seconds after each question is asked to allow time for the test taker to answer.]

20. What is it that the man does not understand?

21. Why does the man feel bad?

22. What will the man probably do?

**Questions 23–25. Listen to a conversation between two friends who have haven't seen one another for a while.**

*(Woman):*    Hi, Ed. Are you in town for another job interview?

*(Man):*    Yes, I'm pretty hopeful this time. I've just finished my second interview with this company.

*(Woman):*    That sounds great. I hope it works out for you. But wasn't it expensive just getting here?

*(Man):*    No, in fact the company is paying all my expenses. They've put me up in a hotel downtown.

*(Woman):*    How nice! How many people are they interviewing?

| | |
|---|---|
| *(Man):* | Well, they interviewed 16 the first time, and now 4 of us were chosen to come back for this interview. |
| *(Woman):* | It sounds like you have a good chance to be selected then. |
| *(Man):* | I hope so. The manager told me he would call us on Monday. |
| *(Woman):* | Well, I hope it goes well. John and I would love it if you came to this area to work. |
| *(Man):* | I would, too, but my girlfriend doesn't want to leave her family. She hopes I find a job close to home. |
| *(Woman):* | Oh dear, what a decision. |
| *(Man):* | I'm trying to convince her of how good it is to live here. But anyway, I've got to wait until Monday to find out whether I even have the chance. |
| *(Woman):* | Good luck! |

[**To the reader:** Pause for 12 seconds after each question is asked to allow time for the test taker to answer.]

23. How does the man seem to feel after this interview?

24. How many people have been asked for a second interview?

25. What does the man's girlfriend want?

**Questions 26–29. Listen to two students as they talk about going to an exhibit.**

| | |
|---|---|
| *(Man):* | Hi, Sandy. How are your finals going? |
| *(Woman):* | Oh, hi, Michael. I finished my last exam this morning, and I finished my two term papers. I finally feel like I can see the light. |
| *(Man):* | Great. Now how about a change? I've got two tickets for the new modern art exhibit downtown. Do you want to go with me? |
| *(Woman):* | Oh, I don't know. I don't know anything about modern art, and I'm no artist. |
| *(Man):* | You don't have to be an artist to enjoy a good art show! Besides, at least it's something different from studying. |
| *(Woman):* | You're right. Have you seen this exhibit yet? |
| *(Man):* | No, but I've heard that it's great. The exhibit was in New York last summer and in Chicago after that. And next week it goes to Los Angeles. |

| (Woman): | Oh. Well, it ought to be good then. |
|---|---|
| (Man): | And, besides, next door to the modern art museum is a new Asian art museum. So, we could hit both of them if you're up for it. |
| (Woman): | OK, you've talked me into it. Did you want to go this afternoon? |
| (Man): | If you have time. I'm ready. |
| (Woman): | OK. Let's meet after lunch. I'm starving now. I've got to go back home and get something to eat. Shall we meet at 1:30 right here? |
| (Man): | Sounds good to me. See you then. |

[**To the reader:** Pause for 12 seconds after each question is asked to allow time for the test taker to answer.]

26. How does the woman feel at the beginning of the conversation?

27. What was the woman's first response to the man's suggestion?

28. Which city will the art exhibit go to next?

29. What does the man suggest they do after going to the art museum?

**Questions 30–32. Listen to a conversation between two students about enrolling in their university classes.**

| (Woman): | Well, I'm really upset. |
|---|---|
| (Man): | Why? What's going on? |
| (Woman): | I just finished trying to use the new telephone system to enroll in my classes. |
| (Man): | And . . . what's wrong? |
| (Woman): | I couldn't get anything I wanted. First, I had to wait 15 minutes before getting through on the phone. Then the classes I wanted were all full. |
| (Man): | So what are you going to do? |
| (Woman): | I don't know. I'm on the waiting list for two classes, but who knows if I'll ever get in. I don't know what to do. |
| (Man): | Maybe you should see your counselor. |
| (Woman): | I guess I could try that. She might be able to suggest some other classes that would fit my major requirements. I only have a few left to take. It's really frustrating. Have you enrolled yet? |
| (Man): | No, and after hearing you, I'm not sure if I want to, but I really don't think I'll have any trouble. Last semester it was easy. I got most of my first choices. |

*(Woman):*     Well, you're lucky.

[**To the reader:** Pause for 12 seconds after each question is asked to allow time for the test taker to answer.]

30. What is the woman trying to do?
31. What does the man suggest?
32. How does the man seem to feel?

**Questions 33–36. Listen to part of a lecture in a music theory class. The professor has been talking about the history of Western music.**

*(Male speaker):*     Before we continue with our discussion of historical influences on Western music, I'd like to step back a bit and focus on one of the main problems that researchers and historians run into when they study ancient music. This major problem is that there is often nothing tangible to examine. Think of the difference between studying ancient music, for instance, and studying ancient sculpture or architecture. If you want to study ancient sculpture or architecture, you can find remnants of old buildings and statues around to examine—but not so with music. There is no way to hear the ancient music itself. So how do we get our information? Well, we can look for written accounts and also get ideas of how instruments looked by examining ancient mosaics, paintings, or bas-reliefs. We can also get information from scholars of past times. In the Middle Ages and the Renaissance, for instance, scholars studied ancient Greek and Roman music, so we can look at their records. But even they had trouble. It was especially difficult for them to get information about ancient Roman music. In fact, musicians of the Middle Ages did not have a single example of Roman music to study. So you might ask: why wasn't there evidence of Roman music when there was at least some evidence of Greek music? Well, the main answer is that the music of ancient Rome was deliberately destroyed. The leaders of the early Christian church thought that secular festivals and pagan religious activities, as well as the theater, were abominations, and should be exterminated. And it was precisely at these activities that music flourished. So, the result was that almost all music died out. Luckily for us, however, a few of the features of ancient music lived on into the Middle Ages. And it is from these that we get most of our historical information today. Though it's not much,

it's all we have. OK. That's a bit about a major problem we have in studying ancient music and especially ancient Roman music. We do know a bit more about ancient Greek music since festivals and religious activities were not banned in Greece. So let's continue now by looking at some particular aspects of ancient Greek musical practice and theory. This will give us a good background for understanding medieval music, which we will study later in the term.

[**To the reader:** Pause for 12 seconds after each question is asked to allow time for the test taker to answer.]

33. What is the main purpose of this lecture?

34. Why does the professor say it is easier to study ancient architecture and sculpture than ancient music?

35. Which two of the following indicate the connection between ancient Rome and the lack of knowledge of ancient Roman music?

   1. Music was banned in church, so it didn't survive.

   2. Music was destroyed since it was associated with pagan festivals.

   3. Music flourished at festivals, so it died out when festivals were banned.

   4. Music was not religious, so the early church leaders did not keep records of it.

36. Which of the following will the professor talk about next?

**Questions 37–40. Listen to a lecture from a U.S. history class. The professor is talking about the history of the White House.**

*(Female speaker):* You all know our U.S. presidents always live in the White House, which is on Pennsylvania Avenue in Washington, D.C. What I'm going to talk about today is some of the changes in White House décor that have occurred over the years. As you may remember, the White House was first built in 1792 on a site chosen by our first president, George Washington. He didn't live there, though. John Adams, the second president, was the first one to live in the White House, even though it wasn't finished when he and his wife Abigail moved in. In fact, Abigail Adams once commented that she used the East Room, which is the room where large receptions are held now, to hang out her washing since the room was still bare and unfinished. In 1814 the house was burned down by the British, but was then rebuilt and renovated. It was at that time that it was painted white. Though it had been called "the White

House" even before it burned down, it wasn't until Theodore Roosevelt became president, at the beginning of the last century, that it was officially named "the White House."

The White House has always reflected the styles of its inhabitants, and sometimes the public has not been too pleased with the changes. In the 1820s, for instance, John Quincy Adams put in a billiard table, and people criticized him for wasting government money on such a thing. And about fifteen years later, Martin Van Buren was criticized for spending too much money on carpets purchased from abroad. There have always been some Americans who have argued that the objects used to decorate the White House should only be American. But in fact, many of the oldest and most elegant pieces are not American. James Monroe, for instance, graced the White House with gilded furniture from France. There is only one object that has been in the White House ever since it was first inhabited, and that is a portrait of George Washington.

[**To the reader:** Pause for 12 seconds after each question is asked to allow time for the test taker to answer.]

37. What is the main topic of this lecture?

38. What did Abigail Adams use the East Room for?

39. What is the argument that the professor mentions?

40. Which of the following is true according to the professor?

**Questions 41 to 44. Listen to part of a lecture from a biology class. The professor has been discussing strategies that lead to survival of young animals in the wild. Today's topic focuses on crocodile survival.**

*(Female speaker):* We begin a new topic today in our course on the survival of young animals, and I'd like to begin with an explanation of a common misconception. Many people have heard that crocodiles eat their babies. Well, in fact, they don't. What happens is that the mother crocodiles take all their newly hatched youngsters into their mouths in order to carry them to the safety of the water. The reason that this is necessary is that the female crocodile must leave the water in order to hatch her eggs. She goes to the beach and digs a hole approximately ten inches deep. She then lays her eggs in the hole and covers them with soil, using her body and tail to pat down the earth. While she guards her nest during the day and night for about twelve weeks, the

sun heats the soil and hardens it. Then, when the baby crocodiles hatch, they find it almost impossible to get out, and they begin yelping and croaking. The mother hears them and rips open the nest. Then she takes the young into a pouch of skin in her lower jaw and carries them to the safety of the ocean water before she releases them.

[**To the reader:** Pause for 12 seconds after each question is asked to allow time for the test taker to answer.]

41. What does the speaker say is the common misconception about crocodile mothers?

42. Where do the young hatch?

43. Why does the crocodile put her babies in her mouth?

44. How long does the mother wait for the young to hatch?

**Questions 45–47. Listen to a lecture from a history class. The professor has been discussing past winners of the Nobel Peace Prize.**

*(Male speaker):*    Norman E. Borlaug was the first agricultural scientist to receive the Nobel Peace Prize and the fifteenth American to do so. He was born in 1914 in Iowa, the son of a farming family. In 1940, Borlaug earned his doctorate degree in plant pathology, and a few years later he was chosen by the Rockefeller Foundation to go abroad to help introduce new agricultural technology to farmers who were growing wheat. Borlaug's goal was to improve the quality of low-yielding wheat that some farmers had been growing for centuries, and he accomplished his goal. He developed new dwarf and semi-dwarf wheat that had stronger stems and could hold heavier heads of grain. In Mexico, for instance, the new methods resulted in doubled wheat yields, helping that country move from having a wheat shortage to being a wheat exporter. For the introduction of these new wheat-growing methods, Borlaug was dubbed Father of the Green Revolution.

[**To the reader:** Pause for 12 seconds after each question is asked to allow time for the test taker to answer.]

45. Which of the following was Borlaug's goal?

46. What helped finance Borlaug's trip abroad?

47. What did Borlaug do when he left the United States?

**Questions 48–50. Listen to a lecture from a geography class. The professor is introducing great rivers of the world, beginning today with the St. Lawrence River.**

*(Female speaker):* This week we're going to begin a new topic in our geography class. We'll focus on the great rivers of the world, and we'll start today with the St. Lawrence River, a major waterway linking the Great Lakes of the United States with the Atlantic Ocean, a distance of about 750 miles. Not all portions of this waterway, which divides Canada and the United States, has been open to large ships. In fact, it's only been since 1959 that a series of canals, locks, and dams has made the river navigable up to the inland cities of Detroit and Duluth.

The St. Lawrence is quite a busy river. Each year it handles some 50 million metric tons of cargo, mostly grain, coal, and iron ore. And it's not only cargo boats that you see on the river. There are pleasure boats and ocean-going freighters as well, especially in the area of the Thousand Islands, near Lake Ontario. If you'd like a beautiful place to vacation, this is one of them. The Thousand Islands is an area of the river that is dotted with tree-covered islands. In fact, there are probably more like 2,000 islands there. This area has been known as a millionaire's retreat since the 1860s and is full of beautiful homes and castles covering the small islands. Well, this has been just a short introduction to the St. Lawrence River. We'll be talking more about it next week.

[**To the reader:** Pause for 12 seconds after each question is asked to allow time for the test taker to answer.]

48. What can you best infer about the speaker's attitude toward the St. Lawrence River?
49. What happened in 1959?
50. Which of the following best describes the Thousand Islands?

**This is the end of Section 1, Listening. Turn off the tape and continue with Section 2, Structure.**

# Test 3 (PBT Style) Listening Script

## SECTION 1

### LISTENING COMPREHENSION

This test is written to represent the PBT in terms of numbers of questions, types of questions, and length of time for each section.

The Listening Comprehension section includes three parts. In Part A, you hear conversations between two people. Each conversation is followed by one question.

In Part B, you hear longer conversations followed by several questions. In Part C, you hear talks given by a single person followed by several questions.

**Now listen to the directions for each part.**

# PART A

*(Narrator):* In Part A, you will hear short conversations between two people. After each conversation, a third person will ask a question about what was said. You will hear the conversation only one time, so you must listen carefully. After you hear a question, read the four possible answers in your test book, and decide which one is the best answer. Then, on your answer sheet, fill in the oval of the answer you have chosen. Answer all questions based on what is stated or implied by the speakers.

| | |
|---|---|
| *(Narrator):* | Now, listen to an example. |
| | You will hear: |
| *(Woman):* | Have you called Pete? |
| *(Man):* | I'll call him as soon as I get home. |
| *(Narrator):* | What does the man mean? |
| *(Narrator):* | You will read the answer choices in your test book: |

(A) He will call Pete before he goes home.

(B) He will call Pete after he gets home.

(C) He called Pete at home.

(D) He will call Pete tomorrow.

| | |
|---|---|
| *(Narrator):* | You learn from the conversation that the man will call Pete as soon as he gets home. The best answer to the question "What does the man mean?" is choice (B), "He will call Pete after he gets home." |
| *(Narrator):* | Now continue listening to the recording and begin the test. |

[**To the reader:** Pause for 12 seconds after each question is asked to allow time for the test taker to answer.]

| | | |
|---|---|---|
| 1. | *(Woman):* | Fred, we should have the car repaired before spring vacation. |
| | *(Man):* | Oh, I'll have Adam fix it. |
| | *(Narrator):* | What does the man mean? |
| 2. | *(Woman):* | Did you hear that Jeff has passed his oral exam? |
| | *(Man):* | Finally. |
| | *(Narrator):* | What does the man imply? |
| 3. | *(Woman):* | How do you like the new librarian at the information desk? |

| | | |
|---|---|---|
| *(Man):* | You mean Ron? He's been here as long as I have! |
| *(Narrator):* | What does the man imply? |

4.  *(Man):*  I sure had trouble understanding that article we had to read for class.

   *(Woman):*  It seemed pretty clear to me. Would you like me to help you with it?

   *(Man):*  Would I!  Please do.

   *(Narrator):*  What does the man mean?

5.  *(Woman):*  I thought you were on your way to the bookstore.

   *(Man):*  I have to go back to the classroom again.

   *(Woman):*  Why? What's up?

   *(Narrator):*  What does the woman want to know?

6.  *(Woman):*  Mary is going to give me a ride to the party.

   *(Man):*  How could she? She doesn't have her license yet.

   *(Narrator):*  What does the man mean?

7.  *(Woman):*  I'm not sure where the Humanities building is. Do you know?

   *(Man):*  Yes, and I'm going that way.  Would you like me to show you where it is?

   *(Woman):*  If you don't mind.

   *(Narrator):*  What does the woman mean?

8.  *(Man):*  Does the campus bookstore accept credit cards?

   *(Woman):*  Only if the charge is more than $15.

   *(Narrator):*  What does the woman mean?

9.  *(Woman):*  I hope I can still register for the speech class.

   *(Man):*  I heard there was a waiting list.

   *(Narrator):*  What does the man mean?

10. *(Woman):*  Your final exam will be next Tuesday.

   *(Man):*  Dr. Jones, is it possible for the exam to be an open-book exam?

       **(Woman):**      Sorry. Department regulations don't allow that on final exams.

       **(Narrator):**      What does the woman mean?

11. **(Woman):**      Could you take notes for me and get copies of the handouts while I'm away next week?

     **(Man):**      Sure. I'd be glad to.

     **(Narrator):**      What does the man mean?

12. **(Woman):**      I just can't stop eating this great pizza.

     **(Man):**      I thought you didn't care for pizza.

     **(Woman):**      Well, I usually don't, but this pizza is really good. I think I'll have one more slice and then that's it.

     **(Narrator):**      What does the woman mean?

13. **(Woman):**      How are you and your roommates getting along?

     **(Man):**      So far, so good.

     **(Narrator):**      What does the man mean?

14. **(Woman):**      The university policy has changed a lot since I've been here.

     **(Man):**      Hasn't it!

     **(Narrator):**      What does the man mean?

15.    **(Man):**      You weren't scared, were you?

     **(Woman):**      Not much! My heart was beating fast and my knees were shaking, that's all.

     **(Narrator):**      What does the woman mean?

16. **(Woman):**      Shall we sit here and talk?

     **(Man):**      There is no better place than here.

     **(Narrator):**      What does the man mean?

17. **(Woman):**      What would you like for your graduation present?

     **(Man):**      A racing bike—that's something I've always wanted.

     **(Narrator):**      What does the man mean?

18. *(Woman):*      I sure did like that sweater.

    *(Man):*      Why didn't you buy it?

    *(Woman):*      If it had been $10 cheaper, I would've.

    *(Narrator):*      What does the woman mean?


19.   *(Man):*      Marie, why did you get up so early today?

    *(Woman):*      I thought the lab started at 8 a.m.

    *(Narrator):*      What does the woman mean?


20. *(Woman):*      Usually, Jim grades all the papers himself.

    *(Man):*      Yeah, but this time he gave them to his assistant to grade.

    *(Narrator):*      What do they say about Jim?


## PART B

*(Narrator):* In this part of the test, you will hear longer conversations between two people and class discussions. After each conversation or discussion, you will be asked some questions. You will hear the conversations or discussions and the questions only once, so listen carefully. After you hear a question, read the four possible answers in your test book, and decide which one is the best answer. Then, on your answer sheet, find the number of the question and fill in the oval of the answer you have chosen. Answer all questions based on what is stated or implied by the speakers.

    *(Narrator):*      Listen to the example.

               You will hear:

    *(Narrator):*      Questions 1 and 2 are based on the following conversation between two friends at school.

    *(Man):*      Hi, Joanie. Where are you going?

    *(Woman):*      Oh, hi, Paul. I'm on my way to the library.

    *(Man):*      Oh yeah? I just wondered if you wanted to go to a movie with me.

    *(Woman):*      I'd love to, but I can't. I can't believe all the work I have this semester. I only have three classes, but in all of them I have lots of reading, term papers, reports, and essay exams. It's incredible! I feel like I'll never get through everything.

    *(Man):*      That's terrible. I felt like that last year when I had term papers to write, but this semester seems easy now. I

|  | spend a lot of time in class, but most of it is in labs doing experiments. I hated writing all those term papers. But can't I talk you into going to the show anyway? I've heard that the movie over at the East Auditorium is really good. It's a murder mystery. |
|---|---|
| *(Woman):* | Oh, now I'm sure I won't go. I might go to a comedy, but I hate murder mysteries. |
| *(Narrator):* | Now listen to sample question number 1. |
| *(Narrator):* | 1. Where is the woman going? |
| *(Narrator):* | You will read the answer choices in your test book: |

(A) To the cafeteria

(B) To the movie theater

(C) To her dorm room

(D) To the library

| *(Narrator):* | The correct answer to the question "Where is the woman going?" is (D), "To the library." |
|---|---|
| *(Narrator):* | Now listen to sample question number 2. |
| *(Narrator):* | 2. Which best describes the man's feelings about his classes? |
| *(Narrator):* | You will read the answer choices in your test book: |

(A) Term papers are easy for him.

(B) He has a lot of essay exams.

(C) He finds lab experiments easier than writing term papers.

(D) He is busier this semester than last semester.

| *(Narrator):* | The best answer to the question "Which best describes the man's feelings about his classes?" is (C), "He finds lab experiments easier than writing term papers." |
|---|---|

**Now listen to the test. Remember, you are not allowed to take any notes or write in your test book.**

**Questions 21–28. Listen to the following class discussion on inventions.**

| *(Male Professor):* | There is an old saying that necessity is the mother of invention. |
|---|---|
|  | What exactly does that mean? |
| *(Woman):* | It means that people are inspired to design and create new things when there is a need for such an item. |
| *(Male Professor):* | That's right. And since the beginning of time, people have been trying to make a better mousetrap, or rather, improve on what they have to better meet their needs. Some of these innovations have been tremendously |

successful, such as the automobile, indoor plumbing, Velcro, the computer. Other ideas have failed to catch on. Well, today I'm going to introduce you to some creative Americans and their inventions, some of which were successful and some that fell flat. First, I'll tell you about a guy who had the idea of using heavy canvas fabric from tents to make work clothes. What do you think? Did people like his product or not?

*(Man):* Probably not. That material is too stiff. Workers would hardly be able to move wearing that stuff.

*(Woman):* I say, yes, the guy was successful. I've seen some work jackets made out of thick material like that. But what's the real answer, Professor?

*(Male Professor):* Well, the real answer to my question is right here in this room. In fact, almost all of you are wearing his invention, or an imitation of it, right now.

*(Woman):* You mean blue jeans!

*(Male Professor):* That's right! And not just any blue jeans, but Levi's jeans, invented in the 1850s by Levi Strauss. He made pants and also jackets out of tent canvas for miners working in the gold mines of Nevada. At first, he used the fabric in its natural, off-white color, but that got dirty too fast, so he began dyeing it a dark blue, just as most of you are wearing in class today.

*(Man):* Wasn't that fabric too stiff and scratchy?

*(Male Professor):* As a matter of fact, yes. But Strauss soon found a softer cotton fabric with similar durability, yet softer to the touch. The fabric came from Nimes in France and was called serge de Nimes. In English, de Nimes is pronounced denim, so that's why we call this type of fabric denim.

*(Woman):* Did the first Levi's jeans have the rivets on the pockets?

*(Male Professor):* Not the very first ones, but miners complained that their pants pockets often tore. And sometimes they lost gold nuggets because of this. So, Strauss began securing all the pockets, front and back, with rivets. But if you're wearing Levi's today, you'll find that your back pockets no longer have the rivets. Any guess as to why?

*(Man):* They were uncomfortable?

*(Male Professor):* That's possible. But actually, Strauss stopped using them in the 1930s because ranchers and cowboys

complained that the rivets scratched their saddles, and schoolteachers said that they scratched the chairs when kids sat down. So, was Levi Strauss successful in building a better mousetrap? You bet! Jeans are everywhere in the world today. And despite the vast number of other brand names and designer jeans, most people just refer to all of them as Levi's.

[**To the reader:** Pause for 12 seconds after each question is asked to allow time for the test taker to answer.]

21. What is this class discussion mainly about?

22. What is meant by the saying, "Necessity is the mother of invention?"

23. What two problems did miners have with the first Levi's jeans?

24. Why did Strauss start using fabric from France to make his jeans?

25. What feature did Strauss later add to his original jeans design?

26. Why did Strauss remove the back-pocket rivets in the 1930s?

27. The professor said that Strauss was successful in building a better mousetrap. What did he mean?

28. Why do many people use the word Levi's to refer to all brands of blue jeans?

**Questions 29–32. Listen to the following conversation between two friends.**

*(Man):* Hi Marsha. Hey, when are you going home today?

*(Woman):* Oh, hi Greg. I have to stay here at the library and study until at least eleven o'clock tonight. Are you studying here, too?

*(Man):* No, I'm not studying. I'm working. I work at the circulation desk until eleven o'clock tonight. Do you want to meet for awhile then?

*(Woman):* OK. Are you working full-time now?

*(Man):* Yeah, I work 40 hours a week, and I'm taking three classes.

*(Woman):* Wow! When do you have time to study?

*(Man):* In the mornings, usually. Some days all I do is eat, study, work, and sleep.

*(Woman):* That sounds terrible. If you ever get some free time, maybe we could get together and watch a movie or go dancing or something.

*(Man):* That would be great. I'll check my work schedule. Why don't we talk about it when we meet later on?

*(Woman):*     OK, see you then.

[**To the reader:** Pause for 12 seconds after each question is asked to allow time for the test taker to answer.]

   29. Where does this conversation take place?

   30. What is the woman going to do until eleven o'clock?

   31. What is the man doing?

   32. What seems to be the main purpose of this conversation?

**Questions 33–35. Listen to the following conversation between two students in a class.**

*(Man):*     Caroline, do you know where Tuskegee is?

*(Woman):*     Sure, it's in Alabama.

*(Man):*     Oh, no. I thought it was somewhere in a foreign country.

*(Woman):*     It's a Native-American name. Do you know what Tuskegee is famous for?

*(Man):*     No.

*(Woman):*     It's the home of the Tuskegee Institute, where George Washington Carver worked.

*(Man):*     Who was he?

*(Woman):*     He was a great scientist who invented over 200 uses for peanuts, sweet potatoes, and other agricultural products.

*(Man):*     Really? That's interesting.

[**To the reader:** Pause for 12 seconds after each question is asked to allow time for the test taker to answer.]

   33. Where is Tuskegee located?

   34. What does the woman say about George Washington Carver?

   35. What quality most clearly describes the man?

## Part C

*(Narrator):* In this part of the test, you will hear segments read by a single person. After each segment, you will be asked some questions. You will hear the segments and the questions only once, so listen carefully. After you hear a question, read the four possible answers in your test book, and decide which one is the best answer. Then, find the number of the question on your answer sheet, and fill in the oval that corresponds to the letter of the answer you have chosen. Answer all questions based on what is stated or implied in the talk.

*(Narrator):*     Listen to this sample talk.

You will hear:

**Questions 1–2 are based on the following announcement.**

*(Female speaker):*     At this university, we offer three different programs for students who have children. For those of you with very young children, we have a day care program for infants from 3 months to 30 months. We have another program for children between 2 and 5 years of age, and we also have an after-school program for school-aged children. This program offers sports, crafts, outings, and tutoring during after-school hours. Enrollment in these childcare programs is limited, and early application is essential because our programs often have waiting lists. The fees are on an hourly basis. If any of you new students need these services, please let me know right away so I can get you an application form.

*(Narrator):*     Now listen to sample question number 1.

*(Narrator):*     1.  What is the main purpose of this announcement?

*(Narrator):*     You will read the answer choices in your test book:

(A) To demonstrate tutoring techniques

(B) To explain school policies

(C) To recruit childcare workers

(D) To explain a service

*(Narrator):*     The best answer to the question "What is the purpose of this announcement?" is choice (D), "To explain a service."

**Now listen to sample question number 2.**

*(Narrator):*     2.  What does the speaker recommend?

*(Narrator):*     You will read the answer choices in your test book:

(A) Give your child extra tutoring.

(B) Take your child to the program today.

(C) Apply as soon as you can.

(D) Pay next month.

*(Narrator):*     The best answer to the question "What does the speaker recommend?" is (C), "Apply as soon as you can."

**Now, listen to the talks. Remember, you are not allowed to write any notes in your test book.**

**Questions 36–39. Listen to the following announcement given by a professor at the beginning of a class.**

*(Female Speaker):*  Before we get started with the lecture today, I want to share some information I received in the mail yesterday. This letter is announcing a program called "Paleontology with the Smithsonian." It says that Smithsonian Research Expeditions is offering a study trip for volunteer field workers. The volunteers will help explore some current archaeological digs in Wyoming. The trip will last from May 22 to June 5, and the participants will learn about the animals and plants that existed about 150 million years ago near the town of Cody, Wyoming. Volunteers will search for fossil remains of plants and animals while living in tents near the dig sites. Smithsonian paleontologists will teach field skills such as prospecting, mapping, and labeling, and excavation techniques. During the evenings, they will give informal lectures and lead discussions. You need to bring your own sleeping bag. The cost of the expedition is $1,500, and you get class credit from our department here. It sounds like a good opportunity to learn a lot about archaeology and have a good time. If you'd like more information, come see me after class.

[**To the reader:** Pause for 12 seconds after each question is asked to allow time for the test taker to answer.]

36. What class are the students most likely taking?

37. Where will the volunteers go?

38. What will the field workers be doing?

39. How much does the trip cost?

**Questions 40–43. Listen to the following lecture on a famous American artist.**

*(Male speaker):*  This evening we'll continue our lecture series on famous American artists as we look at the life and work of Georgia O'Keeffe. You may be familiar with O'Keeffe's still-life compositions, in particular, her enormous flower paintings, but you may not have known that she also painted landscapes and city scenes.

O'Keeffe was born in 1887 on a dairy farm in Wisconsin, and at an early age, she knew that she wanted to be an artist. She studied at a variety of art schools, including the Art Institute of Chicago and Columbia University. Later, she served as head of the art department for Texas State Normal College, where she also taught art. In 1916, she met the famous American photographer Alfred Stieglitz. He was extremely impressed with her work, and he exhibited some of her paintings at a gallery in New York City. Eventually, O'Keeffe moved to New York, and in 1924, O'Keeffe and Stieglitz were married. In time, O'Keeffe's works were on display in many galleries in New York.

By 1930, O'Keeffe had begun to spend much of her time in New Mexico, and later, after her husband's death, she settled in there. The breathtaking desert vistas, unique vegetation, and characteristic southwest architecture became recurring themes in her artwork. Her adobe home also appeared frequently in her work. "Black Patio Door" and "Patio with Cloud" are two such paintings. Perhaps the most well known of O'Keeffe's works are her many paintings of huge vividly colored flowers. One of these paintings was chosen in 1996, ten years after O'Keeffe's death, as a commemorative stamp. Now let's take a look at some slides of O'Keeffe's work.

[**To the reader:** Pause for 12 seconds after each question is asked to allow time for the test taker to answer.]

40. What is true about Georgia O'Keeffe?
41. What is Georgia O'Keeffe particularly well known for?
42. According to the speaker, what influenced O'Keeffe's artwork?
43. What does the painting "Black Patio Door" depict?

**Questions 44–46. Listen to the following talk given by a tour guide.**

*(Male speaker):*     Los Angeles today is the second largest city in America, sprawling over 464 square miles along the southern California coast. It is the center of the entertainment industry, and it has a balmy climate of mostly sunny days. But there was a time when Los Angeles was nothing more than a tiny Indian village. The Spanish expedition searching for Monterey Bay camped there one night on August 1, 1769. Twelve years later, other Spaniards started a settlement at the village, which remained unchanged for decades. Yankee sea traders used the settlement as a port, and the California gold rush brought some new economic life to the village, but the town remained quite small. It was not until the completion of the transcontinental railroads in 1869 and the discovery of oil in the 1890s that the population began to grow. Later, during the two world wars, Los Angeles experienced more growth, in part, because of

the new airplane industry. At about the same time, the arrival of two New York motion picture producers in search of sunny weather marked the beginning of an entertainment industry that has become a multibillion-dollar industry today. In just the past 100 years, this tiny sea village has grown into the sprawling metropolis that we know today.

[**To the reader:** Pause for 12 seconds after each question is asked to allow time for the test taker to answer.]

44. What is this talk about?

45. What two factors caused the town to begin to grow?

46. Approximately how many years ago did Los Angeles begin growing into a large city?

**Questions 47–50. Listen to the following presentation given by a student in her class.**

*(Female speaker):*  Last year, I was involved in field research, studying gorillas in southwestern Uganda where some of the few remaining mountain gorillas live. I stayed for three months in a community-run camp on the edge of Bwindi Impenetrable National Park. The park consists of about 130 square miles of tropical rain forest surrounded by small farms and grazing land. Bwindi is unique for its biodiversity, and it provides a refuge for many endangered species of plants and animals, including mountain gorillas. Today, there are only about 600 mountain gorillas left in the world, and half of them are found in Bwindi National Park.

There are four separate groups of gorillas that are being studied now in Bwindi, and one group actually comes close to the camp to feed. But the group I was studying generally stays much deeper in the forest. And so, every morning at sunrise I'd get up and leave the camp, heading off into the forest with another American student, two Ugandan researchers, and two invaluable trackers that helped us locate the gorillas each day. We often had to hike all morning to locate them, as they would generally have moved from the previous day's feeding sites.

The Ugandan team had been observing this particular group of gorillas for about five years, so they could provide us with some important background information on each individual, and they helped us identify who was who, until we were able to recognize them on our own. You might think that gorillas all look the same but, in fact, each gorilla has a very distinctive face, as well as personality.

So, let's go to the slides now, and I'll show you some of these fascinating individuals and tell you more about the specific work I was doing.

[**To the reader:** Pause for 12 seconds after each question is asked to allow time for the test taker to answer.]

47. Where did the woman do field research the previous year?
48. According to the woman, what is one unique feature of Bwindi Impenetrable National Park?
49. According to the talk, what can we assume about the researchers and trackers?
50. What can be inferred about the woman's opinion of mountain gorillas?

**This is the end of the Listening Comprehension section for Test 3. Now go on to Section 2, Structure and Written Expression.**

# Test 4 (PBT Style) Listening Script

## SECTION 1

### LISTENING COMPREHENSION

This test is written to represent the PBT in terms of numbers of questions, types of questions, and length of time for each section.

The Listening Comprehension section includes three parts. In Part A, you hear conversations between two people. Each conversation is followed by one question. In Part B, you hear longer conversations followed by several questions. In Part C, you hear talks given by a single person followed by several questions.

**Now listen to the directions for each part.**

## Part A

| | |
|---|---|
| *(Narrator):* | Now, listen to an example. |

**You will hear:**

| | |
|---|---|
| *(Woman):* | Have you called Pete? |
| *(Man):* | I'll call him as soon as I get home. |
| *(Narrator):* | What does the man mean? |
| *(Narrator):* | You will read the answer choices in your test book: |

(A) He will call Pete before he goes home.

(B) He will call Pete after he gets home.

(C) He called Pete at home.

(D) He will call Pete tomorrow.

| | |
|---|---|
| *(Narrator):* | You learn from the conversation that the man will call Pete as soon as he gets home. The best answer to the question "What does the man mean?" is choice (B), "He will call Pete after he gets home." |
| *(Narrator):* | Now continue listening to the recording and begin the test. |

[**To the reader:** Pause for 12 seconds after each question is asked to allow time for the test taker to answer.]

| | | |
|---|---|---|
| 1. | *(Man):* | I didn't expect Lisa to spend so much of her time helping me. |
| | *(Woman):* | She really has a tight schedule this semester, doesn't she? |
| | *(Narrator):* | What are the speakers saying about Lisa? |
| 2. | *(Woman):* | Guess what? I'll be a teaching assistant for Chemistry 1B. |
| | *(Man):* | I thought your major was computer science. |
| | *(Narrator):* | What had the man assumed about the woman? |
| 3. | *(Woman):* | Mark sure smokes a lot when he studies hard. |
| | *(Man):* | Not anymore, he doesn't. |

| | *(Narrator):* | What does the man mean? |

4. | *(Man):* | I heard that the workshop was a disappointment. |
| *(Woman):* | Dozens of people signed up for it. |
| *(Man):* | But only a few showed up, didn't they? |
| *(Narrator):* | What does the man imply? |

5. | *(Woman):* | Has your brother finished his studies yet? |
| *(Man):* | Steve won't graduate until this summer, but did you know that he has already started his own computer consulting company? |
| *(Woman):* | Boy, he's really using what he's learned. |
| *(Narrator):* | What does the woman say about Steve? |

6. | *(Man):* | I need to take a break. |
| *(Woman):* | Let's go to the movies tonight. |
| *(Narrator):* | What are the speakers going to do? |

7. | *(Man):* | Would you please drop this book at the library for me when you go to school? |
| *(Woman):* | I would if I was going, but I have to work today. |
| *(Narrator):* | What does the woman imply? |

8. | *(Man):* | Excuse me, but is this seat taken? |
| *(Woman):* | No, somebody just left. |
| *(Narrator):* | What is the man probably going to do? |

9. | *(Woman):* | The professor seems exhausted after that long lecture. |
| *(Man):* | So am I. |
| *(Narrator):* | What does the man mean? |

10. | *(Man):* | You don't want to start graduate school right after graduation, do you? |
| *(Woman):* | Well, actually I do. |
| *(Narrator):* | What does the woman mean? |

11. | *(Woman):* | Why haven't you completed your registration process? |
| *(Man):* | Two of the classes I want to take have conflicting schedules. |

| | | |
|---|---|---|
| | *(Woman):* | Then you need to make a decision. |
| | *(Narrator):* | What does the woman suggest the man do? |
| | | |
| 12. | *(Woman):* | You've already read this book, haven't you? |
| | *(Man):* | I wish I had. |
| | *(Narrator):* | What does the man mean? |
| | | |
| 13. | *(Woman):* | Bill, I think I'll ride my bike to school today. You want to go with me? |
| | *(Man):* | Sure, the exercise will do me good. |
| | *(Narrator):* | What does the man mean? |
| | | |
| 14. | *(Man):* | Uh-oh, these two books are due tomorrow. |
| | *(Woman):* | Already? |
| | *(Narrator):* | What does the woman mean? |
| | | |
| 15. | *(Man):* | This is the second time my machine has broken since I started working five minutes ago. |
| | *(Woman):* | Let me try to fix it for you. It's probably a bad connection. |
| | *(Narrator):* | What does the woman mean? |
| | | |
| 16. | *(Man):* | Excuse me. Did you drop this? |
| | *(Woman):* | Oh, thanks. |
| | *(Narrator):* | What does the woman mean? |
| | | |
| 17. | *(Man):* | Do you know how to get there? |
| | *(Woman):* | I think so, but give me the directions, just in case. |
| | *(Narrator):* | What is the man probably going to do? |
| | | |
| 18. | *(Woman):* | Mark, the university library is hiring now. Are you still looking for a job? |
| | *(Man):* | I've found one, but thank you anyway. |
| | *(Narrator):* | What does the man mean? |
| | | |
| 19. | *(Man):* | I'm usually on the job Tuesday and Thursday from 1 to 5. |
| | *(Woman):* | Do you work on weekends, too? |

| *(Man):* | Yes, but the hours are different. |
|---|---|
| *(Narrator):* | What does the man mean? |

20. | *(Woman):* | Jill is very excited about her new project. |
|---|---|---|
| | *(Man):* | But is it feasible for her to complete it within a year? |
| | *(Narrator):* | What is the man's concern about Jill's project? |

# PART B

*(Narrator):* In this part of the test, you will hear longer conversations between two people and class discussions. After each conversation or discussion, you will be asked some questions. You will hear the conversations or discussions and the questions only once, so listen carefully. After you hear a question, read the four possible answers in your test book, and decide which one is the best answer. Then, on your answer sheet, find the number of the question and fill in the oval of the answer you have chosen. Answer all questions based on what is stated or implied by the speakers.

| *(Narrator):* | Listen to the example. |
|---|---|

You will hear:

**Questions 1 and 2 are based on the following conversation between two friends at school.**

| *(Man):* | Hi, Joanie. Where are you going? |
|---|---|
| *(Woman):* | Oh, hi, Paul. I'm on my way to the library. |
| *(Man):* | Oh yeah? I just wondered if you wanted to go to a movie with me. |
| *(Woman):* | I'd love to, but I can't. I can't believe all the work I have this semester. I only have three classes, but in all of them I have lots of reading, term papers, reports, and essay exams. It's incredible! I feel like I'll never get through everything. |
| *(Man):* | That's terrible. I felt like that last year when I had term papers to write, but this semester seems easy now. I spend a lot of time in class, but most of it is in labs doing experiments. I hated writing all those term papers. But can't I talk you into going to the show anyway? I've heard that the movie over at the East Auditorium is really good. It's a murder mystery. |
| *(Woman):* | Oh, now I'm sure I won't go. I might go to a comedy, but I hate murder mysteries. |

| | |
|---|---|
| *(Narrator):* | Now listen to sample question number 1. |
| *(Narrator):* | 1.  Where is the woman going? |
| *(Narrator):* | You will read the answer choices in your test book: |

    (A) To the cafeteria
    (B) To the movie theater
    (C) To her dorm room
    (D) To the library

| | |
|---|---|
| *(Narrator):* | The correct answer to the question "Where is the woman going?" is choice (D), "To the library." |
| *(Narrator):* | Now listen to sample question number 2. |
| *(Narrator):* | 2.  Which best describes the man's feelings about his classes? |
| *(Narrator):* | You will read the answer choices in your test book: |

    (A) Term papers are easy for him.
    (B) He has a lot of essay exams.
    (C) He finds lab experiments easier than writing term papers.
    (D) He is busier this semester than last semester.

| | |
|---|---|
| *(Narrator):* | The best answer to the question "Which best describes the man's feelings about his classes?" is choice (C), "He finds lab experiments easier than writing term papers." |

**Now listen to the test. Remember, you are not allowed to take any notes or write in your test book.**

**Questions 21–24. Listen to the following conversation between two friends.**

| | |
|---|---|
| *(Woman):* | Hi, Sid. I loved your concert last night! How are you? |
| *(Man):* | I'm a little bit tired. We didn't go to bed until five o'clock in the morning. And I injured my ankle before the show, but I feel better this afternoon. I slept all morning. How did you like the show? |
| *(Woman):* | I loved it. You were singing great. When are you playing next? |
| *(Man):* | We have our next show here in New York at the Roxy Theater this Thursday. |
| *(Woman):* | I would love to go, but I have to stay and work here at the store. |
| *(Man):* | Well, maybe you can see us next week when we play in Washington. |

| | |
|---|---|
| *(Woman):* | Yeah, maybe. I'm planning to go on vacation to San Francisco in April, so I may not be able to travel to Washington. |
| *(Man):* | Really! We were invited to play at the Rock Music Festival in San Francisco in April, but we don't have a way of getting there. It's a long drive from New York. |
| *(Woman):* | Well, a friend and I are driving across the country in a big van, and we might have room for you and the band. |
| *(Man):* | That would be great! Let me talk to the band members, and I'll call you later this week. |
| *(Woman):* | OK. I'll look forward to hearing from you. Do you need any help looking for any records in the store today? |
| *(Man):* | Yeah, I was looking for an album featuring John Coltrane and Miles Davis. Do you have any in stock? |
| *(Woman):* | No, I'm sorry we don't. We can order one for you, or you might try down the street at one of the other record stores. |
| *(Man):* | OK, I'll just try down the street. I'll give you a call later this week. |
| *(Woman):* | Good, see you later. |

[**To the reader:** Pause for 12 seconds after each question is asked to allow time for the test taker to answer.]

21. What was the man doing the previous night?
22. Where will the man play next week?
23. Where is the woman working?
24. Where is the woman going for her vacation?

**Questions 25–28. Listen to the following conversation between two students.**

| | |
|---|---|
| *(Woman):* | Hey, Tom. |
| *(Man):* | How's it going, Mary? |
| *(Woman):* | Great, I just finished my last exam for the semester, and now I'm going home to get ready for summer break. What about you? |
| *(Man):* | I'll finish my last exam this afternoon. I'm on my way to the library to finish studying for it. Where are you going this summer? |
| *(Woman):* | I'm planning to work in Woods Hole, Massachusetts, at the Woods Hole Oceanographic Institute. I'll be studying whales. |

| | |
|---|---|
| *(Man):* | That sounds like a great job. I'll be working nearby on the coast at Nantucket. |
| *(Woman):* | What are you planning to do on the coast? |
| *(Man):* | My uncle owns a restaurant there, so I'll be working as a waiter at night and then helping him do some accounting a few days each week. I have to save a lot of money for the next school year. Maybe we can get together and go to the beach this summer since we'll be living near each other. |
| *(Woman):* | That sounds good. I'll be working on a boat during July, and I won't return to shore for the entire month. But in June and later in August I'll be working in the laboratories, and I could drive up and see you in Nantucket. |
| *(Man):* | OK. My uncle tells me June is the best time to go there before the town gets too crowded with tourists. Call me before you leave tomorrow, and I'll give you a phone number where I can be reached this summer. |
| *(Woman):* | All right. I'll talk to you later. Good luck with your exam! |
| *(Man):* | Thanks! |

[**To the reader:** Pause for 12 seconds after each question is asked to allow time for the test taker to answer.]

25. Where is the woman going to work for the summer?
26. Where will the man be working during the summer?
27. What is the woman going to study?
28. Why can't the woman visit the man in the month of July?

**Questions 29–31. Listen to the following conversation between two teachers.**

| | |
|---|---|
| *(Man):* | Hey, Jean. How's it going? |
| *(Woman):* | Oh, the same old thing, I guess. I have to go to Washington next week to meet with my publisher, and I don't know how I'll manage with exams coming up. I'm looking forward to the break this summer. |
| *(Man):* | Yeah, me too. How's the book coming? |
| *(Woman):* | Pretty well, I think. I just have to meet with the publishers to talk about the format for my last chapter. It's almost done. |
| *(Man):* | What's the last chapter about? |

| | |
|---|---|
| *(Woman):* | Well, the book is about the poetry of Edgar Allen Poe, and the last chapter just focuses on "The Raven" as one of his most significant poems. |
| *(Man):* | If you weren't so busy with going to Washington and all, I'd love to have you come to my American literature class and discuss Poe with them. We've been going over poetry and prose of the nineteenth century. |
| *(Woman):* | I'd love to, Jim, but I don't know what my schedule is going to be like when I get back next Thursday. When does your class meet? |
| *(Man):* | Tuesdays and Thursdays at three. |
| *(Woman):* | I might be able to do it. Let's talk when I get back next Thursday, and I'll let you know. |
| *(Man):* | Thanks, it would be great if you could come. |

[**To the reader:** Pause for 12 seconds after each question is asked to allow time for the test taker to answer.]

29. What field of study are these two speakers most likely teaching?

30. Why is the woman going to Washington next week?

31. What favor does the man ask of the woman?

**Questions 32–35. Listen to the following class discussion on genetics.**

| | |
|---|---|
| *(Female Professor):* | Before we move into the topic of genetic engineering, I'd like to answer any questions you have up to this point on the basic structure of DNA and make sure you understand the terminology. **\*\*\*PAUSE\*\*\*** Yes, John? |
| *(Man):* | I'm still not clear on the difference between a chromosome and a gene. |
| *(Female Professor):* | Well, you can think of the chromosome as packaging, so to speak, or the container for the DNA molecule. And a gene is a segment of that DNA molecule that carries genetic information. The whole DNA molecule is made up of thousands of genes, and it's twisted around inside of the chromosome. |
| *(Woman):* | So does the term double helix refer to the DNA? |
| *(Female Professor):* | Yes, but specifically "double helix" refers to the shape of the DNA molecule. The DNA molecule is shaped like a long ladder twisting around itself in a spiral. And, just like a ladder, it has many rungs, or crosspieces. |

*(Man):* Then can we say that one gene is like a small section of the twisted ladder?

*(Female Professor):* Exactly. And genes come in various lengths, so one gene may be a long segment of the ladder or a shorter segment. Remember, we're using the analogy of the ladder just to help us picture the DNA molecule. Another way to look at it is like a spiral staircase with one section of the staircase representing one gene.

[**To the reader:** Pause for 12 seconds after each question is asked to allow time for the test taker to answer.]

32. What is this discussion mainly about?

33. How does the professor describe a gene?

34. Why did the professor use the analogy of the ladder?

35. Which of the following is true about DNA?

# PART C

*(Narrator):* In this part of the test, you will hear segments read by a single person. After each segment, you will be asked some questions. You will hear the segments and the questions only once, so listen carefully. After you hear a question, read the four possible answers in your test book, and decide which one is the best answer. Then find the number of the question on your answer sheet, and fill in the oval that corresponds to the letter of the answer you have chosen. Answer all questions based on what is stated or implied in the talk.

*(Narrator):* Listen to this sample talk.

You will hear:

**Questions 1–4 are based on the following announcement.**

*(Female speaker):* At this university, we offer three different programs for students who have children. For those of you with very young children, we have a day-care program for infants from 3 months to 30 months. We have another program for children between 2 and 5 years of age, and we also have an after-school program for school-aged children. This program offers sports, crafts, outings, and tutoring during after-school hours. Enrollment in these childcare programs is limited, and early application is essential because our programs often have waiting lists. The fees are on an hourly basis. If any of you new students need these services, please let me know right away so I can get you an application form.

*(Narrator):* Now listen to sample question number 1.

*(Narrator):*          1.   What is the main purpose of this announcement?

*(Narrator):*          You will read the answer choices in your test book:

(A) To demonstrate tutoring techniques

(B) To explain school policies

(C) To recruit childcare workers

(D) To explain a service

*(Narrator):*          The best answer to the question "What is the purpose of this announcement?" is choice (D), "To explain a service."

### Now listen to sample question number 2.

*(Narrator):*          2.   What does the speaker recommend?

*(Narrator):*          You will read the answer choices in your test book:

(A)  Give your child extra tutoring.

(B)  Take your child to the program today.

(C)  Apply as soon as you can.

(D)  Pay next month.

*(Narrator):*          The best answer to the question "What does the speaker recommend?" is choice (C), "Apply as soon as you can."

**Now, listen to the talks. Remember, you are not allowed to write any notes in your test book.**

**Questions 36–39. Listen to a lecture in a literature class.**

*(Female Speaker):*   The first book we're going to read in this class is James Joyce's *Dubliners*. Please start reading it immediately since we'll be discussing it next week. Today I'd like to begin with a bit of background about James Joyce. He was born on February 2, 1882 in Dublin and grew up in a very large family of 17 children. He attended Catholic Jesuit-run schools, including the boarding school Clongowes and later Belvedere College in Dublin. He went on to study languages and philosophy at the Royal University. After graduation he left Ireland and went to Paris, supposedly to study medicine, but instead he wasted time and squandered most of his money. Later he returned to Ireland to care for his mother, who had become very ill. After she died, Joyce stayed for a while in Ireland, doing some teaching and writing. In 1904, he met Nora, the woman with whom he would live, and later marry, and they left Ireland to live in Zurich and Trieste. Joyce continued writing and

he held a few jobs, but for the most part he and Nora were extremely poor. In fact, Joyce's brother paid many of his bills.

The book we're reading in this class, *Dubliners*, was the first book Joyce wrote. It's a collection of 15 short stories that reflect life of the Irish lower middle class. Joyce spent a frustrating 8 years trying to get this book published, but it was continually rejected in Ireland. Finally, in 1912 it was published in London. As an adult, Joyce rarely returned to his native country; he spent most of his life in continental Europe. In his later years, he lived in Paris, often in poverty, but he continued to write. He published *Ulysses* in 1922, and in 1939, *Finnegans Wake*. Joyce died unexpectedly in 1941 at the age of 59. ***PAUSE*** OK, let's stop for now. Next week we'll go over more details of James Joyce's life as we focus on his book *Dubliners*.

[**To the reader:** Pause for 12 seconds after each question is asked to allow time for the test taker to answer.]

36. What is the main purpose of this lecture?

37. What does the professor say about the book *Dubliners*?

38. What does the author imply about Joyce?

39. Where did Joyce live in his later years?

**Questions 40–43. Listen to this lecture at an Institute of Natural History.**

*(Female Speaker):*  Good afternoon. I am pleased to welcome you to the Institute of Natural History for our Wednesday afternoon lecture series. As you know, this month our focus is on paleontology, and I am especially pleased today to introduce our guest speaker, Dr. Charles Sawyer. Dr. Sawyer and I met many years ago as undergraduates at the University of Colorado where we were both biology majors. He later went on to the University of Cambridge to study paleontology, while I stayed in the U.S. We continued to keep in touch, however, meeting over the years at professional conferences, and working together to co-author a few articles.

Dr. Sawyer's research in paleontology has been extensive. He is recognized the world over for his contribution to our understanding of prehistory through fossil research. He has documented fossils in sites that range from Antarctica to Australia, Egypt, and

Kazahkstan. His latest finds are from a new site in southern Kazahkstan where he has found some late Cambrian assemblages, and that is what he will discuss today.

Dr. Sawyer's work is at the cutting edge in our field so we are extremely fortunate to have him here today. Let us hear now from my good friend and colleague, Dr. Charles Sawyer.

[**To the reader:** Pause for 12 seconds after each question is asked to allow time for the test taker to answer.]

40. What is the main purpose of the talk?
41. What does the speaker say about himself and Dr. Sawyer?
42. What does the speaker say that Dr. Sawyer is famous for?
43. What will probably be discussed next?

**Questions 44–46. Listen to an announcement by a university official.**

*(Male speaker):* On behalf of the university and the town, I would like to welcome all of you to the University of North Carolina. This is the oldest public university in the United States, and we are proud to say that we offer one of the best public education opportunities anywhere in the nation. We have quite a heritage. Among other things, we were the only university in the United States to graduate students in the eighteenth century. Our school was founded in 1792, and in 1793 the cornerstone was laid for the first building. That building, which came to be called "Old East," is still standing. It is now designated a National Historic Landmark and is the oldest state university building in the United States. Our university began with this single two-story brick building and only 41 students. And from this small beginning, we have grown to a total of 16 campuses and to the large student population that you see today. We are proud of our excellence, as demonstrated through faculty research and teaching, our diverse student population, and our broad curriculum of study. And now, we are very excited to have you here and are looking forward to getting to know you. If you have any questions about getting settled and beginning classes, please contact our staff. I will introduce them now.

[**To the reader:** Pause for 12 seconds after each question is asked to allow time for the test taker to answer.]

44. According to the speaker, which of the following is true about the university?

45. What is the speaker proud of?

46. What does the speaker say about the building called "Old East?"

**Questions 47–50. Listen to an announcement by a teacher.**

*(Male speaker):*  Before I start with today's lecture on Einstein's theory of quantum mechanics, I'd like to invite anyone who is interested in making a bit of money this summer to see me about working at a summer camp for high school students. The camps will be science camps, one each month, focusing on introducing students to cutting-edge technologies such as particle accelerators, micro-wave communications, and electron microscopes. The science camps need college students to help as camp counselors and to live with the students in dormitories. Each counselor will be assigned 10 campers and will have his or her own room. Your room will be free. Counselors will also get the chance to use some of the equipment and meet internationally known scientists who will be visiting the camp over the course of the summer. In addition, the entire group will travel to Washington for a week in July. If you are interested, please see me after class.

[**To the reader:** Pause for 12 seconds after each question is asked to allow time for the test taker to answer.]

47. What type of summer camp is announced?

48. Where is this discussion most likely taking place?

49. Why does the camp need college students?

50. Where will all campers travel in July?

**This is the end of the Listening Comprehension section for Test 4. Now go on to Section 2, Structure and Written Expression.**

# Appendix

## TOEFL WORD LIST

Most of the words on the following list have been used in past versions of the TOEFL. Some of them have been the selected words in vocabulary questions, and others have been used as answer choices. All of them represent the typical level of words used on the TOEFL. It gives you an idea of the type of words that you might encounter. When you study the words, make up your own sentences to help you remember the meanings.

| | |
|---|---|
| abhor (verb) | to hate or think of with disgust<br>The man abhorred the feel of snakes. |
| accelerate (verb) | to increase the speed<br>This car accelerates quickly. |
| accessible (adj.) | able to be reached; convenient<br>Elevators in tall buildings make the top floors accessible to everyone. |
| accurate, accuracy (adj./noun) | exact; correct<br>In order to get 100 percent on the test, you must be accurate. |
| adjacent to (adj.) | next to; near, but not necessarily touching<br>Our garage is adjacent to our house. |
| advantageous (adj.) | profitable; helpful<br>Sometimes it is advantageous to own a car. |
| advocate (noun/verb) | a person who supports or speaks in favor of something; to support<br>Our group is an advocate of equal opportunity for men and women. |
| aforementioned (adj.) | said or written before<br>The aforementioned topic is one of great interest. |
| alert, alertly (adj./adv.) | fully awake and ready to act; in an alert manner<br>The guard watched alertly as the people appeared. |
| amass (verb) | to collect or pile up<br>The rich man had amassed his fortune over several years. |

| | |
|---|---|
| ambrosia (noun) | food that has a delightful taste or smell; "food of the gods" <br> This fantastic dish tastes like ambrosia. |
| anomaly (noun) | something abnormal or unusual <br> A bird that cannot fly is an anomaly. |
| anxiety (noun) | an emotional condition of fear and uncertainty <br> Her family waited with anxiety for the news of her safe arrival. |
| appall, appalling (verb/adj.) | to fill with fear; shocking <br> The number of people who starved in the famine was appalling. |
| appear (verb) | to come into view; to become visible <br> At dawn the sun appears on the horizon. |
| appropriate (adj.) | suitable; proper <br> A wedding dress is not appropriate to wear to a beach party. |
| apt (adj.) | likely; appropriate; relevant <br> The mischievous child is apt to get into trouble. <br> Your statement is not apt to this conversation. |
| arouse (verb) | to awaken; to cause to become active <br> The alarm clock used to arouse us at 6 A.M. |
| as of late (conj. + adj.) | recently <br> I've been feeling tired as of late. |
| astute (adj.) | clever, quick <br> The astute student answered all the questions correctly. |
| attribute (verb) | to consider something as the result of something else <br> I attribute my success to my hard work. |
| authoritative (adj.) | having authority; commanding <br> The authoritative manner of the general made us respect him. |
| back and forth (adv.) | movement: first one way and then the other <br> The anxious man walked back and forth across the room. |
| barely (adv.) | only a bit; hardly <br> I barely know my new neighbors; they just moved in. |
| barter (verb) | to exchange goods or property for other goods or property <br> Ancient societies bartered food before they had money. |
| behold (verb) | to look at; to observe <br> The clear blue-green lake is a lovely sight to behold. |

| | |
|---|---|
| beneficial (adj.) | helpful<br>Fresh air and good food are beneficial to your health. |
| bind (verb) | to tie or fasten; to hold to an agreement<br>If you bind the package with rope, it will be easier to carry. |
| bizarre (adj.) | very odd or unusual<br>The costumes for this play are bizarre. |
| blunder (verb) | to move with uncertainty; to make foolish mistakes<br>The candidate for president was careful not to blunder in his speech. |
| border (noun) | the edge; the line or the boundary between two places<br>The lake is on the border of two countries. |
| breach (noun) | a breaking or neglect of a rule or agreement<br>Fighting in the streets is a breach of the peace. |
| bump (noun/verb) | a swelling; to move with a jerking motion<br>I have a bump on my arm from the bee sting.<br>The old car bumped down the dirt road. |
| bush (noun) | low-growing plant with many stems<br>The trees, bushes, and flowers in the park are beautiful. |
| by degrees (adv.) | gradually<br>Their friendship grew by degrees. |
| by rights (adv.) | if justice were done<br>This property is mine by rights. |
| candid (adj.) | frank, straightforward, truthful<br>I'll be candid with you; you did a poor job. |
| care (verb) | to feel interest or sorrow; to be willing; to look after someone by providing food, medical assistance, etc.<br>He doesn't seem to care whether he passes or fails. |
| carve (verb) | to form something by cutting away wood or stone<br>The statues by Michelangelo were carved from granite. |
| celebrate (verb) | to do something to show that a day or event is special<br>We celebrated my birthday by having a party. |
| chart (noun) | a map; a paper with diagrams, tables, or visual information<br>The sailors looked at their charts to find out where they were. |
| circulate (verb) | to move from place to place freely<br>The teacher circulated around the room as the students studied. |

| | |
|---|---|
| classify (verb) | to arrange in classes or groups<br>One of the secretary's jobs is to classify the new information. |
| colleague (noun) | a partner or associate working in the same profession<br>Her colleagues assisted her when she needed help. |
| collusion (noun) | a secret agreement or discussion for a dishonest reason<br>The robbers were in collusion before the robbery. |
| command (noun) | a position of power<br>The general was in command of the army. |
| commonplace (adj./noun) | normal, ordinary, obvious, not interesting<br>It is a commonplace event to eat dinner in the evening. |
| compromise (noun/verb) | a settlement of a dispute by which each side gives up something it wants; an agreement; to make concessions<br>This hotel is a good compromise; it's near the lake for me and near the mountains for you.<br>To settle the argument, each person compromised a bit. |
| conceal (verb) | to hide; to keep secret<br>The robber concealed a weapon under his coat. |
| confidential (adj.) | secret<br>Some military information is confidential. |
| conform (verb) | to stay in agreement with rules<br>People who don't conform will be discharged from the group. |
| congregate (verb) | to come together<br>After the speech, the audience congregated around the speaker. |
| conserve (verb) | to save or to keep from destruction<br>During a drought, everyone needs to conserve water. |
| considerably (adv.) | much, a great deal<br>I have considerably more work this year than I did last year. |
| conspicuous (adj.) | easily seen<br>You look conspicuous in that large purple hat. |
| contemporary (noun/adj.) | belonging to the same time; of the present time, or modern<br>George Washington and Benjamin Franklin were contemporaries.<br>I live in a contemporary house. |
| contrast (verb) | to compare so that differences are made clear<br>Her words contrast with her actions. |

| convenient (adj.) | easy to use, easy to get to, or easy to do<br>It is convenient to have a washing machine in your house. |
| --- | --- |
| counter (noun/verb) | a table surface on which goods are shown or food prepared; to oppose; to return an attack<br>You can pick up your food from the counter.<br>My argument was countered by my friend's argument. |
| craggy (adj.) | with high, steep, or sharp rocks<br>The mountain climbers slowly ascended the craggy slopes. |
| critic (noun) | a person who gives judgment, usually about literature, art, or music<br>After his new play was performed, he was anxious to read what the critics said about it. |
| crush (verb) | to press so that there is breaking or injury<br>His leg was crushed in an automobile accident. |
| curious (adj.) | eager to learn and to know; having an interest in something<br>Children are usually curious about the world. |
| cut (noun/verb) | a reduction in size, amount or length; a style of clothes or hair; a remark that hurts a person's feelings; to remove from something larger, to stay away from or be absent from class<br>I don't like the cut of that dress. (style)<br>He cut the dead limb from the tree. |
| damage (noun/verb) | harm or injury; to harm or injure<br>The insurance company will pay for the damages to your car. |
| decay (verb) | to go bad; to lose power or health<br>Fruit decays quickly in hot weather. |
| defeat (noun/verb) | loss; to cause to fail<br>After five victories, the soccer team suffered its first defeat. |
| deficit (noun) | a condition of spending more than you have<br>The only way to decrease the deficit is to increase taxes. |
| den (noun) | a secret place; an animal's hidden place; a room for studying<br>The fox's den is in the bushes. |
| desolate (adj.) | ruined, barren, neglected, lonely, or sad<br>The small town looked desolate after the storm. |
| detachable (adj.) | able to be removed, unfastened, or taken apart<br>The legs of this table are detachable. |
| deter (verb) | to discourage<br>A locked door will deter thieves. |

| | |
|---|---|
| dig (verb) | to use a tool to move earth<br>To get ready to plant the tree, you must dig a hole. |
| dim (adj.) | not bright, not seen clearly<br>A small light is too dim for reading. |
| discerning (adj.) | able to see clearly<br>A discerning eye can tell the difference between planets and stars. |
| discord (noun) | disagreement, conflict<br>Quarrels over money have brought discord into the family. |
| disseminate (verb) | to distribute; to spread widely<br>The news of the new king was disseminated over the whole country. |
| distinct (adj.) | easily seen or heard, clearly marked, separate<br>She has a distinct accent. |
| draft (noun/verb) | an outline of something to be done; a current of air in a room; to select a person for the armed forces<br>Before I submit an essay, I always write a first draft.<br>My brother was drafted into the army. |
| due to (prep.) | because of, caused by, attributed to<br>The accident was due to slippery streets. |
| duplicate (noun/verb/adj.) | a copy; to copy exactly; to make exactly alike<br>Please make a duplicate of this letter for me. |
| earmark (verb/noun) | to set aside for a special purpose; an identification mark to show ownership<br>The boss has earmarked this money for Christmas decorations. |
| elaborate (verb/adj.) | to work out with much care; worked in detail<br>We have made elaborate plans for New Year's Day. |
| eligible (adj.) | suitable, having the right qualifications<br>You must pass the TOEFL in order to be eligible for entrance into many Canadian and American colleges. |
| emancipate (verb) | to set free<br>Abraham Lincoln is famous for having emancipated people from slavery. |
| embrace (verb/noun) | to take someone into one's arms to show affection; to include<br>When the soldier saw his family after the war, he embraced his mother and father.<br>This speech embraces all the major ideas of the president. |
| emit (verb) | to give or to send out<br>A volcano emits fire from the earth. |

| | |
|---|---|
| encourage (verb) | to give hope, confidence, or support<br>I encourage all my children to study hard in school. |
| enhance (verb) | to add to the value or importance of something<br>Keeping your house clean and well-cared for enhances its value. |
| entangle (verb) | to become caught or involved in something so that escape is difficult<br>The kitten cried when it got entangled in a ball of string. |
| entitle (verb) | to give a right to something<br>As a student here, you are entitled to use the services at the health center. |
| epoch (noun) | a period of time in history<br>Henry Ford's automobile began a new epoch in the history of transportation. |
| erode, erosion (verb/noun) | to wear away, usually by rain, wind, or acid; a wearing away<br>Acid eroded the metal under my car.<br>Water erosion from the heavy rains has caused damage to the land. |
| essential (adj.) | necessary<br>To enter many colleges, it is essential that you get 550 on the TOEFL exam. |
| evacuate (verb) | to leave empty; to withdraw<br>If there is a fire, evacuate the building quickly. |
| exceed (verb) | to do more than enough, to go beyond, to be greater than<br>His success has exceeded all our hopes. |
| excerpt (noun) | a part of a book or article<br>In the magazine, you can read an excerpt of his latest book. |
| exhilarating (adj.) | filled with high spirits, lively, exciting<br>I have some exhilarating news: We won the national game! |
| expanse (noun) | a wide open area<br>To raise cattle, you need a large expanse of land. |
| extend (verb) | to make longer<br>The teacher extended the deadline for our essays for another week. |
| extravagant (adj.) | wasteful; excessive<br>Rich people are sometimes extravagant with their money; they spend a lot. |
| face (verb) | to meet confidently, to recognize, to turn in a certain direction<br>I don't want to face my friend after what I did to her.<br>Please face the front of the room. |

| | |
|---|---|
| fame (noun) | the condition of being known or talked about; good reputation<br>Unfortunately, his fame as a composer did not come until after his death. |
| fancy (adj.) | very decorated, not plain<br>For the party, you should wear fancy clothes. |
| faucet (noun) | a device for controlling the flow of liquid (usually water) from a pipe or tank<br>To make the water come out, you must turn on the faucet. |
| feature (noun/verb) | the appearance of something, distinct or outstanding parts, an attraction or main part; to emphasize the main part<br>One of the main features of Yellowstone National Park is Old Faithful. |
| fellow (adj.) | having the same ideas or position, in the same condition, or associated<br>My fellow workers and I are all going on a picnic together. |
| fictitious (adj.) | untrue or invented<br>The writer published under a fictitious name. |
| final analysis (adj. + noun) | at the end, in conclusion<br>In the final analysis, the Northern team won the prize for Team of the Year. |
| fizz (verb/noun) | to make a bubbling hissing sound, as when gas escapes from a liquid; a bubbling sound<br>Soft drinks like Coca-Cola fizz when they are poured into a glass. |
| flaw (noun) | a fault, an imperfection<br>The store is selling clothes that have flaws at half price. |
| flicker (verb) | to burn or shine unsteadily<br>The candle flickered in the wind and then went out. |
| forbidden (adj.) | prohibited; ordered not to be done<br>It is forbidden to enter the compound after dark. |
| foster (verb) | to help to grow or develop; to bring up with care<br>A relaxed environment can foster creative ideas. |
| fragrance (noun) | a pleasing smell<br>I like perfume with the fragrance of fresh flowers. |
| frightening (adj.) | filled with fear and alarm<br>A frightening nightmare can cause a child to wake up and cry. |
| fuel (noun) | a material that produces energy or heat<br>Some cars run on diesel fuel, and some run on gasoline. |

| | |
|---|---|
| fund (noun/verb) | a supply of necessary things, money; to provide money for support<br>Our group raised money for the scholarship fund. |
| gain (noun/verb) | an increase in power or wealth; to obtain something<br>The boss is interested only in gain. He wants to gain power. |
| gemstones (noun) | precious, valuable stones or jewels<br>Some people keep gemstones in a safe. |
| glistening (adj.) | shining brightly, sparkling<br>In the morning, the flowers are glistening with the dewdrops. |
| goods (noun) | things that have worth or are valuable<br>After you count the goods, lock them in the warehouse. |
| graphic (adj.) | described in clear images<br>The man gave a graphic account of the fight. |
| grave (adj.) | serious, requiring careful consideration<br>Her illness is grave. |
| grumpy (adj.) | bad-tempered<br>Grandpa is always grumpy when he first wakes up. |
| hardly (adv.) | only just, scarcely<br>When I was sick I could hardly talk. |
| hatch (verb) | to break out of an egg; to produce a plan<br>The chicks are hatching today. |
| hearty (adj.) | strong, in good health<br>After a good breakfast, I feel hearty. |
| hostile (adj.) | unfriendly<br>The enemies were hostile toward each other. |
| huge (adj.) | very large<br>I just ate a huge dinner; I can't eat anything more. |
| hybrid (noun) | an animal or plant that is the offspring of two different parents or species<br>The mule is a hybrid animal, a cross between a donkey and a horse. |
| ignore (verb) | to refuse to notice someone or something<br>When people are angry at each other, they sometimes ignore each other. |
| imitate (verb) | to copy something or use it as an example<br>By imitating great artists, young artists can learn good techniques. |
| imperceptible (adv.) | slight, gradual, unnoticeable<br>The improvement, though imperceptible, was still there. |

| | |
|---|---|
| increase (verb/noun) | to make larger; growth<br>There is an increase in the number of students in school this year. |
| indefinite (adj.) | not fixed; vague<br>The factory will be closed for an indefinite period of time. |
| indicative (adj.) | an indication or sign of something to come<br>The blossoms on the fruit trees are indicative of spring weather. |
| induce (verb) | to cause; to produce; to influence<br>Her illness was induced by a poor diet and overwork. |
| ingenious (adj.) | very clever and skillful<br>The professor was ingenious at solving problems. |
| inhibit (verb) | to restrain or suppress; to hinder<br>Being very tired inhibits studying. |
| insatiable (adj.) | something that cannot be satisfied<br>My father has an insatiable desire for candy. |
| inspiring (adj.) | uplifting; stimulating<br>After the inspiring speech, the audience was filled with confidence. |
| insult (verb) | to speak to in a way that is intended to hurt a person's feelings<br>When the child was insulted, he cried. |
| intense (adj.) | deeply felt, high in degree<br>The explosion from the bomb caused intense heat for several miles. |
| intricate (adj.) | complicated, difficult<br>The beauty of the painting is its intricate design. |
| inundated (verb) | flooded<br>The rains inundated the fields, washing away the crops. |
| invent (verb) | to create or design something not already existing<br>The brilliant man invented a new technique to speed up his work. |
| landmark (noun) | an object that marks the boundary of a piece of land; an object that is easily seen and can be used as a guide; an event that marks a turning point<br>The first hotel built in our city is still a landmark to progress. |
| lateral (adj.) | from or at the sides of something, from side to side<br>Earthquakes usually cause a lateral movement in buildings. |
| legendary (adj.) | from an old story told to people from generation to generation<br>The legendary travels of ancient Greeks are well known in literature. |

| | |
|---|---|
| liberate (verb) | to free<br>The victorious army liberated the prisoners. |
| limited (adj.) | restricted, narrow<br>There is a limited number of books on this topic<br>for sale. |
| literally (adv.) | exactly, corresponding word for word to the<br>original, lacking in imagination<br>If you translate an idiom literally, you probably<br>will not get the correct meaning. |
| locale (noun) | an area, the scene of an event<br>This is the locale of the accident. |
| ludicrous (adj.) | ridiculous, absurd<br>It is ludicrous to say that it is easy to become<br>fluent in all languages. |
| lyrical (adj.) | full of emotion, like a song<br>The lyrical words of the poem made me feel<br>almost like crying. |
| magnificence (noun) | splendor, imposing beauty<br>The palace is famous for its magnificence. |
| mandatory (adj.) | required<br>It is mandatory that you take basic science courses<br>before entering college. |
| mar (verb) | to injure or damage<br>Nothing could mar the happiness of the newly wed<br>couple. |
| mature (verb/adj.) | to be fully grown, to be ready for use; perfected<br>A 10-year-old child is not mature enough to leave<br>her family. |
| merchandise (noun) | things to buy or sell<br>The ships brought new merchandise in to the city. |
| minuscule (adj.) | a tiny bit<br>There was a minuscule amount of iron in the<br>chemical solution. |
| misleading (adj.) | causing a wrong impression; deceiving<br>The police were given misleading information<br>about the crime. |
| moderately (adv.) | reasonably; to a limited degree<br>It is relaxing to swim in moderately warm water. |
| motionless (adv.) | still, having no movement<br>The bird stood motionless so that it could hardly<br>be seen. |
| muscular (adj.) | having many muscles, strong<br>The lifeguards on the beach were all muscular. |
| mutation (noun) | a change, an alteration in the genes of a plant or<br>animal that can be passed on to its offspring<br>The strong X-rays caused a mutation in the plant. |

| | |
|---|---|
| naked (adj.) | without clothes, bare; without protection<br>Babies are all born naked.<br>I can see it with my naked eye (without a microscope or telescope). |
| nominal (adj.) | very small<br>A nominal fee is charged to enter the museum. |
| nourishment (noun) | a source of strength and support, food<br>Food is nourishment for my body, but love is nourishment for my heart. |
| now and then (adv.) | occasionally<br>Now and then I like to take a nap. |
| oath (noun) | a promise or vow to tell the truth<br>Before giving evidence before the court, you must take an oath. |
| obstacle (noun) | a hindrance, something that prevents you from doing something<br>Arguments and fighting between nations are obstacles to world peace. |
| ominous (adj.) | threatening<br>Ominous black clouds on the horizon indicate a rainstorm. |
| on the spot (prep.) | immediately, at the place one is needed<br>He was killed on the spot. |
| operation (noun) | a process of doing something; a surgical procedure<br>My father had an operation to remove his appendix. |
| option (noun) | choice<br>You have the option of taking biology or chemistry. |
| outlawed (verb) | made illegal<br>Guns are outlawed in many countries. |
| overlap, overlapping (verb/adj.) | to cover part of something else; covering part of another thing<br>The roof consists of overlapping tiles.<br>When building a roof, you overlap the tiles. |
| overwhelm (verb) | to defeat; to exhaust; to cover completely<br>All the work I had to do overwhelmed me. |
| panacea (noun) | a remedy for all troubles<br>There is no panacea that will bring everlasting happiness. |
| particle (noun) | a small piece, a part<br>Chew carefully so that you don't get a particle stuck in your throat. |
| passing (adj.) | not lasting, going by<br>The passing years are becoming more difficult for the sick old man. |

| | |
|---|---|
| path (noun) | a place made for walking<br>There is a path through the woods. |
| penetrate (verb) | to go into or through; to spread<br>The terrible smell penetrated the whole house. |
| perennial (adv.) | continuing through the whole year; lasting;<br>perpetual<br>I like perennial plants because they don't die in<br>the winter. |
| perjury (noun) | a false statement after giving an oath to tell the<br>truth<br>The woman was put in jail for perjury. |
| perplexing (adj.) | confusing, complicated<br>It is perplexing to read the laws of the nation. |
| phenomenon (noun) | something that can be perceived by the senses,<br>something remarkable or unusual<br>If you are interested in a phenomenon like how<br>mountains are made, take a class in earth science. |
| plot (verb/noun) | to plan secretly; the main story of a book or play;<br>a small piece of ground<br>The enemies of the government plotted to over-<br>throw the government.<br>I don't understand the plot of the play.<br>I planted my vegetable garden on a small plot of<br>land by my house. |
| point out (verb) | to show or call attention to something<br>The teacher pointed out my mistakes so that I<br>could correct them. |
| poll (noun) | a survey of public opinion made by questioning<br>people<br>The people took a poll to see which candidate<br>might win. |
| posthumously (adv.) | after one's death<br>The poet was awarded the honor of Best Poet<br>posthumously. |
| praise (noun/verb) | an expression of approval or esteem; to give<br>approval, admiration, honor, or glory to someone<br>A teacher should praise students who do well. |
| precision (noun) | the state of being exact, correct, accurate<br>A skilled engineer works with precision. |
| predominantly (adv.) | most frequently or most noticeably<br>The students in our school are predominantly from<br>the North. |
| prevail (verb) | to gain victory over something; to be the usual<br>thing, commonly seen or done<br>The South prevailed over the North in the last war.<br>The prevailing winds are from the West. (adj.<br>form) |

| | |
|---|---|
| primitive (adj.) | of early times; of an early culture, pretechnical culture<br>In primitive times, human beings lived in caves. |
| private (adj.) | concerning one person or group rather than for people in general; secret; secluded; isolated<br>I don't want my boss to know my private affairs. |
| profitable (adj.) | useful; bringing in money or gain<br>We made a deal that was profitable to everyone. |
| promotion (noun) | advancement to a higher rank or position<br>After working for two years in my company, I was given a promotion. |
| propagate (verb) | to increase the number of plants or animals by natural means; to spread information<br>Some farmers and botanists propagate plants. |
| prospect (noun) | something hoped for or looked forward to<br>The prospect of getting a new job excites me. |
| pulp (noun) | the soft part of fruit; a mass of soft material such as wood fiber<br>To make paper, wood is soaked and mashed to a pulp. |
| puzzling (adv.) | hard to understand or answer<br>It is puzzling that my friend quit his job. |
| range (noun/verb) | a row of things; a large area; maximum distance; the limit; a stove with an oven; to travel over or roam<br>The Himalayas consist of a large range of mountains.<br>The cows feed on the range.<br>The range of colors in the rainbow is limited.<br>I bought a new range when I rebuilt my kitchen.<br>The deer ranged in the woods in search of food. |
| reach (verb) | to stretch; to extend; to come to<br>The government wanted the new tax information to reach all citizens. |
| rebel (verb) | to act against something; to show resistance; to fight<br>The child rebelled against his parents' demands by running away. |
| recipient (noun) | someone who receives something<br>I was a recipient of the award for best singer. |
| recycle (verb) | to treat waste materials such as paper, glass, or metal so that they can be used again<br>We save all our old newspapers and take them downtown to be recycled. |
| refrain (verb) | to hold back; to keep oneself from doing something<br>Please refrain from smoking while in the elevator. |

| | |
|---|---|
| regrettably (adv.) | sadly<br>Regrettably, I won't be able to come to your wedding next month. |
| relate (verb) | to tell a story; to have a connection with something<br>Grandfather likes to relate stories from his childhood.<br>Scientists are trying to relate the illness to possible causes. |
| release (verb) | to let go; to set free<br>The prisoners were released from jail. |
| reluctantly (adv.) | unwillingly<br>The man reluctantly admitted that he was guilty. |
| remote (adj.) | far away, distant<br>This new robot is operated by a remote switch. |
| repair (verb) | to restore to a good condition<br>When my bicycle broke, I repaired it. |
| research (noun) | an investigation to discover new facts or information<br>As a graduate student, you are expected to do research. |
| resort (noun/verb) | a place one goes to for fun, relaxation, or health; to turn to something for help to gain one's purpose<br>I'd like to visit a health resort on my vacation.<br>The teacher resorted to threatening the unruly students with additional homework. |
| restore (verb) | to bring back to the original condition; to repair; to make well<br>A good carpenter can restore old furniture. |
| revere (verb) | to have a deep respect for; to regard highly<br>Some people revere their grandparents. |
| rewarding (adj.) | satisfying; giving pleasure in return for something<br>It was rewarding to see the smiles on the children's faces when they received their gifts. |
| rise (verb) | to appear; to get up; to come to life; to become greater in intensity or volume<br>After a heavy rainstorm, a river might rise several feet. |
| rudimentary (adj.) | elementary, undeveloped<br>In ages past, humans had rudimentary ideas of economics. |
| run-down (adj.) | not cared for; weak and exhausted; fallen into disrepair<br>That old vacant house has become run-down.<br>My watch is running down; it needs a new battery. |
| scarcely (adv.) | hardly, barely, almost not<br>We have scarcely any money left this month. |

| | |
|---|---|
| scenery (noun) | the general appearance of a place; features of the landscape<br>It's nice to stop while driving and look at the scenery. |
| scrupulously (adv.) | done very carefully, paying attention to detail<br>He does his work scrupulously. |
| secretly (adv.) | not known to others<br>My friend secretly told me that he was going to get married. |
| seek (verb) | to look for<br>When it started to rain, the hikers began to seek shelter. |
| sensible (adj.) | reasonable, practical<br>It is sensible to dress warmly in cold weather. |
| shade (noun/verb) | something that cuts off the sunlight; a screen or curtain; to protect from light or heat<br>It's cooler to sit in the shade.<br>On hot days I often close the shades.<br>An umbrella will shade you from the sun. |
| sheer (adj.) | complete or absolute; of transparent cloth<br>It is sheer nonsense to listen for an echo in a crowded noisy place.<br>For her bridal veil, the woman chose a sheer lace. |
| shield (verb/noun) | to protect; a piece of metal, plastic, or other material that protects<br>Motorcycle riders wear leather jackets to shield themselves from the wind. |
| silently (adv.) | making no sound<br>If you sit silently, you can hear the birds sing. |
| single-story (adj.) | having one floor<br>My friends live in a tall apartment building, but I live in a single-story house. |
| site (noun) | a place where something was or will be<br>This looks like a good site for a picnic lunch. |
| sketch (noun/verb) | a rough plan; to make a rough, quick drawing or outline<br>The artist made a sketch of the mountain so that he could paint it later. |
| slim (adj.) | small, insufficient; slender<br>She has slim hopes of getting the new job.<br>She should become slim if she eats less. |
| socket (noun) | a hole or space into which something fits<br>Before you can turn on the lamp, you must plug it into the socket. |
| solitary (adj.) | living alone; without companions; seldom visited; lonely<br>The prisoner was put in solitary confinement.<br>Sometimes I like to take a solitary walk. |

| | |
|---|---|
| sophisticated (adj.) | a lack of simplicity or naturalness; cultured; with the latest improvements<br>After living in a big city, she became quite sophisticated. |
| spacious (adj.) | having a lot of space<br>In our new house we have a very spacious living room. |
| split (verb) | to break into two or more parts; to divide<br>In order to eat a coconut, first you must split it. |
| stain (noun/verb) | a mark that doesn't wash out; to permanently change the color of something<br>Blood can stain your clothes if you don't wash it out.<br>In my house, I stained the wooden doors light brown. |
| static (adj.) | in a state of balance, not increasing or decreasing; electric charges in the atmosphere; crackling noise in radio or television<br>We could not listen to the radio because of all the static. |
| strengthen (verb) | to make something stronger<br>If you add an introduction, it will strengthen your essay. |
| strict (adj.) | demanding obedience; clearly and exactly defined; precise<br>My boss is very strict; we have many rules to follow. |
| stripe (noun) | a band of material of a different color, pattern, or material<br>My socks have three red stripes on them. |
| stubborn (adj.) | obstinate; difficult to deal with; determined<br>The stubborn mule would not pull the farmer's plow. |
| style (noun) | a manner of writing, speaking; a quality of being superior; a general appearance<br>I like Hemingway's writing style.<br>The fashionable woman always bought her clothes in the latest style. |
| subtle (adj.) | difficult to perceive or describe<br>The subtle effects of the artist's use of color make her work fascinating. |
| supernatural (adj.) | spiritual; unexplainable by physical laws<br>Ghosts and angels are supernatural. |
| surpass (verb) | to do better than someone or something else<br>On the last test, I surpassed my previous score. |

| | |
|---|---|
| suspicious (adj.) | having an idea that something bad is about to happen; thinking someone may be guilty<br>I have a suspicious feeling that he may be telling a lie. |
| swift (adj.) | fast, quick<br>The swift runner won the race. |
| symphony (noun) | a long musical composition<br>Beethoven's symphonies are well known throughout the world. |
| take place (verb) | happen<br>The first scene of the play takes place before the hero and heroine have met.<br>The party will take place at my house. |
| temperature (noun) | a degree of hot or cold; a body fever<br>The child has a high temperature; she should stay in bed. |
| tension (noun) | strain<br>When my parents are angry with each other, there is a lot of tension in the house. |
| terrifying (adj.) | frightening<br>I had bad dreams after seeing that terrifying ghost movie. |
| theory (noun) | an explanation of a general principle; an opinion, not necessarily based on logical reasoning<br>Darwin's theory of evolution is important in the study of botany.<br>My friend has a theory that rubbing the scalp will cause hair to grow. |
| timid (adj.) | shy, easily frightened<br>The timid child hid behind his mother's skirt. |
| tolerate (verb) | to put up with; to allow without protest<br>I can't tolerate loud, angry people. |
| touching (adj.) | causing sympathy<br>It was very touching to receive letters from all my friends when I was in the hospital. |
| trace (noun/verb) | a very small amount; a mark showing that someone has been in a place; to draw or sketch; to copy; to follow a line<br>There is only a trace of iodine in the water.<br>The archaeologists found traces of an ancient civilization.<br>By tracing the line in the sand, we could follow the path of the insect. |
| transplant (verb) | to transfer; to move to a new place<br>The tiny plants were transplanted from little pots in the kitchen to a sunny place in the yard. |

| | |
|---|---|
| treasured (adj.) | valued, loved<br>I keep my treasured jewels in the bank. |
| trickle (verb/noun) | to flow slowly; to move little by little; a slow, small flow<br>The accident on the highway caused traffic to slow to a trickle. |
| tropical (adj.) | of the part of the earth around the equator<br>Many people like to spend their vacations on tropical islands where the weather is always warm. |
| turbulence (noun) | the state of being violent, uncontrolled, disorderly<br>After the rainstorms, the turbulence of the water in the river caused damage to the farmer's fields. |
| unaccustomed (adj.) | not used to something<br>I am unaccustomed to eating dinner at midnight. |
| unbearable (adj.) | not tolerable; causing much sadness<br>It is unbearable for me to see you go away for a year. |
| uncalled-for (adj.) | undesirable, unnecessary, not justified<br>That remark was rude and uncalled-for. |
| unquenchable (adj.) | not able to be satisfied<br>I have an unquenchable thirst. |
| vacillate (verb) | to waver; to be uncertain<br>I have a difficult time making decisions; I vacillate among all the options. |
| vandalism (noun) | deliberate destruction of a work of art or private property<br>Because of possible vandalism, guards have been posted at the doors of the museum. |
| verify (verb) | to test the truth or accuracy of something<br>Can you verify this answer? |
| vigorous (adj.) | having strength or energy<br>He works in a vigorous way. |
| vivid (adj.) | lively; intense; bright; clear and distinct<br>I had a vivid dream last night about my parents. |
| warn (verb) | to inform someone of possible danger<br>Fire alarms warn people that something is burning. |
| wed (verb) | to marry<br>He will be wed next June. |
| widespread (adj.) | occurring over a large area<br>Widespread damage was caused by the earthquake. |
| willing (adj.) | ready; agreeable<br>I am willing to help you finish your work. |
| withhold (verb) | to keep or refuse to give<br>Don't try to withhold the truth from me. |

# NOTES

# NOTES

# NOTES

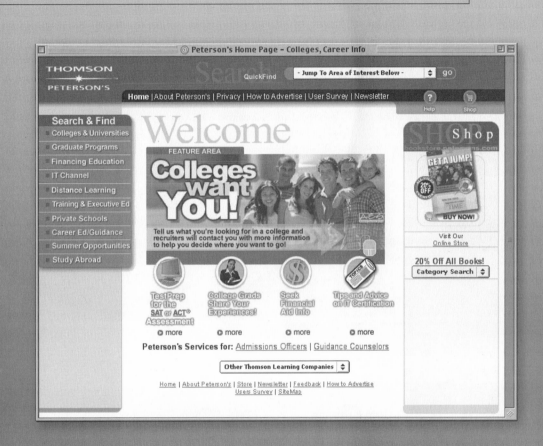

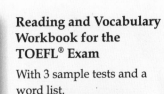